WITHOUT RESERVATION

"*Without Reservation* is a wonderful representation of the personal struggles Native American people often find themselves in. The conflicts between societal viewpoints and self-determination cause many to evaluate and reevaluate themselves on a continuous basis. There are often internal power struggles between the European viewpoints of what an Indian should be and the mirror of our ancestors that shows us who we are—by our mere existence. We are all subconsciously drawn to communications from the spirits of our ancestors, the environment, and the animal and plant relatives. We only have to open our ears, hearts, and minds to receive these messages from the great web of life."

CHIEF DON STEVENS, NULHEGAN BAND OF
THE COOSUK–ABENAKI NATION

"*Without Reservation* is a surprising treat for a curious, open, and scientifically trained mind. The story of Coy-Wolf is a delightful fusion of engaging storytelling, anthropology, philosophy of biological science, and findings from recent DNA studies. It is a new and exciting way to understand and ~~~~~~ ~~~~~~~~~~~
both scientific rationality and indigen

ALEH CHERP, PROFESSOR
UNIVERSITY (AUSTRIA) AND]

"Randy's work and experience are at the right time for all of us to explore our inner and outer medicine world for our true renewal. As Randy has seen and felt with his writing, all of us should truly learn to 'live' again in our own way and come together as one universal circle. The old ones called it 'the way of right relationship with all things.'"

"We are all native of Mother Earth. Many of us in the 'developed world' are hauled out of our roots by the modern industrial culture's dream of separation from nature and community. *Without Reservation* is a very personal and skillful reminder to guide us back to reconnect with our soul's yearning to be one with nature. It inspires us to reconnect with our spirit helpers and our ancestors to gain real knowledge, wisdom, and wholeness."

WITHOUT RESERVATION

Awakening to
Native American
Spirituality
and the Ways of
Our Ancestors

RANDY KRITKAUSKY

Bear & Company
Rochester, Vermont

Bear & Company
One Park Street
Rochester, Vermont 05767
www.BearandCompanyBooks.com

Text stock is SFI certified

Bear & Company is a division of Inner Traditions International

Cataloging-in-Publication Data for this title is available from the Library of Congress

ISBN 978-1-59143-384-2 (print)
ISBN 978-1-59143-385-9 (ebook)

Printed and bound in the United States by Lake Book Manufacturing, Inc. The text stock is SFI certified. The Sustainable Forestry Initiative® program promotes sustainable forest management.

10   9   8   7   6   5   4   3   2   1

Text design and layout by Virginia Scott Bowman
This book was typeset in Garamond Premier Pro with Cheddar Gothic used as the display typeface

To send correspondence to the author of this book, mail a first-class letter to the author c/o Inner Traditions • Bear & Company, One Park Street, Rochester, VT 05767, and we will forward the communication, or contact the author directly at **www.randykritkausky.com** or **randykritkausky@hushmail.com**.

To the two most influential women in my life,
Mother Earth and Carolyn Schmidt,
both of whom patiently guided and nurtured my awakening.

Mother Earth gifted me with visitations bearing
insights that I treasure.

Carolyn Schmidt gifted me with her presence at,
participation in, and witness to the events
documented in this book.

CONTENTS

INTRODUCTION

Reflections

Mirror, mirror on the wall, am I really an Indian, after all?

I can't count the number of times in recent years that I have been before a mirror and asked this question. The face that stares back at me always has hazel eyes, light brown hair, light skin, and northern European bone structure. I am continually reminded that I look more like my adopted family's Lithuanian ancestors than my biological family's Potawatomi ancestors.

This ambiguity surrounding my identity is undoubtedly due to the fact that most of the mirrors around me are not flat and objective glass surfaces. They are social reflections, in the spirit of sociologist Charles Horton Cooley's term *looking glass self*. Cooley argued that who we think we are is a composite of reflections of our personhood provided by the world and people around us. These reflections may be accurate, or they may be distorted, like carnival mirrors that make us look ridiculously tall and thin or impossibly short and fat. They may be idealized versions of what we should be, or negative images of what we should avoid becoming. In any case, the experience of sorting through multiple and often competing social identities is universal. In that sense my tale is a common one.

However, another dimension of my experience is somewhat distinct and is rooted in the legacy of indigenous peoples across the globe. Millions of us are but a few generations removed from millennia spent living in intimate contact with the natural world and in close communion with ancestral spirits. Who we are and who we think we are is not merely a social construct rooted in the fleeting here and now. Who we are and who we think we are is rooted in historical connections with those who have walked on but continue to be with us. Our identity is rooted in our relationships with the land and with a sentient natural world that shares an active understanding with us. When we wander too far from our roots, our ancestors and kin in the natural world call us home, sometimes with gentle whispers, and sometimes in loud voices sounding alarms.

When I have looked in the many mirrors around me since my awakening began, much more than a mere passive reflection has greeted me. Something has reached out, grabbed me, and pulled me through the looking glass. That is when things got interesting and I began to write. It is why I continue to write.

I write with the hope that the universal part of my awakening will resonate with a broad audience. Then, standing on that common ground, I hope that readers will trust me to be their guide so that we may together explore the possibility that some significant part of the more distinct nature of my awakening, the Indian part, may also be made accessible to others.

Surely those who do not have my Potawatomi ancestry are not going to be visited by the spirits of my ancestors. However, I am convinced that ancestral connections and intimate communications with the natural world are not restricted to those with indigenous cultural roots. If we remove the obstacles, we can all let ourselves explore these dormant but beckoning connections. Then we will better understand our relationship to the past, present, and future. We will begin to imagine and create a more positive road map for what is ahead. We will escape from the torturous burden of hyperpresentness inflicted by social media and the diminished selves reflected in the small screens of smartphones. We

Fig. I.1. The statue "Alice Through the Looking Glass," on the grounds of Guildford Castle, England.

may even begin to recover a sense of personal and cultural authenticity, for which there is a desperate hunger.

With such high hopes, I begin my storytelling.

Guided Wanderings

Journeys in the modern world are generally carefully scheduled, scripted, planned, and coordinated. They unfold in linear, chronological time. Our destinations are typically selected with considerable forethought; advance reservations are made after consulting travel magazines, brochures, websites, and even algorithms that purport to know our interests and needs better than we do. GPS coordinates in our cars and handheld electronic devices keep us on our chosen paths and eliminate disturbing surprises. Watches or other electronic devices help to keep us on normal everyday time.

While most of our journeys take us away from our immediate daily setting, the journey described in this book has not been a journey away from home. It is a journey, as yet incomplete, homeward.

I have not plodded, or sped along, in linear chronological time. I have not turned pages on the calendar or been able to consult dates on a travel schedule to prepare for what comes next. Instead, I have often strayed from the here and now. I have revisited the present from the perspective of a very distant past, with one of my weary pilgrim's feet firmly planted in the now, and the other tugging toward a receding distant horizon, my next steps tossing me momentarily even further into the future or past. It has been like a theme park ride that loops and spirals back on to itself until forward, backward, upward, and downward all become breathlessly conflated.

No itinerary was developed. The destination was initially unknown. No hosts or hospitality staff awaited me upon my arrival along the way. Instead guides—familial, nonfamilial, and totally unfamiliar—appeared and sent me hurling in new directions.

With a few momentary exceptions, the journey described here was made without hesitation, invoking one sense of the book's title *Without Reservation*.

Without Reservation conveys another reality. This is a tale about a collective journey, one being taken by Native American descendants who are without reservation—those of us who do not live on a reservation and have, at most, occasional exposure to reservations' cultural richness as well as their challenges and pitfalls. Like me, many Native Americans have spent a lifetime off reservation. We are separated by generations from life on the reserves (as they are called in Canada), or reservations (as they are called in the United States), that European colonists forced upon indigenous peoples of North America. In fact, 70 percent of all Native Americans now live in urban areas—geographically and culturally far from the rez.

This account does not purport to speak for or on behalf of those Native Americans whose lives are deeply embedded in reservation life, those who are currently "on the rez." Nor does my story pretend to reflect the realities of those whose lives have been connected with the unique and diverse experiences of living within the social, cultural, legal, and geographic bounds of an Indian reservation but for whom this is no longer a daily reality, because they have left. Such itinerant indigenous people are often caught between two worlds in a struggle I cannot adequately capture or represent. Their experience is well documented in a growing body of Native American biographies and in popular fiction produced by Native American authors.

How many Native Americans are there in North America? United States census data for 2010 indicates that 5.2 million people self-reported such status.[1] Of these, about 2 million are officially enrolled in federally recognized tribes. In Canada, 1.7 million people self-reported indigenous status in the 2016 census.[2] Of those, three quarters of a million people have recognized treaty rights. Nearly six hundred thousand Métis—a uniquely Canadian official indigenous status reflecting a legacy of colonial intermarriage—are now also gaining some legal rights and autonomy. However, the Métis often struggle with their ambiguous status within the world of indigenous people.

So I am one of seven million people living north of the Mexican border who claim Native American ancestry. I am one of the three million people who have a government recognized claim to be called an "Indian."* That is because, in the United States, unlike in Canada, tribes have pretty much been allowed to write their own rules for enrollment. Enrollment status sometimes depends on a documentable ancestral link to historical tribal membership, as with my tribe, rather than on minimum "blood quantum" (a calculation of percentage of "Indian blood"). This process has led to acrimonious disputes within some tribes, especially when treaty settlement claims produce funds to be divided, or when casino earnings are to be divided among tribal members. Canadian Métis have an even more fraught status. Having no quantum requirement, they must document continual historical and current involvement in indigenous community life.

These ambiguous designations of tribal membership have placed many of us in the middle of a long historical struggle about what it means to be an Indian. The matter has been further complicated by the fact that the U.S. government has tried repeatedly to challenge our claims of Indian status and tried to deny our ability to share in treaty rights and enjoy benefits. They would be happy if we just collectively faded away, like some digital image whose pixels fall off the screen one by one until the image finally vanishes.

As off-rez, European-looking, marginal members of the indigenous world, we are sometimes viewed with ambivalence by other Native Americans, especially those with stronger blood quantum or social and cultural connections with Native American tradition. However, I believe that we may prove to be critical allies in the struggle of all

---

*I use the term *Indian* throughout my writing, interchangeably with *Native American*. *Indian* is the term that my family and tribe most often use to refer to themselves. It is a familiar term throughout the world. Canadians use the term *First Nations*. I embrace the implications of the Canadian designation, but have concerns that most American readers would stumble over the name. Similarly, *indigenous people* is widely used, but lacks the geographic and historic specificity I seek to address.

indigenous people to preserve their sovereignty, to preserve and revive threatened cultures. As my path of discovery suggests, we may paradoxically even prove to be an underappreciated and unexpected contribution of spiritual rebirth that is so vital to renewal and revival. Being far from the turmoil of life on the reservation, insulated from the temptations of striking financial deals for casino construction and management of lucrative resource extraction agreements, we often inhabit that much maligned, and also envied, space of comfortable middle-class life. This is not the public's image of an Indian.

Life in mainstream America is certainly easier than life on the rez. However, our middle-class lifestyle too is threatened, not by swashbuckling men in metal armor bearing swords and guns, but by those who would conquer and control all they touch as they parade about in their fine suits. Our lifestyle is threatened by growing economic inequality, increasing burdens of holding multiple jobs, an opiate crisis, and technology that often fragments and distracts rather than uniting us. Many of the more recent and insidious forces of cowboy capitalism present challenges for the mainstream middle class that were once seen as unique to indigenous populations or marginalized racial minorities, such as colonization and marginalization, with mortality rates increasing among the most seriously displaced.

A growing sense of a shattered past and uncertain future in mainstream culture may explain a white middle-class obsession with the image of the "Vanishing Indian." This widely held historical narrative is a tale that the once triumphant white settlers tell themselves over and over. This is done in a desperate effort to find stories that help them to understand their own increasingly uncertain present and fraught future. If this is the case, perhaps Native American pushback on the Vanishing Indian narrative offers a story of spiritual renewal for the mainstream middle class.

Despite the growing uncertainties of middle-class life in the twenty-first century, the comfort and security of mainstream life may continue to offer many Native Americans like me peace of mind and economic security for some time. With this gift comes an extraordinary, possibly unprecedented, opportunity for self-examination, reflection, and reinvention as we stand with our feet planted in two worlds. But this gift is not only a gift. It is also an awesome responsibility, to be used well and wisely for the benefit of indigenous people as well as the general population.

As my personal journey suggests, the simplest gift, such as sleeping nightly for five months a year on a screened-in porch in a quiet Vermont forest, opens doorways to a world that many thought had vanished. Certainly my twenty-first-century middle-class experience is not to be equated with a lifetime, and even generations, of continual living in intimate contact with a vast and unspoiled nature, as was the case in the precolonial woodlands of North America. However, since the vast majority of my tribe has been forced to abandon those woodlands and live in an arid Oklahoma desert, it may just be that we distant cousins of those Indians have a unique opportunity and responsibility to listen to the whispers of kin and ancestors that are still to be found in the last fragments of a natural world that once covered the Earth and was home to our people.

The subtitle of my journey's record needs a bit of explanation. I use the word *awakening*. But my adventure is more than a mere gentle rising from slumber. There is a dimension of urgent desire to recapture something lost, and in my case, enlightenment nearly missed when offered. I see my awakening as a form of rekindling, giving life to smoldering embers nearly extinguished. This image is more than mere metaphor. It touches on the very origins and meaning of my tribal name, the Potawatomi.

Our name dates to the eighth century AD, when three upper midwestern nations of Native Americans—the Ojibwe or Chippewa, the Odawa or Ottawa, and the Potawatomi—formed a Council of the Three Fires. It is part of a larger upper midwestern and southern Canadian confederation of tribes often known today as the Anishinaabe people.

From that confederation came our tribal name, Potawatomi

(Bodewadmi), which means "Keepers of the Fire." Fire may have multiple connotations, just as it does in the Greek myth of Prometheus, which describes how fire was stolen from the gods and given to humans. Over millennia, fire in this myth has been construed in various ways: literally, as controlled combustion; as technics or technology; and as knowledge or enlightenment. These three interpretations of fire suit the narrative of our tribal origin. Fire was critical to the survival of forest dwellers, as was passing along traditional knowledge and the techniques of hunting and agriculture.

The exact mechanics of how the Potawatomi "kept" fire, in its simplest and physical form, are uncertain. But I have been told that embers may have been transported in birds' nests, which are often lined with dried mud and would serve as an excellent fire-resistant container. The actual ember may have been a tinder fungus (*Fomes fomentarius*), which can remain smoldering for many hours. The five-thousand-year-old Otzi the Iceman, found in the Alps in 1991, carried four pieces of tinder fungus.

For me, the embers of ancestral connections were nearly extinguished. I did not grow up in a household that made a conscious effort to continue ancestral ceremonies and cultivate ancestral sensitivities. We were not very good keepers of the fire.

My childhood home was in a suburb of Binghamton, New York. The adjoining neighborhood houses were built on an Indian burial ground that was excavated with an indifference that disturbed me even at age four. But neither our family nor neighbors raised any concern over this affront to sacred ground. No archaeological experts were alerted, as would be the case today.

I now cringe at the fact that we played Cowboys and Indians in a group of boulders left by glaciers millennia ago across the street from our house. The boulders were literally a stone's throw from the burial remains. "The Rocks," as we called them, were probably used by Native Americans as a marker for their burial ground. I used them to hide from imaginary "Injuns," and I would shoot my cap gun at them in imitation of Westerns I saw on television and at the reenactment of an Indian attack on a stagecoach that my family paid to see at Frontier Town, near our summer cottage in the Adirondack Mountains.

So it was that my uncle and cousins recently had to guide me on my often bumbling path of fanning the embers of ancestral memories that were nearly extinguished, but which began to glow unexpectedly when a passing wind touched my nest. As a result, for this attenuated middle-class Native American, reclaiming my status as a keeper of the fire has been a process of recovery.

Perhaps somewhere in the past, many generations ago, a relative was charged with the duty of tending the sacred bird's nest that held smoldering tinder fungus. He or she may have been neglectful and exposed it to rain, or simply delayed feeding the trace of sacred fire. A sense of panic and failure must have seized this person upon realizing the consequences of breaking a long and uninterrupted chain of trust. I envision this keeper of the fire, bent on knee, desperately blowing on the fading embers and cautiously feeding dry leaves or some other fuel in an effort to avoid extinguishing the chain of fire keeping. So too I imagine my role as a somewhat lapsed fire keeper rekindling connections.

1

BOZHO, BONJOUR, HELLO, DEAR READER

Because the reflections and stories that follow are so personal, and because I wish to invite readers to participate in a journey of discovery with me, I find myself searching for an appropriate greeting.

It is common for members of the Potawatomi tribe to greet one another, as well as outsiders, with "Bozho." Using our native tongue signals respect for a culture. It supports efforts to keep an endangered indigenous language alive. Speaking an "Indian word" before all else, before uttering the language of the settler colonialists, helps to identify a speaker as an authentic tribal member.

Or so I thought. Then, like everything I am encountering, my simple notion of a tone-setting greeting grew complicated, rich, and more revealing of my own tale than I could have imagined. It turns out that *Bozho* encapsulates much of the complication of twenty-first-century "Indianness," my own particular blended Indianness, and my family's Indian history.

My family connection with the Potawatomi began in the eighteenth century, when a French Canadian *voyageur*, or fur trader, named Jacques Vieux married into the Potawatomi. When he first encountered the soon to be indigenous branch of our family tree, he probably greeted them with *Bozho*, or maybe the more Ojibwe version of the greeting:

Boozhoo. Or maybe with *Bonjour,* as he was a native French speaker. Or quite possibly he uttered some scrambled combination of all of the above greetings. From my own frequent foreign travels, and often awkward efforts at learning at least a few words of my host country's language, I am fully aware that my foreign-language greeting is probably quite often a mishmash of English and an inadequate grasp of pronouncing a new language. But the effort is appreciated nevertheless.

In addition to confronting the challenges of correct pronunciation, I quickly discovered that the very origins of the greeting are complicated. Searching print and online sources for the origins of *Bozho* produced results that are unclear and controversial, like so much in Native American history. For example, Native American authors who speak some form of Algonquin such as Potawatomi or Ojibwe, and have some linguistic credentials, routinely note that *Bozho* is derived from the French *Bonjour.* I have read this bit of linguistic history so many times that I began to accept it unquestioningly. But in a fit of historical due diligence, I realized that I had better check out the alleged origins of the word from an authoritative source in which a definitive answer could be grounded. I could find none.

I did find an intriguing alternative explanation of the origins of *Bozho,* written by Native Americans who take the preservation of indigenous language and culture very seriously. While their explanations vary, there is a common element suggesting that *Bozho* is a contraction of *Giin inna Nanaboozhoo?* This Anishinaabe phrase translates as "Are you Nanaboozhoo?" The origins of this question are given various explanations. One is that the greeter is inquiring if the person greeted is of the people of a common ancestor and spirit guide, Nanaboozhoo or Wanaboozhoo.[1] Other explanations are more elaborate, suggesting that Nanboozohoo is a trickster who promises to return in disguise. Anishinaabe people thus greet strangers by asking, "Are you Nanaboozhoo?" which was abbreviated as "Boozhoo?"[2]

I have been unable to find a definitive historical source for the claim that any form of the Bozho greeting has Native roots predating

European contact. Putting this observation into print may invite an avalanche of letters and emails attempting to persuade me otherwise. Perhaps in time someone will present a seventeenth-century source indicating that *Bozho* was uttered by indigenous people upon first contact, uncontaminated by European culture and language. But for now there is something important to be extracted from this confusion.

We must be wary of efforts to resolve issues of Native American authenticity by defaulting to matters of origin, as if such determinations were possible, and as if there were an official referee out there who can determine what is truly rooted in indigenous culture and what is not. Whether it be matters of blood quantum, ceremonial regalia, or indigenous spirituality, we need to be careful both of claims of authenticity and of rejections of aspects of modern Native American life as mere impositions of settler-colonial culture.

I am perfectly satisfied with the murky origins of *Bozho*. Regardless of whether the greeting was used prior to any European contact, using the term is now considered by many Native Americans of Algonquin descent to be a gesture of respect and an acknowledgment of respect for traditions, even if they be fairly new and hybridized ones. That matters most.

I personally find the notion that the greeting I use may reflect both my French Canadian and Potawatomi ancestries to be profoundly satisfying. And while this perspective is my own relatively unique take on a small and obscure linguistic controversy, I think it should serve as a reminder of how much we need to be open-minded and embrace cross-cultural influences in examining current and historical accounts of Native American culture and spirituality, and their richness.

In that spirit I greet you, dear reader. Bozho.

2

THE AWAKENING

It is midnight, heading ever deeper into darkness—and into enlightenment.

Fireflies are dancing on the outside of the screen encapsulating the porch where we sleep nearly half of the year. These annual visitors normally come all too briefly. This year they have come very early and have stayed an unusually long time.

Tonight they have awakened me, taunting me with a mystery that has been presenting itself almost nightly for the last few months—the last months of my mother's life—which have been both an ordeal and an awakening. This journey ended, in part, for my mother yesterday, but I now recognize that it has actually only begun for both of us. She pointed out a pathway. Now lit with fireflies, it is ever so slowly becoming clearer.

The dancing fireflies are dots I have been struggling to connect, not just since my mother's death yesterday, but for some months quite intensively, and intermittently and unconsciously for many years. Tonight I began to recognize some semblance of a pattern in the chaos of the little points of dancing light. But the pattern does not consist of clear and simple lines connecting dots to form a two-dimensional image, like in a children's coloring book where you draw a line from one numbered dot to another, in their numerical order, and then an image is revealed.

Instead I see a wondrous matrix of many scattered dots, which could be connected simultaneously in multiple ways, and through dimensions in the air and in time so complex that I am only beginning to grasp the possibilities. This matrix, or web, is like a three- or four-dimensional dream catcher changing through time. You may be acquainted with Native American dream catchers, which consist of a circle with a web inside and small feathers hanging below. These sacred objects have become commercialized trinkets, sold as key chains, earrings, and rearview mirror bangles in gift shops. But tonight the dream catcher's web of firefly trails has caught me up and swept me away, just as my mother's illnesses caught her up and swept her away yesterday.

This newly intense twist in my journey began a little over a year ago, in Montréal.* It started innocently enough. Carolyn Schmidt, my wife, and I had developed a fondness for visiting Montréal, staying at a bed-and-breakfast west of the city center, and bicycling into the old port along the historic Lachine Canal. We would walk the city's cobbled streets and peer in the windows of souvenir shops and art galleries, visit museums, or attend a concert.

On one trip we came upon a collection of art kiosks in an open square in the old section of the city, a tourist section called Vieux Montréal. Standing out amid a collection of small displays of tourist kitsch, jewelry, and cheap caricatures, we came upon a dazzling display of paintings done in brilliant colors, executed with great care and feeling. Quietly sitting in the small shelter that housed the cheerful paintings was a smiling Sikh with a long gray beard and a colorful turban. We expressed our joy at the quality of his work, embarked upon an unexpectedly lengthy and intense conversation about art, and learned how the artist's roots in India shaped his view of art, both technically and philosophically. The artist presented his card, and we learned his name: Manjit Singh Chatrik. We also learned that Manjit was a poet and that lines of his poetry were embedded in many of the paintings. More significantly, the spirit of his poems was embedded in the artwork.

---

*As a convenience to readers who are not Native American, I use the French name Montréal for unceded territory known to the Haudenosaunee as Tiohtiá:ke and to the Anishinaabeg as Mooniyang.

Fig. 2.1. Native American portrait, mixed media
Painting by Manjit Singh Chatrik

As we chatted, I noticed several paintings of American Indians. All were images of bold individuals made unusually vibrant by a palette that I recognized as distinctly South Asian Indian. I explained that my interest in the Native American images was aesthetic, but also personal, as I have Native American Indian heritage. We exchanged chuckles at the irony of a North American Indian discussing portraits of Indians with an Indian Indian.

Over the course of a summer we returned many times to Manjit's kiosk. On hot summer days, it was an oasis of beauty and inspiration. Eventually we began to collect his art. But since we biked into the old town and the paintings we purchased were much larger than our backpacks, we nearly always left our purchases with Manjit. He encouraged us to come to his house to pick them up, to continue our conversations, and to see other paintings he kept there. Manjit and Manjeet, his wife, became friends, and our visits a kind of spiritual renewal.

One of my first thoughts upon seeing Manjit's art was that my mother would love his paintings. The increasing collection of Manjit's Native American paintings in the house Carolyn and I have in Vermont did indeed capture my mother's attention. When she visited for holidays, she sat and admired his portraits.

So it was that Manjit's paintings became colorful dots suggesting a pathway forward for my spiritual wanderings. They were also points of awakening, hanging on and beckoning from our walls.

As I look back, it now seems ludicrous that I was so slow to recognize the significance of the fact that the timber frame cathedral ceiling room where Manjit's paintings hang is full of religious art. I have collected these objects from around the world during decades of travel. I always thought, and rather emphatically claimed, that *I* was collecting the objects because of their transcendent beauty. I now believe that, no mere inanimate objets d'art, *they* have been collecting around me.

To the right of and below an Indian portrait is a large stone Buddha statue. It found me in a Chinese antiques flea market and shows signs of prolonged submersion in water and muck at the bottom of a pond or well. It was probably tossed there for safekeeping during Mao's Cultural Revolution in the 1960s, when owning such items was forbidden and dangerous.

A few feet away from the Buddha is a one-meter-tall wooden Lithuanian statue of St. Rokas (St. Roch) that found me in Vilnius. To judge by his weathered gray patina, he stood outside, only partly sheltered in a roadside shrine, in Lithuania's countryside for decades. A few feet away from Rokas is a Chinese Sung Dynasty ceramic "Buddha House," in which sits a three-inch-tall, glistening, green-glazed gem of a Buddha. And next to it sits a Chinese wooden Buddha, countless centuries old and so dried out that it is almost weightless. Its deeply weathered and eroded surfaces, echoing Rokas's life as a weather-exposed object of adoration, now present only a vague suggestion of a human form. At first glance, this Buddha looks more like a piece of driftwood than a statue. Except for the face, which has been restored and preserved in great detail with applied and carefully modeled clay. The statue stares out at all present before it. Visitors from eastern Europe have always found this Buddha frightening, its aura simply too overwhelming.

Such objects have been finding me for decades and assembling in our cathedral-ceilinged living room, which one visitor likened to a chapel.

Did I mention that in the space below Manjit's painting of Native Americans a giant, two-meter-long, wooden Advent calendar appears at Christmas? I spent many months making it. It resembles a medieval altar piece. My mother enjoyed seeing it and opening its doors during her annual Christmas visits. At that time of year our living room really does resemble a chapel. Additional Christian images populate our walls—crucifixes from Lithuania and Spain, Russian icons, paintings and batiks of saints.

You get the idea, probably more quickly than my rational secular mind did.

Back to the dots, those dancing fireflies, points of enlightenment that have been appearing faithfully year in and year out, which I had been ignoring as little more than beautiful light shows put on for us by an obliging Mother Nature.

Tonight the dots spoke to me. For the first time I listened. I suddenly sat up, bolt upright, in the middle of the night in my bed on the porch and realized that in all my musings and reflecting on my mother's illness and approaching death these last months, I had forgotten the other dot, the one marking the starting point in the most recent sequence of events that has taken me on my journey of reconnecting with Mother Earth and ancestors.

I am referring to the peaceful night that was upended by a phone call telling me that my mother was not answering her phone, the lights of her townhouse were out, and the police had broken her door down and found her on the floor. She had had a stroke, and this was the beginning of the end of her life.

What I saw then as an approaching ending, I now understand as a beginning. The dots of enlightenment were beginning to emerge even then and to connect slowly. Only later would they appear more frequently and more clearly, and be connected by me.

Sunday, June 4, emerged as a pivotal moment, the next emerging dot that alerted me to the fact that discrete events were pointing somewhere. This early June dot was actually more like a great lighthouse emerging out of the fog in a storm at sea, or from the clouded consciousness of someone lost in a sea of uncertainties.

It began as an evening of entertainment and ancestral reconnection. Robin Wall Kimmerer gave a presentation at the Middlebury Bread Loaf Environmental Writers' Conference. The event was up in the beautiful Green Mountains near Ripton, Vermont. My wife, my mother, and I attended. Kimmerer was scheduled to read from one of her award-winning publications combining a scientific perspective on nature with a Potawatomi view of the world of nature as profoundly spiritual and animate.

Although she had been having difficulty processing complex cognitive relations, my mother had been reading one of Kimmerer's books prior to the Sunday event. She had slowly read *Gathering Moss* as she sat on the couch facing west, where each night she alighted in anticipation of watching the sun set over the Adirondack Mountains. This had become part of her end-of-day routine since taking up residency with us after her first stroke. At her invitation, and sometimes insistence, we all began to slow down at this time of day and would sit with her and watch the sunset colors change, often until the very last traces vanished. I think we all understood the greater message of participating in a sunset.

While other presenters at the conference read from their printed texts to the audience that Sunday night, Kimmerer spoke directly to us and told us stories, in the tradition of many indigenous people steeped in oral history. She was engaging, spellbinding, and gentle. She did not attempt to overwhelm the audience with self-consciously crafted literary technique or words displaying a profound depth of academic vocabulary.

Her words were carefully chosen. Hints of a writer's self-conscious crafting, if evident at all, were delicate and employed as a means to a greater end rather than as a display of literary acumen.

Kimmerer first told us a creation myth of Native American people and let this story reveal the fact of our reciprocal relationship with nature. Within the tale lay a powerful call to action and message about global warming. It was a strong yet gentle message. She then told a simpler, more personal tale of gardening and the plenty and love that natural things give to us, in expectation that we will acknowledge that gift and reciprocate the loving activity.

Mom, the elder member of our clan, was enthralled. It was an awakening to our tribal heritage, which she, like many of us, had probably never experienced so deeply.

I will always remember this night as my mother's brightest end-of-life moment. I don't know where her energy, enthusiasm, and clarity of mind came from, but it was astounding. It was like the burst of light that ends a meteor's ephemeral appearance in a summer sky.

Two days later, my mother had a second stroke. I wrote the following message to our multigenerational family as part of my updates about our mother, aunt, grandmother, and sister.

> When we returned home [Sunday after Kimmerer's talk], as I got out of the car, one of the owls that nightly calls in the distance was this night just a few feet from the car. "Who cooks for you, who cooks for you," it called with almost deafening intensity. The intensity shocked me, but I also had memories of a movie Carolyn and I saw in the 1970s about a dying priest in a northwest Kwakiutl village. He learns about native culture, its belief that the owl calls one's name at the time near one's death. The priest ultimately learns of his own impending death when he hears the owl call his name. I knew who cooked for me during my early life, and worried.
>
> Today as Mom lay on a gurney in the ER, motionless and

unresponsive, she raised both arms several times and reached out as if grasping something or being called. Twice she did this and clutched ever so gently at the air with her fingertips, as if she were gathering apple blossoms or butterflies so gentle they must not be squeezed.

A time of sadness and discovery. Our elders teaching us even as they fade, maybe because they are fading and see where we cannot?

Randy

My cousin Barb wrote back to me:

Mno gzhep Cousin Randy,

My mom was very moved by the words in your email, so moved that she forwarded them on. I empathize with you and your siblings, and families. This is a difficult time, full of a storm of emotions, concerns and stress. I will put my semaa* down for all of you and my sweet auntie as well. Please let me know if there is anything I can do from a distance. I carry a prayer pipe for the women of our Nation. It is my responsibility to help.

I wanted to share with you a teaching about Koo-koo-o-koo (owl). Koo-koo-o-koo is a protector for our people and a helper to grandmother moon and the spirits. Our ancestors' spirits come back to earth in the spring with the Thunders. Their day is our night. Koo-koo-o-koo flies silently and swiftly all night long, protecting our families while we are sleeping . . . keeping the spirits from the dark side away while bringing love. She has acknowledged you and your momma, protecting you both and sharing love. That is all I can share via cyberspace . . . I hope these words are of value and comfort.

With love,

Your cousin Barb

---

*Ceremonial tobacco

Barb's support continued through email communications.

Subject: Full moon pipe ceremony
To: Randy Kritkausky
Hello Cousin, Boozhoo Nitaawes,

Last night I sat in the silver light of D'bik Giizis, Nokmis, our Grandmother moon and I lifted and lit the Nokmis Pwaagan (grandmother pipe). Prayers were said for my auntie (your mom) and her impending journey home. The Nokmisag and Mishomisag (Grandmothers and Grandfathers) said they will help her find her way, as she hasn't had our teachings. They will greet her with love and a great feast.

Watching the night sky and the clouds flow across the moon I caught glimpses of your mom joyfully soaring above the earth. I sang the Koo-koo-o-koo song and three others. Your mom has done good work here on the earth. She embodies love.

Holding you all in my heart and in my prayers,
Barb

Grateful, yet dazed, I wrote back.

Barb,

I can hardly describe the impact of your message and Kimmerer's talk last Sunday here in Vermont.

You see, about a week ago, after learning once and for all that she could not drive, and finally beginning to accept that she could not ever return to her townhouse, Mom asked us and her doctor, "What do I have to look forward to?" I tried to answer this question by suggesting that she could show us, once again, something we did not know how to do, and that which only an aging mother can teach: how to end our lives. Perhaps she is showing us to how to live, not just end, our lives.

I think that your prayer is being answered and that all of us, sometimes clumsily and belatedly, are beginning to learn the meaning of finding our way home, back to Mother Earth.

Kimmerer's tale last Sunday at the Bread Loaf Writers' Conference, which moved Mom and all of us beyond our ability to express, was about her experience with a turtle along the Hudson River, and then with many turtles at the school in the Adirondacks where she teaches. In the Adirondacks, multiple turtles "invaded" the volleyball court to lay their eggs in the sand because the nearby waters had risen as a result of extreme weather and climate change, and the normal nesting ground was unavailable. The turtles needed our help, as an exchange, or reciprocity for what Mother Earth did in our native Turtle Island creation myth.

So well-timed, this lesson. Today, as I left to go into town to see Mom again and say goodnight for the evening, a box turtle was in the middle part of our sandy upper driveway. Then I noticed that she was laying eggs. My first thoughts were "How stupid, another turtle in the road!" But she forced me to stop and to think. I remembered Kimmerer's stories. And I erected a barrier to protect the nest, planning to move it later.

Carolyn has been asking, "So what do we do?" after hearing Kimmerer's talk. Her second talk began to give answers. And today your message and the turtle are providing more answers. As Kimmerer said, "All we need to do is listen and learn from nature and our kin." Sometimes our kin find it necessary to park themselves rudely in the middle of the road and stop traffic. Especially when we are obtuse. It is a kind of civil disobedience. Like native people blocking the road to stop a pipeline.

I think we need to leave our upper drive blocked until the turtles hatch. It will be a small inconvenience and a great new beginning of an altered journey and redirection.

I have been secretly praying for such enlightenment for some time. I admit to the secrecy as I hesitate to fess up to anything resembling the sometimes too mechanical actions of those who demand instantaneous gratification from the saints for little problems not worthy of their attention.

The object, or inspiration, of my seeking has been a giant ancient Chinese ancestor painting hanging over our entryway doorway. It came to me as a kind of gift at a Chinese flea market. I had just bought three ancient wooden Bodhisattva (human incarnations of Buddha) statues and the antiques dealer wrapped one in this giant cloth painting, treating it as no more than a useless rag. It was musty and mildewed. I have restored and preserved it. Every time I walk under it during stressful times, I think/pray, "Ancestors and wiser ones, show me/us the way." How appropriate that I hung it over the door, where each day we begin our travels.

In recent days, I noticed that the hundreds of figures in this remarkable painting are arranged into seven rows/generations. From half way round the world, echoes of our native "seven generations."

So Barb, your prayer is being answered, and Mom has been hanging on, even without nourishment or water, which she cannot swallow. She cannot speak. Her spirit cannot let go. But in her silence, she is still teaching us. Now perhaps she can be released from the trap of a worn out body.

And perhaps, thanks to her, and your prayers, we can find our way to restoring Mother Earth, not through the narrow paths we have followed for decades, but through a path of reason guided more strongly by the lessons of Mother Earth all around us.

These days are not, and for me will not be remembered as, an ending. They are a new beginning.

Randy

And we continued.

Mno Waaban, Randy, good morning.

I hope you've been able to get some rest. Your words, read early this morning and just before I went back to sleep for a while, were a catalyst for my dreams and further connecting of the dots of my thoughts and experiences. It is usually early morning, just before sunrise that teachings and understanding come to me. Waabanong, the eastern direction, is the direction of Gikendasswin or Knowledge.

Here is what I came to understand this morning—

The full moon is a time when turtles of all kinds can be observed laying their eggs . . . we are told to plant seeds with the full moon for best results. Nokmis D'bikat Giizis is connected to our women's twenty-eight-day cycles, connected to the tides, water, and all life. When she is full, she is at her peak of physical presence and strength. When she is not visible for that one of twenty-eight days, she is at her peak of spiritual strength as her body has disappeared from sight. We call that time Manidoo Giizis (Spirit Moon).

When our people are put out to fast, the intent is to diminish physical strength to allow for reconnection and strengthening of our spirit as well as the connection with our own spirit and the spirits in general. Our people routinely fast (without food or water, and in quiet isolation) for four days, and the old ones are said to have fasted for seven days, some for twelve days.

These teachings bring me to the understanding that as our *getsijig* (elders) pass, those that are given the opportunity to pass slowly are being "put out to fast" to increase their spiritual strength for the journey ahead. That journey home is a spiritual journey only, not a physical one. That journey home is led by Giiwedinang, the North Star (literally the going-home star).

So, yes, protect that turtle nest, keep seeking enlightenment in whatever way is right for you. Our Ancestors guide us continually, in so many unexpected ways, and we have to be quiet and open to "hear" them. Each day is a new beginning, a new opportunity.

Feel free to pass this along to whomever, and my previous words as well. These "teachings" are given to you with compassion, and they are yours to share as you need to.

Love,

Barb

My mother died on June 14. The circumstances surrounding her final days will remain forever vivid in my mind.

She was in a hospice care room at a small local hospital. She had been unable to swallow water or take food for many days. I had previously understood that a human cannot survive more than three days without water. But hospice care staff informed us that dying patients, who are very inactive, can go many days, occasionally even a week or more, without food or water. Weakened, Mom was barely conscious, at least in the traditional medical sense of the word; she was not reactive, and her eyes rarely opened.

During her last days, Matt, a hospital chaplain, visited Mom. Matt played his harp, and it was calming. During one session, I noticed that a clear plastic cup of water on the table by Mom's bed was behaving strangely. The surface of the water was dancing, jumping upward in a column about one inch high, as if something beneath the surface were erupting. Carolyn suggested that it might be the music causing the pulsing. But the pulsing continued even after the music had long stopped. Carolyn then suggested that it might be Mom's now interrupted and labored breathing that was causing the pulsing. I put a magazine between her and the glass so as to intercept her breath. It had no effect. The water continued dancing vigorously for some time.

As Mom's breathing became ever more interrupted, it was apparent that death was near and that her body was in distress. She was given small doses of morphine, which seemed to calm her a bit, but the distress was agonizing. Her ever-determined physical self just would not let go. It was as if her spirit were imprisoned in a broken body.

I took Mom's hand and put my other hand gently on her forehead. This had previously relaxed her and allowed her to sleep when she was struggling in previous days. But this time I did something different. I tried a *tumo* yoga technique I had acquired inadvertently in my efforts to raise my body temperature during the winter when I was suffering from adrenal exhaustion and felt constantly cold. With this technique, I attempted to conjure whatever physical energy I could tap into and concentrated intensely on making it go to my hands, which were resting upon my mother. And I thought, though I did not say, "Mom, take this energy, and use it to let go of your tired body." Within less than one minute, she took her last breath.

I had no regrets at encouraging Mom to take her final breath. It was a relief. I did, however, soon begin to lament one omission, a thought that had been plaguing me ever since it became obvious that she was dying. I realized that she did not have a Potawatomi spirit name. How could I have let this happen to the oldest and wisest member of our clan? Then even before sharing my concern, I received the following email from cousin Barb.

Boozhoo Cousin,

I hope you and Carolyn and your families are resting amidst the sharing of memories and processing of emotions. I send you all love and good thoughts at this time.

I would like to share something with you. Last night I felt it necessary to light Nokmis Pwaagan, the Grandmother pipe, to assist your mom on her journey home as well to confirm something that was revealed on the full moon. You see, no one has formally requested your mom's Anishinaabe/Nishnaabe/Spirit name, yet it was revealed during that full moon pipe ceremony! (Just so you know, I have been mentored, for the past several years, in the process of seeking, finding, and naming by my husband, a fluent first-language speaker and spiritual elder. He and I worked together to name my father and my sister, and several other Bodwewaadmii Anishinaabe relatives. He assisted me in interpreting what was revealed, and with the proper use of our language.)

If you would like and if you feel it is appropriate I would be happy to write up the story of your mom's name and her name. Please know that it is with humility and love that this is offered up.

Her name was not asked for, or actively being sought. Rather it was a spontaneous gifting.

Sleep well,

Barb

I responded.

Barb,

Once again, the experience of my mother's death involves extraordinary developments that defy what I, until recently, would have called secular "reasoning." Every night since my mother's death, I have had dreams of her, something unfinished, even though we had a wonderful awakening in recent weeks and closure during her process of passing. As I awoke this morning, I told Carolyn about the dreams. At the very same time, I thought of the missed opportunity to give Mom a spirit name and wondered what has gone amiss.

This gap, this incompleteness, was emphasized moments later by a message from the funeral home asking for our family tribal name for Mom's death certificate. I had written both *Caucasian* and *Native American* for race on the form. New York State wants the tribal name. As I provided this information minutes ago, the failure to give Mom a spirit name became painful. And I wondered if it could be done posthumously. Then I clicked on your message. You cannot imagine the relief and joy it brings.

Please share with us her name, and the story of how it came to you. It will bring great comfort.

As for me, I am still processing the awakening of recent years, and especially recent months. I am in the midst of connecting the dots, which appeared last night as flashing fireflies outside the screens of the porch where we sleep. When my tale is completed, I will share it with you, and perhaps then I can begin to think about the issue of my own spirit name. Until then, thank you for the gift you have given and for conveying the gift of our ancestors to Mom.

Randy

Barbara's description of Mom's name

Manidoo Nigiiwehodaasaa
Man/i/doo Ni/gii/weh/o/daa/saa
(Mahn i doe Ni gee way o dah sah)
Spirit Leading Them Home
Inez Joyce Wall Kritkausky

She has taught us much in both her life and her death. Her passing was gentle and peaceful, accompanied by wondrous and spontaneous events, connections, and reconnections. In going home to our Ancestors, she has shown her family the way home.

I wrote to my extended family.

In recent days the fireflies, my awakening points, have diminished and almost disappeared. One or two still appear in this year of their most extended visit ever. Perhaps it is now time for them also to let go. They have labored long and hard and shown the way. I think I can continue to find the dots from this point on, with the help of our ancestors' spirits, those wise ones amongst us, and by observing and acting on the wisdom embodied in the natural world all around us.

So this is how my awakening unfolded. On the one hand, it was a long, slow process of emerging from a kind of spiritual sleep or dormancy. On the other hand, more recently, it was like being jolted out of a sound sleep by some interruption. In either case, *awakening* best describes the subjective experience of being caught between levels of consciousness. When we awaken from a wonderful dream, we long to hold on to it, its richness, which we know too well will be quickly extinguished.

Or perhaps my experience of awakening is more like the metamorphosis of a caterpillar awakening as a butterfly. Does it recognize itself?

Remember its former self? Does it feel free, being able to flutter quickly and agilely through the air after inching slowly upon the Earth for its entire former life?

Whether emerging from a dream or a chrysalis, we are simultaneously something entirely new and a continuity of everything we were before. Ideally we should seize moments of profound transition, of awakening to changed circumstances. In reality, we often only slowly recognize that we are changing, or have changed already, in anticipation of a new world that our intuition has grasped, even if our rational intellects have not yet done so.

This, I think, may be the greater significance of my awakening: it reflects not just an individual journey, but a manifestation of a greater social awakening and cultural revival.

3

BEFORE THE AWAKENING

If you have driven an automobile, you know that your attention is normally directed to the immediate present before you, just down the road or street. You navigate using an idea of the best route to your destination. You make changes as traffic or weather dictates. But most of your consciousness is in the present or anticipated immediate future.

Occasionally, as you drive, you may find yourself glancing briefly into the rearview mirror, checking some memory of an object or event recently left behind. As a result, a journey is a thread connecting past, present, and future. So, in order to make my spiritual journey more intelligible, let me briefly describe what is in my rearview mirror.

As I have mentioned, my childhood was suburban, white, middle class. My neighborhood was probably built over an Indian burial ground. I played Cowboys and Indians as a kid, and never took the role of the Indian. I preferred to shoot imaginary Indians with my cap pistol. My immediate family rarely alluded to our Native American past. There was no shred of a Native American worldview or ceremony in our lives.

Even my grandfather, who had spent much of his youth at three Indian schools, including the infamous Carlisle Indian School, never discussed this part of his life with me. When I sat on his lap as a child, he would tell me fascinating stories of the Wild West, the Oklahoma he grew up in. There were horses, bandits, corpses of bandits "Wanted

Dead or Alive" displayed in store windows. But no Indians appeared in his stories. There were tales of World War I and mustard gas. But my most direct familial connection with our Potawatomi past was silent about it.

My spiritual upbringing was suburban vanilla, like one of those mass-manufactured ice creams found in a 1950s supermarket: colorless, little natural flavor, nothing unique, one artificial ingredient easily substituted for another. I didn't really like ice cream. Therefore I hated the annual town ice-cream social, where we were given half-melted artificially flavored vanilla ice cream in which a too-small piece of prized cake attempted to swim to safety at the edge of a drooping, spilling, soggy paper plate.

I also hated going to church. It was Methodist and boring vanilla. The only redeeming feature was my other grandfather bringing Necco wafers to church and slipping them to me. I remember the minister once criticizing the congregation for singing without feeling. He had previously been associated with a community with many Welsh parishioners. Their religion too was probably vanilla, but at least they knew how to sing.

My neighborhood of Hillcrest was vanilla in other ways. It was all white. I was aware of one Jewish family. No one ever explained their religion to me. There were no Asians. No people of color. And as I mentioned, the only Indians were buried in our backyards.

Our neighbors were mostly unremarkable, with a few notable exceptions. One neighbor had a trucking company, and some of his trucks were vandalized because he did not pay the local Mafia protection money. I did not know who the Mafia were until another neighbor, a state policeman, played a feature role in busting the Apalachin Mafia gangland gathering in 1957, in a small town near where we lived. The gathering involved one hundred mobsters from the East Coast, who met to divide up the gambling, loan-sharking, and narcotics-trafficking operations left in chaos after the death of crime lord Albert Anastasia. At the time, the very existence of a highly organized crime world was barely acknowledged, even by J. Edgar Hoover, the head of the FBI. All of this was big news in my otherwise placid neighborhood.

Another neighbor, almost unnoticed because his family only briefly resided in our midst, attracted my attention because he somehow connived to take away my highly prized lawn-mowing job, my only source of pocket money. I could not at the time figure out how he managed this treachery. It became clearer decades later, when he appeared in headline news as President Nixon's lawyer: John Dean. After badly advising the president of the United States, he turned on him and helped to bring him down during the Watergate scandal. The country was shocked. I was not. I imagined him mowing the White House law(n) as part of his duties.

My conventional upbringing was disrupted by the traumas of my father's bankruptcy and then my parents' divorce. These were shattering experiences. My mother sought and found some comfort in guidance provided by our minister, the quiet Reverend Compton. I only found hypocrisy in that church, as the boring Sunday School class I was forced to attend was conducted by one of the people who, I overheard, had helped to tip my father into bankruptcy because he refused to pay his bills.

After the divorce, my mother experimented with a local Unitarian Universalist Church. When Mom took me there, I couldn't find anything religious. It looked like my middle-school cafeteria: stark and undecorated. I think a large number of the members were divorcées.

When my mother remarried, her husband, Dr. Anthony Kritkausky, brought emotional and economic security to our family, as well as a new last name for all of us. It was a gift. He was a wonderfully kind, generous, and loving man. Since he and his kids were Catholic, we began attending Catholic Mass. Again I was perplexed. My stepfather had been tossed out of the church for marrying a divorced woman. But I went along politely. After all, we had been Methodists and Unitarians. Why not Catholics?

It was the 1960s. *Time* magazine asked, "Is God Dead?" in its

April 8, 1966, issue. I guessed that they waited one week so as to not ask the question on their April Fool's Day edition. I knew the answer to *Time*'s question. Like President Kennedy, who was assassinated in 1963, and truth, which was slowly being killed during the Vietnam War, along with respect for the president, God was just another fatality to be recognized and reported on.

My kindly stepfather paid for my undergraduate education at an Ivy League university, the University of Pennsylvania. I majored in sociology and learned to analyze virtually any form of human behavior in rational secular terms. As an "engaged" 1960s nonhippie, I explored philosophy on my own. I read Camus and Sartre, and delved into metaphysics. I tried to understand Heidigger, Hegel, and Husserl on my own and couldn't figure out "what the H" was going on with these guys. I was so relieved when the most widely read professor I encountered once commented, "If they are so smart, why can't they write so that ordinary intelligent people can understand?" My skepticism toward religion was now slowly being turned against reason. After a few years of graduate studies in sociology at the University of Pennsylvania, I fled academia.

At this time, the darkness of existentialism made some sense for me. But I was spared from falling into the abyss of nihilism by Albert Camus's *The Rebel,* an exploration of post–World War II philosophy that demonstrates the internal contradictions of existentialists, who claim there are no absolutes even as they protest that human society has gone too far astray from basic human decency. In rebelling, Camus noted, even the most extreme nihilists implicitly affirm some limits, some values. This thread of something anchored in the realm of absolutes was to sustain me, sometimes quite marginally and shakily, for decades.

I report on this personal history because I believe that my experience—of being lost in the spiritual wilderness before the trees showed me a way out—is in many ways the story of my generation, and to some degree of many in the late twentieth and early twenty-first centuries. If we want to appreciate where we are headed, sometimes we do need to look in that rearview mirror.

Thus when the ancestral visitors and the cousins of forest and meadow appeared, they probably knew that they needed to come, not as gentle visitors, but with the gusto of intruders determined to occupy my secular, rational, agnostic consciousness. They did not tap on the door dressed in nice suits and in pairs, like the young Mormon missionaries, or Jehovah's Witnesses with their publications. No, they came with flashing lights up the driveway like a SWAT team and entered uninvited, after breaking down the entrance gate, battering in the double-bolted doorway, and leaving it swinging on broken hinges.

For me, the awakening was more like one of those interventions portrayed in documentaries about families confronting another family member and forcing them into rehab. Only in my case, it was the spirits of ancestors and our cousins from the forest and meadow who, in their desperation and determination, intervened as liberators.

And I am grateful.

4

PATHWAYS TO KNOWING

Before digging more deeply into my awakening, it is important to provide readers with a conceptual map of the four types of encounters with the Native American heritage and wisdom that I have experienced and observed around me. I think that such a framework, explaining the variety of ways we come to know and understand things, is often missing from writings by Native Americans. As a result the general public confuses, conflates, and unnecessarily mystifies different modalities of Native American experience. Too much of this experience is mistakenly thought to be beyond the reach, or even full comprehension, of non-Natives. Regrettably, much of the contribution of our indigenous cultures is viewed as too remote and too esoteric to apply to mainstream living. Such distancing and othering of Native Americans marginalizes indigenous people. It relieves those in the mainstream from having to examine their own beliefs in a new and challenging light.

Here then are the four types of encounter I have engaged in during the rediscovery of my Native American heritage.

Visitations and Connections: The most astounding and sometimes the most perplexing encounters involve wonderful, unintended, and typically unexpected, visitations of ancestral spirits. These are great rarities and great gifts. Equally thrilling, but typically more gentle, are direct connections with the natural world, moments when the consciousness of other living beings, flora and fauna, becomes accessible. The psychology, biochemistry, and neurology of such encounters with natural kin are explored in great detail in Stephen Harrod Buhner's works about plant intelligence and teachings: *Plant Intelligence and the Imaginal Realm: Into the Dreaming Earth* and *The Secret Teachings of Plants: In the Direct Perception of Nature.*

Observation: A far more common encounter with the wisdom of Native American culture comes through intended highly conscious, close observation of the world of nature and the lessons that flora and fauna bring, if we take the time to see and listen. A Native American child first taught me to do this, and my cousins have joined as guides and inspirations. It is often difficult to distinguish between wisdom imparted by a visitation and that which arises from careful observation. I believe that these two modes of knowing often overlap. As noted earlier, this mode of experiencing the world around us is exemplified in the writings of Robin Wall Kimmerer, *Braiding Sweetgrass* and *Gathering Moss.*

Reflection: This mode of coming to know and understanding requires time and critical self-examination, even an element of skepticism. It often requires asking ourselves hard questions: "What did I just experience?" "How much did I really see or hear?" "What part of what I experienced was the result of my too willful conjuring out of some personal need rather than receiving an unsolicited gift from outside or by looking beyond myself?" And of course, the most challenging and rewarding question: "What does it mean?"

Black Elk, a famous Sioux medicine man and later in life a Catholic catechist, asked himself these questions over the entire course of his lifetime. Not only was he constantly skeptical of visitations, but his family, elders, medicine men, and priests also questioned and examined Black Elk's visions. Such reflection was a routine part of living in a Native American community. The questioning became more intense when Native American culture encountered, and sometimes collided with, Christian settler culture. *Black Elk: The Life of an American Visionary* by Joe Jackson navigates these culturally sensitive issues with great respect and sophistication. The 2008 annotated edition of John Neihardt's *Black Elk Speaks* is also a rich source of information on spirituality at the intersection of indigenous and European cultures. This edition contains Raymond J. DeMallie's notes on Neihardt's embellishments and deletions from the original stenographic record of interviews with Black Elk.

Storytelling: This mode of coming to know is profoundly social rather than introspective and private. By sharing or publishing knowledge and wisdom we have been given, we become teachers and conduits of culture. As every teacher knows, we only really begin to deeply grasp what we think we know when we see if and how our experience resonates with others as we attempt to speak of it. Our friends, families, and communities challenge and confirm us. For Native Americans with

Fig. 4.1. Ways of knowing

millennia-old oral traditions, storytelling comes naturally. For others, this is nearly a lost art form. If we are all, Natives and non-Natives, to rediscover our past, understand our present, and create a better future, we must become better storytellers and better story listeners.

These four ways of knowing intersect, overlap, and inform one another. I struggled with various diagram shapes in an effort to portray the interconnections visually. I first experimented with a pyramid. It did not work, because that image suggests a rigid hierarchy of knowing. Nor does a pyramid allow each of the four modes of knowing to intersect, as they do continually.

Appropriately, the wheel came to me as the best pictorial representation. It is also an image from my ancestral heritage—a medicine wheel or a sacred circle and fire used in ceremony. The result pictured below does not include the four directions, sacred plants, or colors traditionally associated with a medicine wheel. That will not all fit in one image, so I leave it for fertile imaginations to embellish my image and complete my work.

5

WHAT COY-WOLF TAUGHT ME

The following narrative reflects the entire spectrum of engagement with Native American sensibilities, knowledge, and spirituality. This includes visitations, connections, observation, reflection, and storytelling. I hope that readers can share in my sense of wonder and begin to understand how different modes of knowing link with one another. Perhaps then we can all begin to understand the path to Native American cultural revival, and even move toward a long overdue spiritual awakening in mainstream culture.

The First Coy-Wolf Visitation

Two days before the supermoon of January 1, 2018, Carolyn and I watched a documentary on Native American history. Behind the TV screen, a giant, bright moon shone in the window. The digital world's light pixels and sound jolted our intellects and emotions, while the silent moonlight begged for our attention on another, quieter, more subtle level.

The intensity of this moon's brilliance was a rarity. It resulted from the approach of this celestial body at its closest point, or perigee, to Mother Earth in a decades-long cycle. This year's supermoon near approach began in late 2017 and will be followed by an even rarer second January blue moon supermoon, which will also be a lunar eclipse at the end of the month. The last time the full moon came so close to Earth was in 1948, the year of my birth, an astronomical fact that would prove to be the least of our surprises and just one of many wonderful synchronicities.

As the lunar event approached and I read about it widely in the news, an intriguing fact kept appearing. A January moon is popularly known as the Wolf Moon, a designation widely attributed to Native American calendars. I did not seriously question this fact, since my cursory online searches all claimed that "the Algonquians called January the Wolf Moon." Had I reflected more seriously, with my usual skepticism, and then investigated even one authoritative source on my tribal language, I would have discovered that the root source of this misinformation was the *Farmer's Almanac*. Online sources authoritatively claiming knowledge of Native American culture had simply lifted the information from this popular compilation of folk wisdom and repeated it, using the exact same seven words over and over, which should have alerted me to a problem.

My tribe in fact refers to the January moon as the Bear Moon, as I was reminded by a knowledgeable elder, who rescued me from being yet another conveyer of online misinformation and falling into a semantic origins trap like the one surrounding *Bozho*. However, that correction happened long after I spent an entire month looking at the January moon, thinking it was Wolf Moon. Like many mainstream Americans, I was just too taken with the allure of a wolfish designation for a bright midwinter moon appearing in cold darkness. I now forgive Wolf Moon for being coy. It was trying to tell me something.

But that is getting ahead of my story. Wasn't this particular story supposed to be about watching a documentary? The question might well be posed by a careful and perhaps increasingly impatient reader. The answer is yes. But that documentary's impact only makes sense when set against the background of a window behind a TV screen. That rich background wrapped itself around a digital image in a spiral of time, which, as I often note, leaves me caught between past, present, and future. And Native storytelling need not be linear, indeed should not be, since enlightenment often comes from taking a circuitous journey.

So before returning to the documentary that precipitated this tale, I must take you a bit more deeply into our culture's intimate relationship with the four-legged, as this story is ultimately about such relationships, which anthropologists often call *totemic*.

Potawatomi clans are named for animals, such as deer, bear, and wolf. Clans and totems are closely related. I have long been familiar with them, having taught college sociology and anthropology courses and having read widely about Native American life. However, until a few days ago they were concepts about which I had only an intellectual and somewhat distant understanding. That has now changed profoundly, as an abstraction has come wonderfully alive.

A bit more background is useful here. We live in a forested area of Vermont, not high in the Green Mountains, but in the flatter Champlain Valley clayplain. There is as much farmland as forest in our area. It is ideal habitat for deer and other wildlife that like living on forest-meadow boundaries, where biodiversity flourishes and protective cover can be quickly found.

A relatively recent arrival in this habitat is the Coy-Wolf. Just a few decades ago, the appearance of such mammals was discussed in terms of the rising population of coyotes. However, wildlife biologists soon began to take note of the size of these predators and observed characteristics not typical of coyotes. For example, their larger skulls and teeth more resembled those of wolves than of coyotes. With such an anatomical advantage, the new creatures could hunt and devour larger animals than are typical coyote fare.

More recently, with advances in genetic research, it became possible to unravel part of the migratory history of this new addition to New England wildlife. It is now recognized that in the nineteenth century, southwestern coyotes slowly moved north and eastward as white settlers virtually exterminated wolves, who were despised as predators on livestock (which, ironically, had been introduced as a new and alien species in the New World). One of the very first laws in the English colonies, a 1642 law of Ipswich, Massachusetts, mandates a virtual war on wolves.

> Whosoever kills a wolf is to have the skin, if he nail the head up at the meeting-house and give notice to the constables. Also, for the better destroying or fraying away wolves from the town, it is ordered, that by the 1st day of the 7th month, every householder, whose estate is rated £500 and upward, shall keep a sufficient mastiff dog; or if £100 to £500, shall provide a sufficient hound or beagle, to the intent that they be in readiness to hunt and be employed for the ends aforesaid.[1]

The fine for not complying with this order was one shilling each month, until obeyed. Much of North America's indigenous human population and entire swaths of wildlife eventually suffered from the same treatment: demonization, dislocation, and genocide. To mix metaphors, the colonial-era wolf was a furry canary in the coal mine.

With wolves virtually gone in the northeastern United States, coyotes from the Southwest slowly migrated northward into this abandoned ecological niche. In the second decade of the twentieth century, a coyote and one of the remaining gray wolves in southeastern Canada interbred on or about the site of the current Algonquin Park in Ontario. From there, offspring of this new half-breed slowly migrated east until they reached Vermont, where a significant population has been established. The same species has now moved into lower New England and New York State, where these wily mammals have snuck into suburban backyards and even into urban spaces such as New York's Central Park.

Many wildlife naturalists consider this coyote-wolf hybrid to be one of the most adaptable species that they have ever studied. Coy-Wolves survive, even thrive, in an extraordinarily wide range of natural and man-made habitats, kind of like Native Americans.

I first encountered Coy-Wolves around the turn of the new millennium, as we began staying in a small cabin on our land while our house was being built. We were often greeted at night by the howls of what we then understood to be coyotes. At that time we viewed them as little more than part of the charm of our new place of residence. It never occurred to us that the night visitors were *actually greeting us,* and reminding interlopers whose territory this was.

Even then, we knew that coyotes communicated with one another, and we were aware that humans eavesdropped on their conversations. But we did not yet know how to listen—to really listen.

Everything changed with my mother's death and the kind mentoring and guidance of family members more versed in our tribal culture than I am. Consequently, we were prepared both to listen and to understand our encounters with Coy-Wolves as part of a process of awakening.

To return to our January moonlit night, we were watching a segment of a video course on Native Americans.[2] The documentary's historical segments resonated deeply, as they dealt in depth with my Potawatomi tribe and its history in the upper Midwest, its forced evacuations and deadly marches westward, its legacy of countless broken treaties. The experience of children at the Carlisle school, which my grandfather had attended, was repeatedly a topic in the videos. The documentary shed light on my family's experience with the Dawes Act of 1887, which succeeded in breaking up collective land holdings on reservations and relocating Native people onto small, unsustainable individual parcels of land, a piece of which my family still retains in Oklahoma.

Then there was the segment on American Indians and World War I, which reminded me that my grandfather was exposed to mustard gas at that time, when he served in the same U.S. Army that, a few decades earlier, had engaged in genocide against Native people.

This kind of intellectual and emotional onslaught through storytelling was leaving us drained every night after watching each new episode of the series and reflecting on its meaning. One of the mind-boggling questions that surfaced was an intensely personal variation on the core theme of the program we were watching. The narrator, Professor Daniel Cobb, repeatedly claims that Native Americans have not disappeared.

He argues that despite continual betrayals and ignominious defeats and slaughter, Native peoples found ways of adapting and maintaining some continuity, even as many of their lands and cultural practices were taken away, even as they intermarried with whites and assimilated elements of European culture.

Each night this historical conundrum of devastation and revival returned to me in the form of profoundly personal questions and reflection. Is part, or even all, of my Potawatomi ancestral heritage vanishing? To what degree am I a "real Potawatomi," or is anyone a "real Potawatomi" today?

These questions haunted me as we ended our most recent viewing. Carolyn and I went downstairs to play cards in an attempt to get our minds off these perplexing questions and regain our composure.

No sooner had we dealt the cards than we noticed the howls. *THE HOWLS*. Even on a freezing Vermont winter night with doors and windows buttoned up, the sounds of our visitors came through the walls. The Coy-Wolves were closer than ever, a fact I confirmed a few days later, when I located their tracks in the snow just outside of and around our house. Our visitors had demanded attention. But what were they saying? The howls continued for quite some time.

Somewhat shaken, I went to bed, reflecting on the documentary and the visitations. Then, as is so often the case, the answer came in the middle of the night. It was as if a message buried in the documentary's storyline had clarified, had been downloaded into my consciousness, and was churning, seeking expression. It hit me. I am a hybrid like the Coy-Wolf. And like the Coy-Wolves in Vermont, I am many generations removed from my pure-blooded ancestors. Like the Coy-Wolf, I am not a lesser being for the dilution of my ancestral bloodlines. I am an evolutionary manifestation of adaptation. This is what the Wolf Moon and Coy-Wolf were trying to tell me.

Then another connection emerged. I began to visualize the migratory routes of southwestern coyotes as they slowly moved northeast in the nineteenth century, in the exact opposite direction, and in the same time frame, that many of my ancestors were being physically driven out of their homelands and off one temporary reservation after another. I also saw the paths of those small numbers of Potawatomi who had escaped from these forced death marches and who had fled to Canada, where their descendants live today. Then I wondered if the spirits of my ancestors forced westward had perhaps found inspiration in their kin who had moved northward to safety and freedom. Had the spirits of those driven into the desert journeyed northward, back home, and then to Canada? Had they cleverly done so in an animal form that no white man would recognize as human, and in a manner that no soldiers could prevent? Were the Coy-Wolves outside my door the embodiment of my ancestors' wandering spirits?

I think so.

I now hope that I will be worthy of more visitations. I hope that I will be better able to listen to the wisdom they bear. I hope that like Coy-Wolf, I can be the conveyor and restorer of my dual heritages, not lessened, but made stronger by the blending.

◙ September 6, 2018 ◙

Observations and Reflections on Coy-Wolf

Last evening we attended a public presentation on the coywolf. This event triggered further reflections on my January encounters with Coy-Wolf and resulted in yet another semisleepless night, during which I attempted to write my way to understanding, to use my storytelling as a tool of self-discovery. A careful reader will immediately notice that the previous two sentences refer to "Coy-Wolf" and "the coywolf." I once would have perceived little difference between these two characterizations. But everything now has changed.

When I first wrote about encountering Coy-Wolf back in January, I described a very personal visitation by living beings with personhood and spiritual gifts. The intimacy and richness of this complex phenomenon lies at the heart of what is happening in my life, in my awakening.

Consequently I now think of Coy-Wolf and capitalize the name out of respect, and in order to acknowledge that the name is one of related kin, with personhood. I have human relatives, Mike, Becky, Bob, Tony. I don't refer to them as "the mike," "the becky," "the bob," or "the tony." If I were to do so, I would be suspected of some kind of relational emotional disorder whereby I depersonalize and objectify humans, rendering them mere objects. I would also be perceived as showing disrespect.

The Animate Pronouns *Ki* and *Kin*

Throughout this book I will occasionally use the animate pronouns *ki* (singular) and *kin* (plural) to refer to the four-legged, winged, and rooted beings with whom we share Mother Earth. The idea was introduced to me by Robin Wall Kimmerer's essay "Speaking of Nature," in which she proposes these terms as an antidote to over objectification or othering our natural kin.[3] I use these pronouns sparingly in order to keep readers from stumbling over unfamiliar terms too frequently. By using the animate pronouns Kimmerer suggests, I seek to convey a sense of my intimate kinship with and sense of animacy about those in the wild or in the garden. I also do this when I simply do not feel comfortable using an impersonal *it*. Ultimately I am hoping to assist the reader in seeing the world in a new perspective. The only other option available to me to avoid "othering" our natural kin is to use Native American names for animals and plants, which are frequently animate. However, I fear that the unfamiliarity of these words would distract from the notion of familiarity and kinship I hope to convey.

So now I stumble over terms like *the coywolf*. Speaking those words is extremely uncomfortable for me. I cannot any longer depersonalize this wonderful member of my extended family who dwells in the nearby forest. I will try to discover Coy-Wolf's Anishinaabe or Potawatomi name, or work to promote the creation of such a new hybrid name if it does not yet exist.

But for now, I can return to last night's events after a brief linguistic detour, which I hope has enabled readers to more easily follow in my tracks, and those of Coy-Wolf.

The public presentation I have mentioned was given by a knowledgeable Vermont naturalist and wildlife tracker, Sue Morse. It was a beautifully photo-illustrated argument for advocacy on behalf of the coyote, according to Morse one of the most persecuted animals in North America. She is qualified to make this claim, because she has spent much of her life studying predators: wolves, cougars, and coyotes.

I was surprised to hear Morse refer to what I understand to be Coy-Wolves as the "Eastern coyote." She explained in detail the origins of Coy-Wolves, confirming the historical and genetic information I have presented here. However, she made it clear that she prefers the term *Eastern coyote* and then almost apologized for occasionally referring to this canid as a coywolf. In support of her hesitation, she asserted that the most up-to-date biological research suggests that this predator is about 60 percent coyote, about 40 percent wolf, and in some instances possibly 10 percent domesticated dog. Throughout the presentation, Morse noted that in the southeastern United States, coyote variations reflecting more interbreeding with dogs are being documented. Consequently, she observed, the genetics of this species are up in the air and constantly changing.

With this muddy but intriguing review of Coy-Wolf's genetics and discussion of ki's name, I realized that the topic had touched a very sensitive personal raw nerve. The hybrid I had come to see as symbolizing my mixed identity and the legacy of my ancestors' forced migrations suddenly came into clearer focus. My kin in the natural world were now suffering the same twisted fate that was inflicted on my ancestors. First and foremost, Coy-Wolf was being subject to a socially constructed determination of identity that was increasingly detached from reality. Despite scientific evidence of strong wolf characteristics, *wolf* was being dropped from the naturalists' lexicon in regard to this animal. An essential part of Coy-Wolf's identity was being scrubbed away.

The renaming process was shaped with good intentions, as with self-proclaimed Native American advocates in the late nineteenth and early twentieth centuries, who took away Indian schoolkids' tribal names to encourage mainstream assimilation. Only now it was happening with well-intentioned biologists and wildlife advocates sensitized to public concerns about "predators" in our midst. These concerns arose in part from the reintroduction of wolves in the Northwest, a process that was quietly and slowly underway as a result of a natural return of wolves well before these predators were reintroduced into national parks by humans. The human initiative, unfortunately, has created a high degree of public backlash in the region, particularly among ranchers whose cattle and sheep were sometimes killed.

My thoughts turned to more human historical conflicts: those between Native Americans and settlers over the control of Western land. History was repeating itself with the same agonizing questions and troubling answers. Who has a right to live on the land? Drive off the wild ones. Well, maybe on second thought, let them have a place to live within the bounds of a small reserve. But they won't be allowed to leave the rez/park, or they will be shot.

A light went on for me. Wildlife advocates were avoiding the use of *coywolf* and even more so *Coy-Wolf* because it set off alarms. Using *coyote* alone had resonance in popular culture, including the famous cartoon in which a wily, anthropomorphized coyote was repeatedly outsmarted by a small, harmless bird, the Road Runner. Indeed Morse's presentation was billed as "Wild Cousins of Our Best Friends," referring to dogs, who were prominently featured. Her presentation also included a humorous poster pretending to be a warning about coyotes. It used the cartoon coyote's failed tricks as indicators of how to identify a coyote: use of dynamite or rocket packs. It was deft public relations and elicited the desired relaxed-audience chuckle of relief over living with a harmless creature.

I understand the good intentions behind this nuanced effort to open minds to embracing predators, who are too often portrayed as red in tooth and claw. Advocates for coyotes have helped put an end to coyote-killing contests: mass slaughters that once filled pickup trucks in Vermont with furry corpses. Wildlife advocates are admirably struggling to correct misperceptions of coyotes as a serious threat to the deer population, and to humans.

I do, however, cringe at repeating the insults inflicted and indignities heaped on my human Native American ancestors and inflicting them on my natural kin. I envisioned a headline in an imaginary newspaper that my human and wildlife kin both cowrite: "Blood Quantum Is Back!" This time my Coy-Wolf kin are the victims. Front and center is the mistaken scientific and cultural notion that a living person or creature is defined first and foremost by their genetic makeup, their percentage of ancestral lineages. Think of discrimination against mixed-race people of African ancestry in the United States, who were legally categorized as mulatto, quadroon, octoroon, and then treated according to their blood quantum. Think of "Coloureds" in South Africa during the apartheid era. Think of "Aryans" versus "non-Aryans" in Nazi Germany. You get the point.

My Native American spiritual sensibilities began to further inform and sharpen my scientific reasoning. My reflection mode of knowing was kicking into high gear. Coy-Wolf's identity struggle, along with news and scientific-journal stories about new applications of DNA matching, and issues associated with reliability of DNA ancestry testing, prompted me to dig more deeply into the specifics of Coy-Wolf DNA. As with other applications of DNA matching and testing, the story of Coy-Wolf's genetics became highly problematic.

The first question I asked myself arose from one of the difficulties of human DNA ancestry analysis. Who establishes the DNA matching baseline for a pureblood? And is *pureblood,* or a pure ecotype (a baseline genetic sample), a reality as opposed to some arbitrary determination?

This question came to my attention when scientists discovered that a new humanoid fossil of a Denisovan found in a Siberian cave contained enough Neanderthal DNA that it was possible to conclude that the mother was more Neanderthal than Denisovan, and that even the father had some Neanderthal ancestry.[4] Although the discovery of Denisovans as a new species of humanoids had made headlines, the subsequent discovery that the new discovery's most famous fossil was not clearly a distinct species only made the news in the inner pages of scientific journals. The public and media like simple stories, not complicated scientific truths. Discoveries about human evolution, race, humanoid species, and recent disclosures that many of us carry Neanderthal DNA have left a lot of people squirming. Many of us are but a generation or two removed from notions of racial purity. Too many of us still cling to the notion.

Revelations about the murky genetics of human evolution prompted me to ask if "wolves" are pure wolf, or if perhaps they are also part "coyote." The answer is astounding. Robert Wayne, a geneticist at the University of California, Los Angeles, and his research team determined that Eastern wolves have between 25 and 50 percent coyote DNA, red wolves have 75 percent coyote DNA, and even gray wolves have traces of coyote DNA.[5] This finding pulls the rug out from under claims that DNA can be relied on solely, or even primarily, to determine the degree of wolf or coyote heritage for Coy-Wolf.

Then I remembered reading multiple articles on the topic by proponents of the term *coywolf*, who examined photos used by defenders of the *Eastern coyote* designation. Often the animals depicted in those photos of "Eastern coyotes" clearly demonstrate body size, ears, and skull structure suggesting a strong genetic wolf presence. It was so obvious that even a layperson with only a glancing acquaintance with wolves and coyotes would see it.

This pathway to knowledge—observation—was kicking in. I was delighting in the clarity of thought that can occur inside of my medicine wheel image of ways of knowing. My awakening was no longer just about my ancestry. It was also about my own thought processes and the joy of discovery that can happen when the scales are removed from our eyes by a shift of consciousness inspired by spiritual awakening. Too often it is claimed that science supplants the ignorance of traditional teachings. The reverse can also be true.

Now that I had returned to the realm of the obvious, I began to wonder how twenty-first-century biological science engages in taxonomy, how it categorizes flora and fauna. *Morphology,* or the detailing of physiological characteristics, was once the primary determinant for categorizing both plants and animals and for locating newly discovered specimens within existing frameworks. During the seventeenth, eighteenth, and early nineteenth centuries, before cameras, the endeavor produced giant and highly treasured artistic portfolios of exotic birds and animals. Natural history museums became repositories of plant and animal specimens. Had this been abandoned, and had the use of DNA analysis entirely replaced morphology? What is the current standard practice and the state of the art of taxonomy? I wondered.

Again the answer is surprising. Both morphology and DNA analysis are routinely used together to substantiate and challenge one another in what is called *integrated taxonomy.*[6] Good science involves both, not just one source of information. In fact, taxonomy often ventures beyond individual species' physiological characteristics. The ecological niche that is occupied, and behavior within that niche, is often considered as well.* How then could Coy-Wolf be named and biologically categorized based on ki's DNA alone?

I returned to my conclusion that Coy-Wolf's name has everything to do with the politics of science. The evidence was right there in the scientific literature. My source of information about wolves having significant coyote DNA is actually titled "Wolf Species Are Part Coyote: Genomic Analysis Reveals Wolves and Coyotes Have Hybridized,

---

*Species behavior, ecological niche occupied, and utility for humans are critical dimensions of taxonomy in indigenous cultures. Biologists have only recently discovered the wealth of information embedded in plant names given by Native Americans.

Potentially Complicating Wolves' Protection under the US Endangered Species Act."[7] The finding that wolves had significant, and in some cases overwhelming, percentages of coyote DNA was greeted with grave concern by those working to protect the wolf as an endangered species. The Endangered Species Act of the United States does not clearly apply to "hybrids."[8] Their protected status is in question and subject to a high level of discretionary decision making. This can change quickly with new political appointees in government and with industry lobbying over concerns about a perceived overuse of the Endangered Species Act. Wildlife naturalists were worried not only about the reactions of suburban residents, but about the reaction of the federal government.

This raises interesting, actually life-and-death, questions. Are these creatures to be relegated to scientifically contrived categories so as to preserve endangered wildlife of few select species, such as wolves? Or should we be asking more fundamental questions? Should we be seeking to better protect all forms of wildlife to the maximum degree possible? Should we be recognizing basic rights of nature for all our natural kin, just as we recognize basic human rights for our human kin? In the future, will our indifference to living creatures, our othering of them, and our lack of recognition of their rights be viewed as barbaric, just as we regard the view of human slaves as property in the not so distant past? Are these behaviors not on the same moral continuum?

Such questions were brought to our doorway in recent days by our kin. Perhaps they were not just welcoming us, but pleading with us for help.

I am reminded that the story of Coy-Wolf begins with the first settlers' war on wolves and that this foreshadowed how the same settlers would eventually treat Native Americans. As I am also attempting to document, something ancient, fundamental, and primeval is now awakening within me. Something within my nature is erupting and desperately struggling to reassert itself. So too it is with Coy-Wolf.

If the ultimate goal of wildlife advocates is to have the public accept wildlife on terms that actually respect wildlife, we need to call our kin by their correct names, just as my ancestors sought to be called by their "real" names, even as their names were being taken away from them at residential schools. Perhaps we can take a page from Native American history and apply it to wildlife conservation.

We could begin by noting that my tribe is reviving the practice of naming ceremonies. The tradition is rooted in a notion that the Creator could not recognize someone until they had their spirit name. What, then, is to be the name of the canid that stealthily migrated from the Southwest and interbred with a surviving wolf in Ontario a century ago, then moved east back onto ancestral Native American woodlands? If my hunch—that this biological phenomenon is the return of my ancestors' spirits—is correct, then the name of this kin shall be Coy-Wolf. (Dear God. I need to learn the correct Anishinaabe name for Coy-Wolf so that the Creator can recognize ki, and so that wildlife biologists correctly name ki.)

Perhaps our collective encounters with Coy-Wolf can help us realize that the struggle over wildlife names and the rights of wildlife to live in their native habitat are both rooted in our desire to dominate, not to live with nature. Most of us can still barely open our minds to this lesson. Our desire to dominate nature is based in our lack of ability to tolerate diversity, especially when it brings aliens, unlike us and our domesticated canids, right into our communities. Especially when those aliens require that we change, even slightly, some of our cultural practices, attitudes, and behavior.

I am not being coy when I suggest that there is more at stake here than a name.

◎ September 2018 ◎

The Story of Coy-Wolf:
Visitations and Reflections Become Myth

I imagine one of my ancestors having an experience like those I have had surrounding the visitations of Coy-Wolf and then using it, after reflection, as the basis for a story she or he would tell family and tribal members on a long winter's night. Such a story might be remembered and become embedded in oral tradition, its origin and association with the original storyteller eventually lost. For those of us with European heritage, loss of authorship might be considered loss of information. But for me and my Native American ancestors, it is the story that matters. Furthermore, for these ancestors, the giver of knowledge in this tale is not the storyteller. It is Coy-Wolf, and ki is duly recognized and immortalized by the tale.

What matters most is capturing wisdom and conveying it when it is offered. I give, in return for this story, my gratitude to Coy-Wolf, who has also reminded me that we need alternative, positive, stories to tell ourselves about ourselves.

Nanim'ewé (coyote) remembered the time when the two-legged Keepers of the Fire first appeared in his territory in the arid lands. They came bearing bitter tears and broken spirits. Nanim'ewé at first did not understand the sadness of these beings. But as he and his kin crouched invisibly near their fires on cool nights, they slowly learned the language, not the spoken one, which the two-legged yelped and which is unintelligible, but the more important one they spoke from their souls, expressed in their dance and song, and carried on their sad faces. This is the universal language that all who listen can understand.

Eventually Nanim'ewé and his kin came to understand that the two-legged Keepers of the Fire had been forced to leave their homes far away, in the direction of the cold winters, where the trees grow dense. The Keepers of the Fire had been forced to leave by other two-leggeds, the Chimookmaan (big knives) with fire sticks, the pain of which Nanim'ewé and his kin had also come to know too well. Nanim'ewé and his kin understood that the Fire Keepers would not be able to return to their ancestral homeland for some time, if ever.

But Nanim'ewé and his kin began to scheme in the manner of their trickster character. If the two-legged Fire Keepers could not return home now as humans, perhaps their broken spirits and those of their ancestors dying in the land of Nanim'ewé could go home another way.

And so it was that Nanim'ewé began a dialogue with the spirits of the Fire Keepers, both the living and those who had walked on. Together they came to understand that it would be possible to return home disguised as Nanim'ewé. The Chimookmaan would not recognize the Fire Keepers when they reappeared as four-legged, fur-covered creatures.

So it was that Nanim'ewé and his new friends began the long, slow journey to the ancestral homeland of the Fire Keepers. Some of the two-legged remembered parts of the path they had walked from their forest home to the grasslands, and then from the grasslands to the dry lands after they were once again expelled. But none of the two-legged remembered the complete route home.

However, the winged creatures who traveled with the Fire Keepers on their long journey many generations ago had kept the memory. Some had accompanied the two-legged, who had shared their meager corn rations with winged friends in a year of very little food. In reciprocity, the winged creatures memorized the route of migration of the two-legged, as such mapping is their wisdom. Winged creatures collectively share such memory of their migratory paths with their descendants, who must make the return trip home yearly, even after some of the original individual travelers have walked on. Just as the small, colorful butterflies remember the return route home after those who made the outward trip have disappeared.

So it was that some of Nanim'ewé's kin set off with the spirits of the Fire Keepers, accompanied by their winged guides. As they traveled north year by year, Nanim'ewé's kin began to suffer from the cold. But they persevered, warmed by the spirits and fires of the Keepers of the Fire and guided by the winged ones.

When they finally arrived in the land of many trees, they found the land now occupied by the Chimookmaan. The Keepers of the Fire knew that this was their ancient homeland because mnomen (wild rice) grew there. But they were not welcomed by the two-legged and felt insecure. So they continued their journey deeper into the land of many trees. And the days as well as the nights grew colder. When they reached the great waters of the north, Nanim'ewé and his kin felt that they could not cross the endless water. But the spirits of the Fire Keepers explained that the water would become hard in the winter and that they could cross.

So it was that one full-moon night, in the month of the Bear Moon, Nanim'ewé and the spirits of the Keepers of the Fire crossed a narrow section of the frozen lake and arrived in the country of the far north.

Nanim'ewé and his kin shook with cold. And they trembled with fear when they first saw Ma'iingan (wolf). Ma'iingan looked somewhat familiar, like a larger version of Nanim'ewé, but with teeth more like the knives of the two-legged who had driven away the Keepers of the Fire. Nanim'ewé wondered if he should turn about and go back to the dry lands. But the spirits of the Keepers of the Fire explained that Ma'iingan was their brother, sent by the creator, Gitchie Manitou, to help them live on the coldest parts of Turtle Island.

The spirits of the Fire Keepers gathered the kin of Ma'iingan and Nanim'ewé around a ceremonial fire where the two-legged placed kinni-kinnick (tobacco, sage, cedar, sweetgrass) in the embers, and it made a wonderful scent of peace. Ma'iingan and Nanim'ewé made peace with one another and agreed to live together.

Before many summers came and went, Ma'iingan and Nanim'ewé had offspring that were neither one nor the other, but something new. The new Nanim'ewé had thicker fur, which was welcome in the cold lands of the many trees. They also had the jaws and teeth of Ma'iingan, which they needed to hunt the larger game of this land of many trees. Ma'iingan realized that his large head was now full of new ideas and new wisdom about problem solving—ideas brought from a warmer place, wisdom that was useful in the summer and useful in hunting the small game that was arriving in the land as the seasons warmed.

Useful also was Nanim'ewé's omnivorous scavenging habit, something at first seen as silly and ridiculous to devoted carnivores and hunters. Ma'iingan grew stronger eating berries, insects, and small rodents, food that Nanim'ewé considered to be his traditional summer meal. "Hmm," thought

Ma'iingan, "other people's special food so often looks disgusting. But then it becomes normal, and then quite appetizing!"

In time, neither Ma'iingan nor Nanim'ewé called themselves by their tribal names any longer. They were given a new spirit name by the spirits of Fire Keepers, who, as they resettled in their homeland, revived their ancient ways. The name of the new creature was Coy-Wolf. The name, it was explained, was more than just a combination of two old names. It came with another meaning: the adaptable ones. The Fire Keepers had been given a prophecy when they were given the new name for Ma'iingan's and Nanim'ewé's combined families. The prophecy was that Turtle Island would change: the winters and summers would become warmer. The waters and forests would change. The two-legged Chimookmaan would visit plagues upon themselves and lose their way as they endangered Turtle Island and all who lived there. For good or for bad, all of the two-legged and all of the creatures on Turtle Island would share one and the same fate.

If the creatures of Turtle Island were to survive, the two-legged would have to gain the wisdom of adaptability.

So it was that the spirits of the Keepers of the Fire sent Coy-Wolf into the world to show the two-legged the meaning of adaptability. Coy-Wolves were dispatched to the far reaches of Turtle Island, as far as the shores of the great water in the direction of the rising sun, and as far as the legs of Turtle Island, where it is wet and hot. Coy-Wolf was warned by the Keepers of the Fire that the two-legged are fearful and would at first hunt them down, just as they had hunted down the two-legged Keepers of the Fire. But the Keepers of the Fire added words of wisdom: become one with the two-leggeds' furry companion, Dog. If you confuse the two-legged and they cannot figure out what you are, but they think you are not Ma'iingan, then they will accept you. They will study you, and they will learn that interbreeding does not necessarily weaken; it can strengthen and bring wisdom.

Thus it was that Coy-Wolf began his migration into the world of the two-legged with some fear and uncertainty. And just as the descendants of wolves of the far north accepted the burden of pulling the two-leggeds' wooden sleds in the land of ice houses so that they could survive, Coy-Wolf accepted the *even greater burden of bringing wisdom to the two-legged, who lived in trees piled high into giant beaver houses and lodges with square corners. The spirits of the Fire Keepers explained that the two-legged who live in such places are slow to listen and to learn, and that they would need to be shown the way many, many times.*

6

THE NEXUS OF TIME

As I grow accustomed to viewing the universe in more animate terms, there seems to be a progression in my thinking. First it was possible to grasp the notion that other beings in the animal kingdom have spirits or souls. Then my mind was opened to the very real possibility that beings in the plant kingdom have spirits. The notion that thingy things, concrete objects, both small (stones) and large (mountains), and moving things such as water or the moon could also be animate—well, that came more slowly, until the following event.

▣ February 19, 2018 ▣

Grandfather's Watch

The gold pocket watch danced under its little glass dome, where it was suspended from a small hook at the top of the tiny glass vitrine. We were listening to a collection of Johnny Cash recordings titled *Bitter Tears: Ballads of the American Indian*.

This occurred two days ago, when a visiting Potawatomi elder, my wife, Carolyn, and I were discussing how memories of Indian ancestors had been passed down to us and what we were doing to keep traditions alive, or even to renew them.

We had just been discussing my grandfather's involvement in World War I and how a gold pocket watch, sitting on the windowsill nearby, had mysteriously come into his possession at that time. This inspired me to play *Bitter Tears,* as our visitor had not heard about the recording. The connection to our discussion was one of the songs in the collection of sad tales about Native American history: a ballad about Ira Hayes, a World War II war hero and a Native American of the Pima tribe, who was involved in the famous hill attack on Iwo Jima. The event is immortalized in a Pulitzer Prize–winning photo by Joe Rosenthal, commemorating Marines planting a U.S. flag after most of the attacking force had died taking a strategic hill near the end of the Pacific war. The campaign on Iwo Jima began on February 19; the hill was captured in a few days. Ira Hayes later died ignominiously of alcoholism and neglect.

As the music played, I reached for and opened my grandfather's watch, and then read the engraved dedication (see page 62).

Robert E. Christie was a friend of our grandfather. He worked for the War Department during World War I, was a friend of James Forrestal (later the first Secretary of Defense), with whom my grandfather had some mysterious connection, and was involved in high-level inspections of troop preparedness in Europe. According to my grandfather's diary, he reconnected with Bob Christie in Scotland on his way to the front in France in early 1918, when Christie was apparently on an inspection tour.

Grandfather Asa's gold watch had sat, unwound and unanimated, on the windowsill in our dining nook behind our table for many months.

As the music played, I brought out a box of family Indian artifacts: pottery, wampum, and weavings, which I placed a few feet away from the watch.

I am honored to be the temporary caretaker of these family artifacts. But I am also pained. Every time I look at the watch, I think of Native Americans like Ira Hayes, fighting in two world wars, wearing the uniform of the army that not so long ago had been active in genocidal practices against our people.

Asa E Wall

from

R E Christie

February 19 1917

Fig. 6.1. At left, the engraving on the back of Asa's watch and, above, a photo of the watch

As the *Bitter Tears* collection played, and then as "The Ballad of Ira Hayes" came on, I noticed that my grandfather's gold watch began to move. It became ever more animated by the minute. I called Carolyn. Pointing at the watch, I observed everyone's astounded faces. Carolyn initially suggested that the watch was pulsing to the beat of the song. Johnny Cash does have a powerful voice with rich, deep tones, and Carolyn's explanation was a reasonable interpretation of what we were seeing. However, the watch's movements continued long after the music ended.

I compared this event to the dancing column of water in the cup by my mother's bedside during the last hours of her life. Matt the harpist had just finished playing for my mother, who was comatose. At that time Carolyn had also suggested the strange motion was resonance with the music. However, even long after the harp music ended, we sat in silence, spellbound, staring at the glass as the water continued to dance.

When I wrote to family about this amazing event, my cousin Barb had written: "Nibiseh Manidoosag, Little Water Spirits . . . what a blessing and wonderment to have witnessed, to have been with your mom helping her on her journey home."[1]

So once again we observed the energy of ancestral visitations manifested in a very material form, channeled through time, animating a timepiece, Asa's watch.

We momentarily left the table and the pulsing watch to examine the nearby items that had once been in the trunk of my grandparents' attic. But we could not turn our attention fully away from the dancing watch.

Among the items we were examining were handwritten notes from my grandfather's cousin, known as Aunt Emma, to my mother and her siblings. An educator of Native Americans, she had written often to Asa's children and had sent them objects, such as pottery and small weavings, illustrating Native American art. They were gifts that Emma's students had given to her. In the spirit of giving, she had passed them along to her kin.

Emma was one of the Red Progressives, who formed the first Native American advocacy organization created by and for Native Americans, the Society of American Indians, at the beginning of the twentieth century. Aunt Emma had an illustrious career that included a presentation of her work at the Chicago Exposition in 1893.

When the Indian elder held Emma's notes explaining the origins and meaning of the objects on our table, her hands trembled. She explained that she felt intimately connected to an individual whom she had previously known only by name and as a historical figure. Perhaps the spirit of this strong woman, Aunt Emma, was also present. The connection that Emma had hoped mere objects could make for our parents suddenly spoke mutely yet eloquently a generation later. It was as if we were experiencing a family gathering in our house.

Holding Emma's gifts in our hands, we turned and looked again intensely at the watch, It was swinging agitatedly. The tribal elder approached it reverently and began to sing in Potawatomi. The watch danced and continued to dance.

It became particularly agitated when, a half hour later, our visitor prepared to return home.

Shortly after the elder's departure, the watch ceased to pulse.

Since these events, I have moved the watch several times, thinking that perhaps its inner spring mechanism had been activated by my movement. But I could not reactivate the motion. The second hand, a delicate watch face within the watch, never moved one iota when I moved it. The watch clearly was not moving as a result of an unwound spring mechanism.

Asa's watch is now hanging once again, immobile in its little glass house, back on the windowsill, an ever ready gateway to times and people of the not-so-distant past.

Today, two days after the events described above, is the 101st anniversary of Robert Christie's presentation of the watch to my grandfather. It is also the seventy-third anniversary, to the very day, of Ira Hayes' landing on Iwo Jima.

Native Americans measured time by moons, seasons, and important historical events. Did our ancestors know, in their time, from their side, of the anniversaries we calculate? Did they sense a gathering of kin at this place, around these objects, these portals of time? So it would seem. And they took this opportunity to send a message: we are present.

7

ROOTS CONNECT IN VIEUX MONTRÉAL

Family trees, like trees in the forest, find ways of connecting at their roots. Botanists know how this happens in groves of our leafy kin: through underground networks of threadlike filaments called *mycelium*. These ethereal fibers are part of fungi that live symbiotically with their aboveground companions. These fungi supply nutrients and moisture to trees and receive nourishment in exchange.

Mycelium also transmit information that flows throughout the forest. When pests such as caterpillars first begin to attack, the forestwide web of mycelium fibers conveys chemical signals from tree to tree warning of a coming threat. The messages even specify the type of threat and the best organic substances for neighboring trees to use as natural repellents.[1]

Trees also share nutrient resources through their underground root connections. That is why sometimes, when a mature tree is cut in the forest, its stump, although unable to engage in photosynthesis, survives for many years, as if nourished by those life-sustaining intravenous drip bags that we see in a hospital. Trees don't use plastics, though; they rely on their interconnected roots and mycelium networks. This inspiring phenomenon becomes visible above ground when we see a ring of new green stems around the outside of an old stump. It is called *crowning* because the new green growth looks as if someone has placed a leafy crown upon the cut stump.

In the same cooperative manner, seedlings from mother trees await their turn to reach skyward, not competing with their elders until it is time for the ancient ones to walk on. Foresters have noticed that seedlings dwarf themselves, biding time for many years with halted growth, then shooting skyward when it is time to take their place among the families of trees in a mountainside ecosystem. As they mature, these younger trees continue the communal efforts. They too become connected, share nourishment, produce information, and share it with others, not only with their own species, but even with distant cousins. Some of these forest communities of interconnected trees and fungi are thousands of years old, functioning continuously as one living organism. Some massive living organisms in the Pacific Northwest of the United States are so old that their existence may predate the appearance of humans in the Western Hemisphere. Who can even begin to guess what stories they could tell, if only we knew how to listen and connect like the fungi?

I experienced the human equivalent of connected ancient tree roots in Montréal, Canada, and in particular in the network I found in Old Montréal, named, appropriately for my story, in French as "Vieux Montréal." For Native Americans, names are important; we are expected to find guidance or inspiration in our names. So it is not surprising that Vieux Montréal lived up to its name for my family.

What is surprising is that the ancient roots of my family tree in Montréal survived for centuries. And then, in their version of a crowning touch, they regenerated and became visible like the ancient cottonwood I discovered along Lac-Saint-Louis, on the Lachine Route Verte bike path.

For me, Montréal's bike path network acts like mycelium in the forest. It creates delicate connections, regenerating a spiritual life that has long lain dormant and is now crowning. Through this network Carolyn and I have discovered nourishment: offbeat cafés, restaurants, healthy neighborhood food markets. We reciprocate, as when we donate to the

Fig. 7.1. Crowned stump

Maison Ronde, a café in a park that we discovered along the downtown section of the bike path. Le Café de la Maison Ronde serves and supports homeless First Nations urban nomads. And it has provided information to us: through posters about exhibitions in Montréal by and about First Nations peoples, with books on First Nations people in its free lending library, and through chance encounters with caring individuals who are helping displaced indigenous people to cope with urban life. Just like the slow communications of tree roots and mycelium, which take hours or days to deliver information, getting connected on the bike route requires getting into the slow lane and taking time to listen in tree time.

◆◆◆

The Montréal part of my journey homeward begins when Jacques Vieux (1757–1852), a French Canadian fur trapper, or *voyageur,* and my great-great-great-great-grandfather, appeared in my life. Like many of my accounts, the unfolding of this sequence of events involves time that is circular or spiral, rather than linear and unidirectional, flowing from past to present and future. Sometimes my understanding unfolds by looping back to previous events and memories in our family history, snatching them up, and then bearing them vibrantly into the present as if they were occurring now. Events in family history can open our minds and spirits to possibilities lying before us now and in the future. Reimagined futures then open doors to reconnecting with and inter-rogating the past, and thus the cycle continues. Having cycled through such a process repeatedly, I can affirm that it is still possible to maintain a rational sense of linear, calendar time, while simultaneously having a wonderful sense of a conflation of past, present, and future.

This chapter in my story begins with an innocuous tourist adventure.

When Carolyn and I moved to Vermont at the turn of the millen-nium, we began to bicycle on back roads for exercise and relaxation. As a result we tuned in to discussions about good, better, and safer bik-ing trails. Then a folk singer at a Vermont coffeehouse we frequented dropped a casual comment about where he was headed after his gig—to a bike trail along the Chambly Canal in southern Québec Province. He made it sound intriguing, safe, and culturally rich.

Some weeks later, we drove north and tried this totally off-road bike route, a former towpath between the Chambly Canal on one side and the Richelieu River on the other. Within a few years we were exploring hundreds of miles of Route Verte, Québec's world-class bicycle network. We remained "just tourists" for over a decade. Canada was our getaway, a disconnect from the demands of home and a home office. We learned that escaping from our daily routine opens gates to connecting with other levels of experience. Being in another culture was enriching and reminded us that there are social realities beyond those we sometimes struggle with.

Eventually one of our favorite destinations became a bike route along another historic Québec canal and river: the Lachine Canal bike route, which runs from the center of Montréal westward to Lac-Saint-Louis, formed by the St. Lawrence River at the *arrondissement* of Lachine. There we found Chez Charlotte, a cozy bed-and-breakfast that became a kind of bicycling home away from home. The unfamiliar was slowly becoming the familiar.

Lachine received its name from the fact that the St. Lawrence rapids nearby stopped the seventeenth-century explorer René-Robert La Salle as he attempted to find a northwest passage to Asia. In mockery of his failure to get beyond the treacherous rapids, the settlement created here became known as *La Chine,* the French word for "China."

Efforts such as those of La Salle, and Columbus, were motivated by economic considerations and a desire to find an alternate route to the Orient. This is how the native peoples of the Western Hemisphere came to be known as *Indians,* a misnomer applied to the people Columbus encountered upon landing in Hispaniola, which he initially mistook for India.

The conflation of American Indians and Asian Indians is an important part of my journey of discovery in Montréal. It became central when we encountered the Asian Indian artist Manjit Singh Chatrik in an open square just off the bike path in Vieux Montréal, at the eastern end of our canal bike route. Manjit is one of many artists who have small kiosks to display their wares for tourists at the center of the Vieux Port tourist destination. Manjit initially attracted our attention because he paints, among other things, marvelous portraits of Native Americans in vibrant colors—true Asian Indian colors from an Indian palette. He was also warm and friendly, and spoke eloquently about his art and its meaning.

On the day of our first encounter with Manjit, we bicycled back toward our bed-and-breakfast in Lachine. It is about an hour ride. As we biked along, I was mulling over images of Native Americans we had seen in his display. I was also thinking about the condominium advertising sign I had seen earlier the previous morning while riding to the supermarket for breakfast supplies. Out of the corner of my eye, I noticed the sign in front of a modernistic building just two blocks from our bed-and-breakfast. It inspired me to imagine having a permanent residence in Montréal, a place we could come to and leave at will, without the hassle of making reservations in a busy tourist season, without working around weather. I persuaded Carolyn to look at the building and investigate just "to keep our minds open to new opportunities." We had stopped by the condo sales office and picked up a brochure. The whole encounter was initially in the spirit of a travel fantasy, like imaginary trips people plan while reading a travel magazine.

With images of colorful paintings and imagined new living quarters spinning through my mind, we neared Lachine and Chez Charlotte. Out of the corner of my eye, I noticed a gathering of people on the steps of a beautiful nineteenth-century stone cathedral, Saints Anges. It is a bit off the bike path, and we would have missed the group of people had we not, for some reason, left the designated trail and taken the less safe sidewalk for the last few hundred meters of our return trip.

Carolyn and I had heard of classical music concerts being held there, but we had never attended one. A crowd on this particular Sunday suggested to me that this might be such a concert, and our opportunity to explore. I stopped rather abruptly, nearly causing a family biking accident, and looked at my watch. It was five to the hour. I asked Carolyn if she would be interested in going to a concert if this was indeed what the crowd signaled. She suggested we check it out.

After chaining our bikes to a sign, we had to run to the entrance and discovered that the concert was free. The music program was wonderfully varied, and included opera excerpts and Beethoven's Fifth performed by a chamber orchestra. This was not just a serendipitous discovery; it was a musical miracle. I love the Fifth, and as often as it is played, I do not tire of it.

We quickly found our seats in a pew and were panting, out of breath from rushing, and for me, partly from the exhilaration. I had just feasted my eyes on beautiful artwork, bicycled along a safe path by a historic canal, which is my recreational delight, and was now about to enjoy great music.

Indeed the youthful chamber orchestra was inspiring, playing a familiar piece of classical music, risking changes in tempo that teased and played on listeners' expectations. The very familiar became fresh and new.

During the intermission, I looked up at the nineteenth-century Baroque-style painted ceiling in the church and pointed out the celestial composition of angels. I commented to Carolyn, "I think they, and this music, are trying to tell us something about that condo." The spontaneous, semifacetious utterance shocked me. I was not having a religious conversion experience, with angels actually talking to me. I was grasping for words adequate to express an overwhelming sense of beckoning that had been building the entire day. Perhaps Carolyn understood, as, surprisingly, I did not receive a rebuke from my very secular companion. She responded with a gentle, tolerant, bemused eye roll.

We were giddy kids, decades younger than our calendar years, when we finally rode the final half kilometer back to our B and B after the concert. The short distance was a delightful affirmation that we could experience world-class music just minutes from our now familiar lodging, and I began to allow myself to secretly fantasize living more than just occasionally in a more permanent home away from home.

The details of how a fantasy became a reality are of secondary importance. What matters is that while we were waiting for the building to be completed and our little apartment to be finished, we more intensively explored Lachine. And that is how we made the French connection. It occurred just a few hundred meters from the church where we had attended our fateful concert. We were bicycling along the familiar path when we noticed a small stone building on the shore of Lac-Saint-Louis, just a few meters off the trail. It was here that we began to discover a more personal version of Vieux Montréal.

The small and ancient building with its welcoming *Ouvert* (open) sign is the Lachine Fur Museum, a wonderful exhibition explaining the history of French colonization and how it initially depended financially on trading furs with indigenous people. It also presented a wealth of information about the lives and challenges facing the voyageurs, the French fur traders. Over the course of several visits we learned about the competing French and English fur companies. I began to resurrect vague memories of my ancestor, who was purportedly a fur trader.

Then I began to really dig into Vieux family history. Almost immediately, bits of family folklore became uncannily real and within my reach. The fur company that my ancestor worked with had operated out of the building that was now the Lachine Fur Museum. It was their warehouse for furs. My voyageur relative had almost certainly spent time working and walking on the grounds we biked over routinely, since in the eighteenth and nineteenth centuries, Lachine was a collection of fur warehouses and trading markets. Then it dawned on me. We had moved into the neighborhood of my ancestor's workplace. I could not help wondering if it was not just the celestial images and classical music that beckoned me home to Lachine, but also his spirit at work.

Details of Jacques Vieux's life prove fascinating. Born near Montréal in 1757, he first became a *coureur des bois** among the indigenous people. Soon thereafter he became a voyageur, attaching himself to a variety of large fur companies. He quickly became a leading figure in this world of commerce, opening new routes and alliances far west of Montréal. In 1786, he married into a family of French Menominee descent. They had familial connections with the Potawatomi, who at the time were established in the Great Lakes region. That is how the European side of our family first established its link with Native Americans.

---

*A *coureur des bois,* or "wood runner," was an unlicensed, freelance, and barely legitimate trader who exchanged goods, often including alcohol, with Indians in order to obtain furs. A voyageur worked for a chartered colonial company, such as the Northwest Company or Hudson's Bay Company.

Vieux Montréal attracted my mother as well. In her final years she sometimes joined us on our trips north, where she delighted in staying in a historic eighteenth-century inn in Vieux Montréal. It was furnished in eighteenth-century French furniture, both authentic and reproductions, including giant four-poster beds. Candlelit breakfasts by a fireplace seemed like a dreamy step into a lost past. My mother even bought a fur coat in Vieux Montréal. She almost never had occasion to wear it; global warming denied her the need, and she also felt a bit awkward displaying this sign of affluence. What might seem like evidence of an older woman's indulgent lifestyle might have been something else. I think it was her connection to our fur trapper ancestor, a gateway that was unconsciously opening for her at the time.

Montréal became my mother's favorite city, eclipsing even her lifelong love affair with New York and the many European cities she had enjoyed as a tourist. I think that in her final years, she too sensed something welcoming and familiar, even familial, about Vieux Montréal.

On her last trip, my mother had a chance encounter with Manjit. It was autumn, well after the tourist season, and we took a short walk after breakfast to the square at the heart of the old port. It was where Manjit sold his art in warmer months. But the artists' kiosks had been closed for many weeks, and I lamented that she would not meet him. As I pointed to the little buildings and explained that this was where the paintings in our house and on her walls came from, we saw an older man in a turban. Manjit had chosen that morning to drive into Montréal and pick up some items remaining in his stall. He was stunned to see me and was overjoyed to meet my mother. He explained that he was there for no more than twenty minutes and was convinced that this was yet another example of how our lives had become entangled by one chance encounter after another.

When my mother died, we were planning another trip to Montréal. Just as I was about to call and cancel our reservations at the inn she loved, I received an email notifying me that the magical hotel would be closing soon. It had been sold. A window in time had opened to welcome my mother, with a touch of her family history, just as Lachine was becoming a doorway for me.

In recent years, Vieux Montréal and its connection to Lachine have proved to be a continual and increasing source of knowledge about my ancestry and also a wellspring of inspiration. Our Lachine location has kept us within range of the Kahnawake Mohawk radio station and its reminders of the struggle to keep indigenous heritage alive. The same radio station allows us to listen to a spoken Indian language and to remember how fragile this linguistic thread is. We hear about events of interest on the station's news, and enjoy interviews with various First Nations artists, musicians, writers, and performers. Because we now drive through the Kahnawake reserve on our way to Lachine, stopping there for a meal or yet another visit to the shrine of Mohawk Catholic saint Kateri Tekakwitha, it has become part of our frequent pilgrimage to Québec. Even when we are not at Kateri's shrine, I can see its church steeple from our balcony and it reminds me of who I am.

The hours, weeks, and sleepless nights I have invested in trying to fully grasp the wonderful mystery of Kateri have opened an illuminating and dogma-challenging window into the fraught world of Christian-Indian relations. Now, as I read about the great medicine man Black Elk, and efforts to make him a Catholic saint, I approach such matters with layers of intellectual understanding and a personally rooted experience of the intersection of distinct cultures.

For me, Jacques Vieux and Vieux Montréal are a critical part of my wandering home. But for others, non-Native Americans, I hope it is an example of how we may all reconnect with our ancestors if only we are willing to open the gates.

8

ENCOUNTERS WITH KATERI TEKAKWITHA

The home territory of my tribe, the Citizen Potawatomi Nation, is in Shawnee, Oklahoma. I describe myself as being "without reservation" because I have never personally visited Shawnee or our own tribal community. What I know about our Citizen Potawatomi Nation Reservation is based on stories and photos in our tribal newspaper, *Hownikan*, and from family members who have visited there. Prior to the events described below, my only direct acquaintance with other reservations and reserves was based on briefly driving through them. Otherwise my knowledge of them was entirely secondhand, derived from books, articles, and stories of friends.

It therefore came as a great surprise when I encountered Kahnawake (Kahnawá:ke), a major Mohawk reserve. Connecting directly and repeatedly with this community brought me into contact with one of its more famous residents, Kateri Tekakwitha. This development left me reeling day and night for months as I attempted to make sense of increasingly mystifying and intriguing visitations, observations, and reflections associated with a young Mohawk woman who died more than three hundred years ago. How and why she was able, repeatedly, to pull me through the looking glass and have me participate in her past so that I might better understand the present is a tale that sheds light, not only on my awakening, but on the spiritual challenges that indigenous people have faced ever since their first encounters with European settler-colonial culture.

◙ September 2018 ◙

First Encounters

In 2012 Kateri Tekakwitha became the first Native North American to be recognized as a saint by the Catholic Church. Although she had died in 1680, the mystery of her life, and perhaps some manifestations of her spirit, have been present in our house on an intermittent basis. On several occasions I have almost felt as if she has checked in as a guest to better raise her gentle voice continually, day and night, in our residence. Such a claim may sound arrogant and self-aggrandizing. As someone who is not Catholic, I cannot claim a long-standing and intuitive understanding of individual relationships with saints. So let me explain how these perplexing developments came about.

My Kateri connection came about when Ed Shoener, a friend who is a deacon in the Catholic Church, visited, and we spent a considerable amount of time discussing my awakening to our family's Native American heritage. Ed mentioned that we might be interested in St. Kateri Tekakwitha, inasmuch as she is viewed as the patron saint of the environment. Ed and I have a decades-long relationship working together on environmental matters locally and globally. Ed had visited a shrine of Kateri and recommended it. He probably mentioned that the shrine was in upper New York State, but if he did, that fact didn't really register.

A few weeks after Ed's visit, Carolyn and I found ourselves in front of the Shrine of St. Kateri Tekakwitha at the St. Francis Xavier Mission on the Kahnawake Reserve near Montréal. We had not gone to Kahnawake looking for the shrine. We were driving through the reserve looking for Moccasin-Jo coffee. Normally we just drive over and through Kahnawake on a four-lane highway and bridge, on our way to and from Lachine, where we live part-time, just across the St. Lawrence River.

While looking for a store that might sell the coffee, we saw signs for a visitors' center, stopped, and parked. It was closed. Then we noticed the Kateri shrine next door. The shrine was also closed on the weekend, so we did not enter. We walked around the ancient stone buildings, gleaning what facts we could from signs and markers. I left wanting to know more about Kateri and began wondering how to put fragments of her story together. Ed's mention of her shrine began to churn in my memory, and it raised questions about where her real shrine was. Did I misremember what Ed had said about its location?

Upon returning home and doing a quick online search, I discovered that there are two major shrines in North America dedicated to St. Kateri. One was the Kahnawake site in Québec Province, which we had just stumbled across. The other is in New York State, near Schenectady, which was apparently the shrine our friend had visited. Who had the real saint in residence? I began to wonder.

To add further complications, being a Native American, I am also sensitive to the controversies surrounding the Christianization of indigenous peoples. Countless questions began to spin in my head. Who exactly was Kateri Tekakwitha? How and why did she become a Christian, and eventually a Catholic saint? Why would Mohawk people living today in Kahnawake embrace a Christian saint, even as the community struggles to protect its own indigenous culture and reverse many of the more extreme effects of colonialism and assimilation? How was Kateri viewed and treated in her own time? I attempted to respond to these questions as a historian while other rumblings began to reverberate in the back of my mind.

While the detour to find coffee had been unsuccessful, another, more intriguing detour was presenting itself, this one far longer and farther afield. As I looked down that path, unassembled fragments of a historical biography beckoned. It aroused my curiosity, like a half overgrown hiking trail leading into a unknown meadow, which invites and tantalizes with mystery and by encouraging further exploration with an array of wildflowers never seen before and with unidentifiable scents. In such circumstances, who doesn't want to know what lies just beyond the immediately visible? I journeyed in, and this is what I found.

◙ October 2018 ◙

An Enigma Wrapped in Competing Narratives

Kateri was born in 1656 in the Mohawk River Valley of what is now New York State. The village of her birth was Ossernenon, near present-day Auriesville. Kateri's birth name was Ioragode; in English that would be *Sunshine.*

Kateri's father, Kenneronkwa, was a Mohawk chief. Her mother, Tagaskouita, was an Algonquin brought up by French settlers near Trois Rivières, Québec, where she had converted to Christianity. Tagaskouita, captured by a Mohawk raiding party in 1653, was taken south to Ossernenon, where she married.

In 1660, Kateri's parents and brother died in a smallpox epidemic. Kateri barely survived the illness; her face was scarred and her eyes so damaged that she was nearly blind. Four-year-old Kateri was then placed under the care of her uncle, also a chief, and lived in his long-house. At this time her birth name, Ioragode, was replaced with a new name, Tekakwitha, which means "she who pushes or feels her way with her hands" or "she who bumps into things." Presumably the name arose from her habit of feeling her way in the village or forest with out-stretched arms.

In some sources, the name Tekakwitha is translated as "puts things in order." This translation appears in histories of Kateri's life created by her hagiographers, who argue that "she put her life in order in a short time."[1] Such translation might be seen as an attempt to make Kateri appear to be a seer rather than as a person with limited eyesight who stumbled in the forest. But before this highly positive translation is dismissed as a yet another gratuitous misreading of indigenous peoples' names, we need to reflect on our inability to grasp Native American names as something more than exotic. For example, they often involve animal associations, such as "Sitting Bull" or "Black Elk," with connotations non-Natives simply cannot access. Other names use adjectives that on a modern school playground might become sources of taunting and teasing, like "Crazy Horse." Native peoples were more accepting of a wide range of behavior than our contemporary society. Deviations from the norm were seen as normal in the natural world, as well as in the human world, where those with ambiguous gender or behavioral abnormalities were often viewed as spiritually gifted. Such tolerance was a part of life in Kateri's village, which consisted of a blended culture of people from many tribes. Her life and spiritual journey can only be understood in this multicultural context and through the freedom of spiritual choice, as well as the confusion, that it likely presented.

As I kept wandering further down the path of Kateri's biography, I became ever more willing to risk getting deeper into the weeds. After all, my elders and kin in the forest have taught me that weeds are often just wildflowers that we have not taken time to understand and appreciate. Many are wild edibles and medicinal plants hidden in plain sight. Is not Kateri's blindness a metaphor for our own?

Some accounts claim that Kateri eventually regained some or much of her sight, and if stories of her skilled beadwork and other craft talents are true, the recovery must have been considerable. Nevertheless, facial scarring remained, and according to some accounts she covered her head with a blanket to protect her eyes from the sun. She may also have been covering her disfigured face.

In October 1667, the Marquis Alexandre de Prouville de Tracy and several hundred French soldiers attacked the Iroquois Confederation settlements in the Hudson River basin, including Kateri's Mohawk village. This was part of a campaign to eradicate the Iroquois, who were trading furs with the English and who were in conflicts with French settlers.

The Mohawk villagers fled before the attacking French army, which burned their longhouses and destroyed the squash and corn the women had grown and were about to harvest. Facing winter, they were without food. The triumphant French erected a cross on the site of the former villages and celebrated by holding a Catholic Mass.

As was typical of the times, conversion to Christianity occurred in the context of military campaigns. The colonizers saw conversion as a redeeming feature of their conquests, as a noble achievement, beyond political and economic gain. Conversion was also part of a clearly articulated and well-documented agenda to undermine indigenous belief systems and weaken native authority. James Axtell's *The Invasion Within: The Contest of Cultures within Colonial North America* details the strategies used by religious orders and colonists to undermine indigenous religions and lifestyles.

As part of what was described as a peace settlement, the French established a Jesuit outpost in the Hudson Valley to continue missionary work. Some of the Mohawk then relocated to a new site a short distance away from Ossernenon and established the village of Caughnawaga, which means "place of the rapids in the river." Jesuit priests, known to Indians as "Black Robes" because of their long, black clerical clothing, took up residence nearby and learned the Mohawk language. They attempted to gain acceptance and convert indigenous people, initially at least, by seeking to find common ground between the two worldviews. This added yet another cultural dimension to the already blended culture of Kateri's world where indigenous cultures had long intermixed.

The growing Christian influence in Caughnawaga created tensions in Kateri's extended family. In 1667, at the age of eleven, she met three Jesuit missionaries. Attempting to understand such encounters challenges a multitude of strongly held opinions on matters of settler-colonial culture. Some in the Native American community today view the missionary priests as colonizing destroyers of Native beliefs, and present Kateri as the poster child of such victimization. But Kateri's mother had become a Christian while most likely also holding on to many traditional beliefs. So the Black Robes were not the young child's first encounter with a new belief system, and their efforts at engagement may have had some resonance.

Kateri's adopted family was torn by the Black Robes' successful conversions of Mohawks to Christianity. Her cousin adopted the new faith and left Caughnawaga to go to the Jesuit-operated St. Francis Xavier Mission at Sault St. Louis, near Montréal in New France, later to be known by its Mohawk name, Kahnawake. During these developments, Kateri's uncle reportedly attempted to prohibit her contact with the missionaries. But his and other efforts to push back against the Jesuits proved to be a losing struggle.

As Jesuit missionary and French secular influence grew, priests became boundary definers, shifting from cultural bridge building to making increasingly clear distinctions between the two colliding cultures on spiritual matters. During Kateri's formative years, the Jesuits started directly challenging specific Mohawk cultural practices and religious ceremonies.

A critical confrontation happened in 1669 when Garakontié, a chief from a neighboring Onondaga tribe, appeared at Caughnawaga to join in preparations for a Feast of the Dead. This Iroquois ceremony occurred approximately every ten years, or when a tribe relocated and wanted to take remains of the dead with them. Part of the ceremony involved exhumation of buried human remains. Native Americans were respectful and even a bit fearful of their dead, as they believed that spirits lingered in both the flesh and bones. Only when the spirit was freed of a fleshly connection could it finally walk on. Consequently, removing the flesh of exhumed remains was an important part of the Feast of the Dead. Cleaned bones were wrapped in animal skins and transported to a new collective burial site.

Father Pierron, a Jesuit priest in Kateri's village, interrupted the Feast of the Dead ceremony and denounced it as superstitious, demanding that it be stopped if the Mohawk wanted to have harmonious relations with the French. With this threat, he was deftly combining his spiritual influence, his association with French traders, who brought wealth, and the memory of French soldiers, who had recently and could again bring coercive power to bear. The Feast of the Dead was stopped dead in its tracks.

Whatever Pierron said or did must have been compelling. Later in the same year, 1669, Garakontié traveled to Québec, where in the midst of great fanfare he denounced his "superstitious" beliefs, promised to discontinue the traditional practice of polygamy, and was given a Christian name, Daniel, at his baptism. Garakontié's was just one of many high-profile conversions to have occurred in Kateri's life; two years later a respected Mohawk warrior and chief, Ganeagowa, returned from a trip north to the Jesuit settlement of Kahnawake and announced his conversion to Christianity.

A Window on the Human Condition

At this point in the narrative of Kateri Tekakwitha's life, important and universal questions about spirituality arose and gave me pause. They were the incentive for me to create my medicine-wheel chart of the ways of knowing and vetting spiritual encounters, discussed in chapter 4. That chart originated with the following questions, which were prompted by digging into the history of this one woman.

- Was the rising tide of seventeenth-century Native American conversions one of genuine religious and spiritual transformation?
- Were the conversions of Native Americans by the Black Robes due more to true revelations or to brilliant public relations and manipulative storytelling?
- Did Native Americans abandon their traditional beliefs upon conversion to Christianity?

Not surprisingly, the very same types of questions are now being raised with respect to the Lakota medicine man Black Elk, currently being considered for sainthood by the Roman Catholic Church.

Even the early Jesuit missionaries asked such questions. More than one despaired at the daunting task of communicating Christian teachings across linguistic and cultural barriers. For example, one Father Lejeune lamented that "our truths are newer to these Barbarians than the operations of Algebra would be to a person who could only count to ten."[2] Other Jesuits, perhaps doubting their ability to compete with indigenous spiritual leaders, used European medicine to display their shamanlike power. Others used their ability to predict eclipses in order to give an impression of power greater than that of holy leaders within the tribe.

Jesuit translators of the Scriptures frequently departed significantly from their literal meaning in order to make foreign notions familiar to indigenous people. Consequently, some of the historical analysis of this period, particularly by some secular sources and indigenous scholars, echoes the questions stated above. Did the Jesuits stray too far and materially misrepresent the new faith? Did many Indians convert for mere convenience, in order to gain social acceptance among increasingly powerful conquerors? Or did they engage in cultural accommodation outwardly, for economic gain, as did no small number of voyageurs and fur traders, including my own French ancestor who adopted Indian ways? The issue of forced religious conversions has been thrashed out for centuries. Think of Moors in Spain who became Christians after the expulsion of Muslims by Ferdinand and Isabella in 1492.

There is indeed some evidence to support all of the above hypotheses. But ultimately each epoch must be examined on its own terms. As many historians argue, if we really want to understand history, we must deal with it as multiple individual biographies and not just with the broad brushstrokes of collective portraiture. The need for such fine-grained historical evidence was a motive behind my decision to describe one person's early twenty-first-century spiritual journey—my own.

Given the lack of documents in Native Americans' voices about their own conversions to Christianity, we should hesitate to give definitive answers for entire populations or deliver sweeping verdicts on the authenticity of their religious experiences. However, if Kateri Tekakwitha's life is any indication, colonial religious conversion was at least sometimes profound and genuine, and it often brought unimaginable solace.

A Counternarrative

The opportunities and attractions offered by permeable cultural frontiers in seventeenth-century North America are most astoundingly documented, not in Indian conversions to Christianity, but in English settler assimilations to French Catholic communities and Native American tribes. English colonists were often abducted by Indians raiding New England settlements. Many hundreds were taken captive. Some captives were killed. However, many of the survivors adapted to their new lives and apparently found comforting new identities and lives among the "savages."

English Protestant settler families were often shocked and dismayed when they had opportunities to ransom and reunite lost family members, only to discover that they typically sought to remain in their adopted Indian communities. For example, in 1704, more than 100 captives were taken from Deerfield, Massachusetts, north to New France. The colony's minister was ransomed, but his daughter was kept by the Mohawks, married into the tribe, had children, and chose to stay with her new family instead of returning to her New England roots. Settler abductions in the later eighteenth century follow a different pattern, with more abductees seeking escape and return to settler culture. But again, our understanding of events needs to be fine-grained and context-specific. Seventeenth-century indigenous culture was still largely intact and coherent. Native American settlements retained much of their ability to be self-sustaining and live close to nature. They were almost certainly far more attractive to Europeans than the disrupted life of Indians in the eighteenth and nineteenth centuries.

But it was not just Indian life that some New England settlers found more attractive than the rigid Puritan society from which they were snatched. English captives originally taken by Indians who were ransomed from the Indians by French settlers and adopted French Catholicism also typically sought to stick with their new lives. This phenomenon has been documented and analyzed by Axtell in *The Invasion Within.**

While Axtell painstakingly examines multiple layers of both spiritual and coercive factors involved in the conversion of Indians to Christianity and other European values, his examination of why white settlers were attracted to Indian spiritual values and lifestyles is less probing. This most likely demonstrates the limitations imposed by a mainstream, Eurocentric cultural perspective. It limits the analyst's historical imagination in fully comprehending indigenous cultural appeal. This is made evident when Axtell's analysis of settler conversions falls short of and even contradicts the rest of his book, which focuses on the nuances of Jesuit and Anglican spiritual conversion strategies. After documenting the numbers of conversions of white settlers to Indian and French culture, Axtell barely questions why some settlers may have found Catholicism and Native spirituality, not to mention indigenous and French lifestyles, more appealing than Puritan culture. This is all the more remarkable given the title and theme of his book: a contest of cultures.

Axtell stresses that the conflict between the settler-colonists and the indigenous peoples was at its foundation a struggle for the hearts and minds of opponents:

> The contest of cultures in colonial North America was far from one sided. Despite superior technologies, aggressive religions, prolific populations, and well-articulated ideologies of imperialism, the

---

*See especially his section on Protestant converts to French Catholicism in the chapter on "The English Apostates," and his examination of settlers who struggled with and often clung to their adopted Native American identity in the chapter on "The White Indians" (Axtell, *Invasion Within*, 287–301; 302–27).

French and English invaders enjoyed no monopoly of success in converting enemies to their way of life. In fact, the Indian defenders of the continent were more successful, psychologically if not numerically, than either of their European rivals. . . . the Indians, despite all odds, succeeded in seducing French and English colonists in numbers so alarming to European sensibilities that the natives were conceded to be, in effect, the best cultural missionaries and educators on the continent.[3]

For me, this paragraph exemplifies both the strength and the weakness of non-Indian academic attempts to understand the Native American experience. On the positive side, a well-honed intellect knows how to answer some questions and brings masses of factual and analytical material to bear. On the other hand, even a honed rational intellect can be blind to certain dimensions of spirituality. Although Axtell tunes in to the appeal of Jesuit Christianity for Indians, he does not even ask about the comparative appeal of Native American spirituality, or for that matter the Catholic faith, for seventeenth-century Anglican and Puritan settler-colonists.

Perhaps the conversion of English abductees can be understood with a simple act of historical imagination. What was the single greatest physical, psychological, and spiritual challenge facing settler-colonists on a daily basis? The answer is obvious and is found in settler journals. Above and beyond the threat of Indian raiding parties or wars involving competing European nations was the ferocity of Mother Nature, the vast and mysterious wilderness. It initially threatened, or destroyed, every colonial settlement effort. Neither Anglican nor Puritan nor Catholic cosmology dealt with this matter. They simply relegated the "desolate wilderness" to a devilish status of chaos, to be tamed and turned as quickly as possible into a replica of European agriculture.

No settler notion illustrates the blind folly of this worldview better than the miserably failed efforts of mid-seventeenth-century English and French colonizers to persuade Indians to give up their sustainable seminomadic practices of hunting and gathering, or settlement agronomy, which was based on growing such traditional foods as the Three Sisters, a traditional interplanting of corn, squash, and beans. The Indians were using hoes made of clamshells. The French and English wanted them to settle down in one place, use plows and other tools they could buy, take on debt (which would be a form of control), and work longer hours to produce food. White settlers were troubled and confounded by the bounty that Indians gained from their "primitive" techniques while the new arrivals often labored to produce enough food.

Equally disorienting for settlers was the fact that their Eurocentric worldview and religion did not adequately acknowledge the magnificent spiritual bounty and natural gifts that Mother Earth offered in the New World. The Earth that the settlers claimed was, for them, merely a resource to be harvested, mined, and exploited. Native Americans, in stark contrast, revered Mother Earth as sacred, viewing flora and fauna as their kin. Native Americans both embraced and felt the embrace of this natural world.

While Axtell states that the Indians "were conceded to be, in effect, the best cultural missionaries and educators on the continent," he fails to inquire about how indigenous peoples came to this knowledge. Had he done so, he would have discovered that it was Mother Earth and the great wilderness, the endless forest. That was the sacred text, the equivalent of the Bible, for indigenous people.

The ability of Native Americans to make the natural world meaningful to the settlers, when it had been illegible and fearsome to Europeans, most likely played a prominent role in settler conversions. Today the same message is bringing people around the globe to a greater appreciation of the wisdom of indigenous cultures. It is no coincidence that this interest grows as natural phenomena are once again seemingly more threatening, more inscrutable, and beyond our ability to manage.

I suspect that a careful rereading of the journals of captive and abducted settlers will eventually reveal a record of spiritual encounters with the natural world similar to that which I am personally documenting in this book. Historians will need to read carefully between the lines, because such sentiments would have been buried beneath layers of cultural blindness and a lack of vocabulary adequate to express engagement with an animist worldview. Only when this chapter of colonial history is finally written will we fully understand the dynamics of the "contest of cultures" that began in the seventeenth century and continues to the present. Only then will we be able to fully benefit from the crosscurrents of such cultural interaction.

Je suis une personne abductée; nous sommes tous des personnes abductées*

How does this apply to me and to my journey of spiritual discovery? I continually ask if, like Kateri Tekakwitha, I am an outsider in my own culture of birth, and if I am on the verge of finding something more meaningful and informative in a spiritually enriching alternative placed before me. How many of us awaken now daily feeling like strangers in a new "desolate wilderness" not of our own creation?

I have also tried to honestly portray my own journey, even referring to the appearance of ancestral spirits and forest kin as something like a SWAT team intervention bursting into my secularly ordered world. It is not a far-fetched leap of imagination to see parallels between my somewhat compelled awakening and the experiences of the seventeenth-century abductees. I will develop this notion in later chapters. For now I will simply state that many are the days when I awaken on the Indian side of the looking glass, and I hesitate to fully leave behind the nighttime peace of the sleeping porch and the sounds of my natural kin to step back into the house and my world of modern conveniences and an impersonal, mechanistic worldview. In such moments I must ask myself if it is my ancestors and natural kin who have abducted me, or if it is my everyday surroundings with their incessant drumbeat of advertising, noise, and bright lights that have abducted my spirit instead.

---

*"I am an abducted person; we are all abductees."

With that heightened sense of self-awareness and sense of kinship with my subject matter, I now return to Kateri's story.

From Stumbling Pathfinder to Visionary Leader

We are stepping back into Kateri's world at a time when conflict over religious beliefs, practices, and affiliations was disrupting the longhouse of her adopted family.

Kateri, then still called Tekakwitha, was adding fuel to the fires of family discontent when she balked at other traditional nonreligious tribal practices. For example, she resisted the idea of a betrothal at age thirteen, when such an event normally occurred. In 1673, when she was seventeen, this conflict reached a boiling point when her adoptive mother and an aunt arranged for another ceremony of betrothal, from which she fled and hid in the forest. Her relatives and community then unleashed a campaign of insults, threats, and punitive workloads in an unsuccessful attempt to compel the independent-minded young woman to comply with their expectations.

In 1674, Tekakwitha began studying the catechism* with a Jesuit priest. Here records disagree significantly. Some accounts, such that of Claude Chauchetière, one of her two contemporary biographers, suggest that she was persecuted for her independent beliefs, especially as they became increasingly associated with Christianity.[4] Some non-contemporaries report that she suffered from accusations of sorcery and even experienced violence for her embrace of Christianity. For example, one standard account reports that "harassed, stoned, and threatened with torture in her home village, she fled 200 miles (320 km) to the Christian Indian mission of St Francis Xavier at Sault Saint-Louis, near Montreal."[5] The *Dictionary of Canadian Biography* states, without citing any sources, that her "conversion brought upon her a veritable persecution. She was even threatened with death."[6] Other accounts suggest

---

*The catechism is a compilation of the fundamental principles of the Catholic faith, in the form of questions and answers.

that there were considerable tensions, but nothing bordering on coercion, from her indigenous family and community.

Even with such uncertainty and ambiguity in historical accounts, it is reasonable to assume that the psychological toll on Tekakwitha must have been mounting. As a result, she journeyed northward in 1676 at the age of nineteen. She joined a growing number of female Iroquois converts at the Jesuit mission of St. Francis Xavier Mission at Sault-Saint-Louis. Here she was baptized and assumed the Christian name Catherine, Kateri in Mohawk.

To understand the process of missionary conversions in the seventeenth and eighteenth centuries, and in particular the case immediately before us, we need to understand Kateri's formal adoption of Christianity within her historical and unique biographical context.[7]

First, the possession and exercise of power in New France during Kateri's lifetime was uniquely, if fleetingly, balanced. Competing French, English, and Dutch spheres of influence kept these aspiring colonial powers in a precarious and ever-changing state, where none were totally secure. Each of the European colonizers sought to use a shifting set of alliances with Native American tribes in order to gain dominance in surrogate struggles for European wars that were fought partly in North America. However, indigenous peoples were more than pawns in a foreign chess game of realpolitik and diplomacy. They too used shifting alliances with foreign allies and adversaries to their own benefit. Eventually these fluid alliances would be formalized and stabilized, with clear spheres of influence and growing European military and cultural hegemony. But during Kateri's lifetime, the kind of settler-colonial domination that came to characterize eighteenth- and nineteenth-century North America did not yet apply. It would be a mistake to project a notion of clear and unambiguous dominance, either military or cultural, backward in time.

Second, before making harsh judgments about the purportedly unilateral imposition of European religious practices upon indigenous spiritual blank slates, we need to recognize that the appeal of foreign notions of spirituality can only be understood in the context of precolonial indigenous religious practices, which were strong and viable.

Such a perspective is called for when we examine the practice of celibacy by some native converts such as Kateri. We can begin by recognizing that many young women in Europe, over many centuries, joined holy orders and took up vows of celibacy in order to escape marriage and other difficulties, such as a high probability of death from multiple childbirths and low social and economic status in a patriarchal world. While the Catholic culture of seventeenth-century French Canada can hardly be represented as a feminist refuge, by comparative standards it may well have been a refuge for Kateri.

Third, we need to look at the harsh realities of Kateri's own life and times. Her mother had been abducted by a Mohawk raiding party. Kateri's mother had purportedly attracted the attention of a potential husband because of her hard work and physical strength. These may have been practical considerations, much as potential mates today quietly calculate the life opportunities (wealth, genetic heritage, social status) presented by various marital possibilities. As is so often the case with such a cold social calculus, the resulting relationships are exploitative and unsatisfying for the exploited. Such discouraging marital realities may have been quite pervasive in Kateri's world.

Furthermore, in a warrior culture wracked by decades of continual brutal fighting and waves of epidemics, we could reasonably expect that the syndrome we now understand as posttraumatic stress disorder (PTSD) may have taken hold in Kateri's world. These communal stressors could easily have spilled over to a further complication: domestic violence. This is not wild speculation. Reading between the lines of Chauchetière's seventeenth-century description of life at the Mission of Sault-Saint-Louis and the Kahnawake community, we can hear subtle hints of interpersonal, intrafamilial sexual violence.

Most significantly, we read over and over how both indigenous people and Jesuits fought to keep alcohol and drunkenness out of the

Indian communities. The theme of pushing back against French colonial government and the fur traders' efforts to introduce alcohol, even to the Sault-Saint-Louis mission community, permeates Chauchetière's account. Alcohol was an unwelcome plague on Native American society, one to which French officials turned a blind eye, or even promoted as a tool for rigging negotiations and trade deals. Drunken Indians could be, and often were, persuaded to sign agreements they barely understood when sober. Drunken Indians frequently recovered from alcohol-saturated trade negotiations to discover that some or all of their bartered goods were gone.

In the seventeenth century, as today, alcohol abuse went hand in hand with domestic violence. But it was not the sole cause, as we have evidence of such violence before the appearance of either alcohol or white settler-colonial culture. Forensic archaeologists have recently been looking at Native American skeletons in a new light. (Their findings are controversial and are currently limited to the Southwest and to a period many centuries before Kateri's lifetime.) Female skeletons frequently display facial and head trauma that was not fatal but suggests a degree of ongoing, normalized, intrafamilial brutality. In addition, there is ample skeletal evidence that many Native American women suffered from physically brutal, occasionally fatal overwork.[8]

We can never know with any certainty what went on in Kateri's adopted family, her longhouse, or her community. But it is reasonable to assume that, even within a matrilineal Native American society such as the Iroquois, high levels of intrafamilial violence against women might well have occurred in unprecedentedly stressful times. Kateri's conversion and her decision to leave her place of birth need to be understood in this context.

Before constructing an idealized image of a cozy refuge within the Jesuit Iroquois community at Sault-Saint-Louis, to which Kateri fled, we need to confront Kateri's religious practices during her time there. These practices were made evident to me just as I felt myself to be on the cusp of a fresh and less emotionally wrenching understanding of her life story, which had become a complicated historical account and spiritual journey for me.

The disquieting revelations appear when we examine what Kateri's hagiographers pointed to as signs of her saintliness in her final years at Sault-Saint-Louis: her practices of mortification of the flesh. These facts have been used as evidence by some who portray Kateri as a young Mohawk woman victimized by Catholic missionary zealots and alien European cultural values. Although today the Catholic Church gives such practices scant attention, and delicately manages their rare continuation, the seventeenth century was very different. Such practices were relatively common. However, the acceptance of these practices in a culture and society a long ocean voyage away does not justify the conclusion that Kateri's rather extreme use of self-mortification came primarily from foreign influences.

Among the Mohawk, various forms of mortification of the flesh, for example using thorns to pierce one's flesh, extreme fasting, immersion in winter ice baths, and self-burning, were quite common among both men and women.[9] Possibly, then, Kateri's self-mortification, which has sometimes been attributed solely to Catholic teachings, was most likely a carryover from her own indigenous culture.

Even so, critics of Kateri's conversion may still ask if her extreme practices of mortification might not have been encouraged to a pathological degree by the Jesuit environment at Sault-Saint-Louis. After all, some accounts of her death suggest a possible connection between her debilitating self-mortification and the illness that took her life. I will admit that I struggled with this possibility myself. But in the end I concluded that such an assertion reveals an unwillingness to let go of dogmatic antisettler and anticolonial narratives.

The answer is clear from the historical accounts. Kateri's mentor priest is on the written record as seeing moderate practices of mortification of the flesh as a sign of Native American spiritual depth. But he also repeatedly cautioned Kateri against extreme and excessive indulgence in self-inflicted mortification, warning that in view of her poor health, such activity threatened her life.[10] There is also evidence that Kateri may have moderated her practices somewhat in response to her mentor's guidance.

Perhaps with this perspective, we can begin to understand Kateri's final three years at Sault-Saint-Louis. In particular, we can better imagine the impact of her attempt to create something approximating a new religious group of Native people on the Île aux Hérons (Heron Island), across the river from the mission. The Jesuits may well have viewed this effort as a challenge to their own religious sodality, the Confraternity of the Holy Family,[11] which was their attempt to create a social network that was one step short of a formal religious order, at the "praying town" of Sault-Saint-Louis.

Kateri was discouraged from creating a competing social structure, just as she was discouraged from overindulging in self-mortification. This is no coincidence. Her Jesuit mentors saw her unusually intense self-mortification practices as a powerful source of her unique claim to purity and hence spiritual authority. Such authority could become a centrifugal force in the Sault-Saint-Louis community, possibly challenging Jesuit control of Christian thought, behavior, and social networks. The level of this perceived threat is revealed in the account of a vision that Claude Chauchetière, one of Kateri's mentors, reported. In the vision Kateri appears and prophesizes the destruction of the community's church.[12]

Kateri and the other female converts at Sault-Saint-Louis may also have been perceived as threatening traditional social and gender roles in Mohawk society. Kateri's example of refusing marriage was just the beginning of what today might be viewed as a feminist challenge to male dominance. Defying her uncle, her tribe, and to some degree the Black Robes, she and others were criticized for their assertiveness.

During this time, such gender norm breaking was also an issue in other tribes. For example, at a tribal council of the Dene Chippewa, or "Montagnais," male leaders blamed women's assertiveness for a host of problems. Montagnais women in turn complained to the Jesuits as follows:

"It is you women", they [the men] said to us [the women], "who are the cause of our misfortunes . . . , it is you who keep the demons among us. You do not urge to be baptized; you must not be satisfied to ask this favor only once from the Fathers, you must importune them. You are lazy about going to prayers; when you pass before the cross, you never salute it; you wish to be independent. Now know that you will obey your husbands."[13]

These smoldering gender power struggles were to some degree an unanticipated consequence of Jesuit teachings. The Jesuits saw patriarchy as a social good and sought to undermine matrilineal traditions in Mohawk society, in which clan mothers appointed chiefs and could play a role in deposing them. Tribal membership descended matrilineally, as did property ownership. However, just as some Mohawk men sought to use their newfound Christian faith to erode female influence, Mohawk female converts used Christian teachings to reassert their traditional influence. They emphasized the central role of the Virgin Mary in Christian worship and took inspiration from numerous female saints. The new faith proved to be a double-edged sword in the struggle of gender politics.

If we examine the evidence of Kateri's life at Sault-Saint-Louis, we may conclude that the Iroquois converts "did not become Christian in the way the Jesuits intended; instead they transformed Christianity into an Iroquois religion."[14]

Kateri Tekakwitha died on April 17, 1680.

Path to Sainthood

Immediately upon her death, what many consider to be her first miracle was reported by Pierre Cholenec, her mentor and biographer, who wrote, "This face, so marked and swarthy, suddenly changed about a quarter of an hour after her death, and became in a moment so beautiful and so white that I observed it immediately."[15] This was announced at once as evidence of her saintliness. The transformation may have been a normal process of facial skin color change upon death. In fact, such questions are usually asked by the Catholic Church's Congregation for the Causes of Saints, which typically takes years to rigorously investigate claims of miracles and petitions for sainthood.

The fact that Kateri's first possible miracle transformed her from a dark-skinned Native American to someone "lily-white," like the French fleur-de-lis, has not been lost on Native Americans who see this as European society's first cultural appropriation after her death. The same discomfort surrounds her title "Lily of the Mohawk." To this day controversy surrounds the claim of lilylike whiteness. It is found even in the souvenir shop and museum attached to Kateri's shrine in Kahnawake, where various images of her, some ancient and some contemporary, sit side by side. Some images portray her as dark-skinned, holding a turtle and a tree. Others portray her as fair-skinned, cosmetically perfect, and airbrushed, like a model on a fashion magazine cover, holding a white lily.

The Catholic Church typically requires verification of two miracles for sainthood. But in 1980, Pope John Paul II waived the requirement in Kateri's case, citing the difficulty of confirming details of an incident said to have occurred hundreds of years ago. The Canadian Conference of Catholic Bishops states, "Kateri was declared Venerable by Pope Pius XII on January 3, 1943, and beatified by Pope John Paul II in 1980. On December 19, 2011, Pope Benedict XVI signed a decree officially acknowledging another miracle attributed to her intervention."[16]

Again we must return to the context of Kateri's death. New France, unlike Europe, did not have an established tradition of saints, nor did it have access to saints' relics. For the faithful, and especially for missionaries, this was a serious problem. For Catholics, saints are intermediaries, potential bearers of messages and prayers to God. Their graves are pilgrimage sites. Their bones, and objects associated with them, become cherished items in ritual and in establishing sacred places.

In this context, the realm of sacred space ultimately depends upon the supply of and access to relics. Kateri died in a spiritual economy of scarcity of relics. Not surprisingly, her bones, dust from her tomb, and objects she purportedly touched all became important first-order relics immediately upon her death. Jesuits and Indian converts working to spread Christianity sought to have a personal connection with Kateri; her history after death includes numerous accounts of which ossuary remains went where. Fragments became smaller and smaller as the demand for her relics grew and her bones were divided.[17] Within four years of her death, a small chapel was erected for her veneration at Kahnawake, and it began to attract pilgrims.

Momentum built over subsequent centuries to advance Kateri Tekakwitha's status from that of just one of many holy people to beatification and then canonization. The process of canonization, official Catholic designation of sainthood, is typically long, drawn out, and bureaucratic. In 1943, Pope Pius XII signed a decree finally declaring Catherine Tekakwitha "Venerable."[18]

The final hurdle en route to sainthood for the Catholic faithful is a certified full-blown second miracle. An opportunity for meeting this requirement for Kateri's case occurred in 2006 with the cure of a young Indian boy in California who was purportedly near death with a facial wound and flesh-eating bacterial infection that medical science was unable to address successfully. Sister Kateri Mitchell, named for Kateri Tekakwitha and who is also a Mohawk, laid a relic of Kateri on the suffering boy's pillow. His surprising turnaround and healing was declared a second miracle by Pope Benedict XVI in 2011.

In 2012, Kateri Tekakwitha entered the pantheon of Catholic sainthood, and the world took notice. The action was widely misreported as the first canonization of a Native American.

In fact, in 2002 the church had canonized Juan Diego, born Cuauhtlatoatzin (Talking Eagle) in 1474 and raised in the Aztec religion. In 1531, he had several visions of a young woman who was later venerated as Our Lady of Guadalupe. He is considered to be the first indigenous American to be canonized. But since he was born in Mexico,

Kateri Tekakwitha is routinely, though inaccurately, recognized as the first American saint.

Welcome Visitations and Guides

When I finally finished exploring Kateri's biography, I expected to get some closure on the questions that kept me awake so many nights writing and researching. But the facts of her biography and the web of analysis I had spun did not provide those insights.

Instead, deeper understanding first began to arrive—as is often the case in my life now—with gentle signals born on the wings of natural kin and expressed in their nonhuman voices. The first visitations occurred while I worked in the garden pondering questions about Kateri. When I wrote that she sometimes seemed to follow me everywhere, I was not exaggerating. Even my downtime activities did not escape unexpected visitations or insights, interrupting my other work. As a result, I needed to occasionally go inside and record what was happening or do a quick online search for a few more basic facts about Kateri that my musings demanded be answered sooner rather than later.

After one such break from harvesting onions, when I went back outside, I noticed two red-tailed hawks soaring above. Round and round they went, making their wonderful calls.

My first thoughts were, "Oh, listen to the bald eagles!" Then I remembered that movie soundtracks use the calls of red-tailed hawks instead of those of the bald eagle when showcasing birds of prey. Apparently Hollywood moviemakers do not consider the eagle's true voice to be powerful and majestic enough to be used as the voice of their country's symbol. As a result, I had once confused the two, and still often do.

The hawks returned several times over the following days, during which time I once again became quite preoccupied with Kateri, even into the middle of the night. As a result of my preoccupation and research, I was buried in a pile of biographical information, much of it fragmented and seemingly contradictory. As I began slowly digging out from under the mountain of stories, tributes, and records, I looked desperately for some facts that would give a deeper understanding of the saint as a whole person, her humanity.

But it was not data that pointed the way to deeper understanding. It was the message of the hawks. They alerted me to the fact that we often want our cultural symbols to be majestic in proportion to our understanding of the power invested in them. This projection of our own values is most disruptive when it is brought to bear on an event or life that is distant in time and place. There are no contemporaries to check facts.

Often we want our heroes and saints to be bold, loud, and commanding, like cymbals in a marching band. As a result we rarely listen to the subtler, gentler voices that speak wisely out of the past, sometimes just whispering as they bring messages designed to nudge us into reconsidering our preconceptions in a quieter, slower, and more reflective way.

In my investigation, the hawks were warning me, Kateri was suffering from the same fate she suffered in her life, and the fate suffered by the eagles. I was failing to hear her genuine voice. I was instead trying to give her the commanding voice of a red-tailed hawk when an eagle's quieter wisdom was drifting in the air. I was imposing my notions of what an outspoken young Native American should be, even as I was confronted with fragments of a quite different story—about a troubled young soul seeking peace amid clashing human cultures by escaping into the forest.

The Canadian Lily of the Mohawk

One day, when Carolyn and I were first exploring the land in Vermont where we would eventually build our house, and before the Coy-Wolves greeted us, we walked around the boundary of wetlands that were part of our property. Among the many plants and wildflowers stood one remarkable white flower that I recognized as a lily. It grew on top of a stem that was two meters tall but no thicker than a pencil. I could not understand how such a delicate plant could stand in the wind. Our guide to Vermont wildflowers indicated that we had a Canada lily or meadow lily (*Lilium canadense*) in a somewhat rare white variation. We have never seen the flower again. The lily had made her glorious ephemeral appearance and then moved on.

At the time I imagined that a bird had transported the seed south from Canada. Or perhaps the plant was the descendant of a long line of ancestors who were slowly carried south on winds, in waters, or in soil moved 15,000 years ago by glaciers that plowed the valley of what would become the Champlain Sea.

Now, after encountering Kateri Tekakwitha, if and when this beautiful cousin ever returns to grace our wetlands, I will think of ki as "Lily of the Mohawk," a fleur-de-lis who refused to be domesticated, and who stood tall because she was so deeply rooted in Mother Earth.

With such thoughts, I returned to the connection that our friend the Catholic deacon had used in introducing us to Kateri Tekakwitha: her role as patron saint of the environment. None of the historical sources I had consulted explained how she was given this attribution. The designation was not made in her Positio, the documents presented to the Vatican in support of her canonization. Kateri's deep personal and cultural connections with the natural world rose to the forefront at the time of her canonization. Then church officials and Catholic ecology organizations decided to signal continuity with indigenous culture by informally declaring her status as patron saint of the environment.[19] It was a spontaneous grassroots development, like the appearance of the lily in our wetland.

But the full implications of her Native origins, of a spirituality deeply rooted in continual connections with nature, still seemed more like an add-on than a core element of the official narrative. Bringing this to the forefront raises the risk of accusations that Catholic belief is being subordinated to Native American animism or pantheism

Fig. 8.1. Canada lily found in Vermont
Photo courtesy of Kate Carter, author of Wildflowers of Vermont

(or vice versa). Catholic doctrine is somewhat ambiguous about the divine status of the natural world. From the Catholic perspective, the flora, fauna, and natural features of the Earth are the creation of God. They warrant reverence because they are God-given. But elevating the natural realm to the status of the sacred in its own right risks glorifying nature on its own, a notion that can make some Catholic theologians uncomfortable.

Native Americans, by contrast, view Mother Earth as sacred. They ascribe spiritual equality to flora, fauna, and natural objects, clearly putting the natural realm on an equal basis with humans, and typically with the Creator as well. Proponents of Native American and Christian perspectives normally avoid emphasizing their differences and instead seek to emphasize common ground. There is nevertheless a difference in worldviews.

For me, this creative tension is the spiritual frontier where Kateri Tekakwitha comes alive. I find myself returning again and again to the names of the two villages where she spent most of her life: Caughnawaga, along the Mohawk River, and Kahnawake, along the St. Lawrence River. Both place names are Roman-alphabet representations of the same Mohawk word for "at the wild water," the turbulent waters of rapids found in the rivers adjacent to both of Kateri's dwelling places. Both place names reflect the power of crosscurrents and the challenges of navigating such turbulence.

Mother Nature was once again acting as my inspiration and guide. Just as names given to Native American people are said to reflect something of their essence, Caughnawaga and Kahnawake reveal a deeper truth. They were places of intense cultural, spiritual, and social crosscurrents. Such currents are capable of knocking one off firm footing, as I discovered at age twelve when I attempted to cross knee-deep rapids in the Moose River near my family's summer cottage. I was nearly knocked off my feet and swept away. Kateri must have experienced such a struggle to remain on her own two spiritual feet many times.

A brief escape from being knee-deep in the undercurrents of crosscultural encounters must have been a cherished moment in Kateri's life. That gift was given to her on a ten-day journey from her place of birth northward to Kahnawake. She traveled by canoe through the entire length of what is today Lake George and Lake Champlain. The journey would have been breathtakingly beautiful and peaceful—a pilgrimage more than an escape.

Pilgrimages typically are ordeals, acts of self-abnegation and purification, undertaken en route to a destination where a transformative spiritual experience is anticipated. But in Kateri's case, her journey toward a religious community may have been part of her spiritual destiny, both a delight and an important contribution to her emerging identity as both a Christian and Native American religious leader.

Dual Spirituality in Native American Religion

Native American history written both by indigenous people and European descendants typically discusses assimilation, and religious encounters in particular, in terms of absolute conversion, as if the process were, for good or bad, a one-way street, or, more appropriately, a toll highway with a high admission price. That price is complete and total renunciation of traditional beliefs so that a new worldview can take root unchallenged. Indeed for many Native Americans, assimilation and conversion were akin to being dipped, or nearly drowned, in a bath of chlorine bleach, from which they emerged, as is alleged with Kateri Tekakwitha, miraculously and entirely whitened. This is the assumption behind the dictum of American Indian school founder Captain Richard Henry Pratt: "Kill the Indian and save the man."

However, careful reading between the lines of indigenous biography suggests a different and far more complex tale—one of dual spirituality. While the assertion is superficially contradictory, more often than not Native Americans assimilated or converted while continuing to boldly affirm much of their traditional spirituality. Privately, out of the reach of the spying eyes of Bureau of Indian Affairs agents, they continued to practice and embrace traditional ways. When Charles Eastman, the most famous late nineteenth- and early twentieth-century Native American, grew old, he returned to his Canadian cabin in the woods and the spiritual context of his Indian youth. Chicago's model success story of assimilation, Dr. Carlos Montezuma, returned to his reservation to die. Black Elk, the great Lakota medicine man, continued to engage with his traditional spirituality while acting as a Catholic catechist.

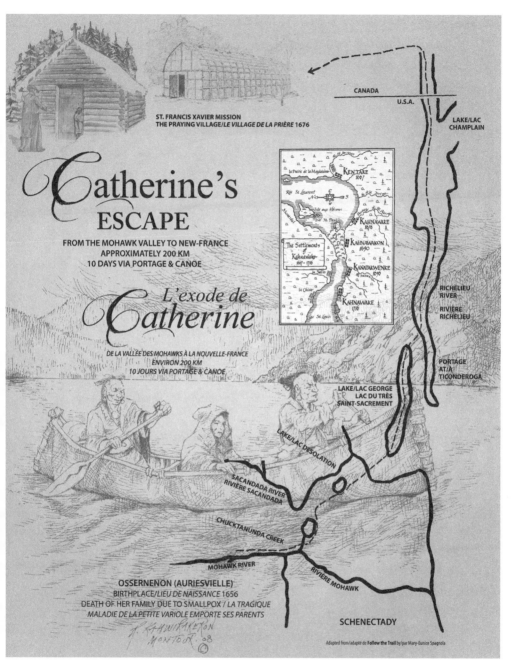

Fig. 8.2. Kateri's journey north
Depiction courtesy of St. Kateri Tekakwitha Interpretative Center, Kahnawake

Indeed, as I reflected on the rapids that run near Kateri's Kahnawake shrine and our residence across the St. Lawrence, I was reminded of just how much of her world and that of the settlers in seventeenth-century New France and New England was shaped by the natural environment. Three centuries later, insulated from the natural elements by modern technology, we can easily fail to understand how the lives of Native Americans and settler-colonists were shaped and dominated by their natural surroundings.

This realization reminded me that intellectual training, although a useful analytical tool, can serve as blinders. For months, I had been looking at Kateri Tekakwitha's world as if it were shaped primarily by social forces. If there were crosscurrents, they were cultural. Despite my work on environmental issues, I was slow to recognize that one of the most important parts of Kateri's message to us in the twenty-first century is about our continuing dependence on and subjugation to the forces of nature.

I struggle daily to free myself from the prevailing culture, which suggests that we control Mother Nature. Living across the St. Lawrence River, opposite Kateri's shrine in Lachine, is a reminder that recent human history is built on our aspiration to dominate nature. Every time I go bicycling along the Lachine Canal, I am aware of the fact that humans eventually built transport routes around the barrier rapids in the St. Lawrence River at Kahnawake. The Lachine Canal, dug and built along the north shore of the St. Lawrence in the early decades of the nineteenth century, was an enormous effort that came at the price of many lives. The opening of the St. Lawrence Seaway on the south shore in 1959 was heralded as a modern engineering marvel. Unfortunately, it was constructed partly on land taken from the Mohawk Reserve at Kahnawake in exchange for meager payments on appropriated land and a swimming pool as compensation for miles of lost riverfront and beaches.[20] The Mohawk lost direct access to their fishing grounds. Today, as you stand at the entrance to the Kateri shrine, you may see giant ships passing, a stone's throw away.

Some of us are slowly returning to a worldview recognizing that forces of nature are not overcome without a great cost. It is a lesson that Kateri Tekakwitha, the Mohawks and the other indigenous peoples, and the European settlers of her day would have easily understood. They negotiated continually with Mother Nature. They traveled in birchbark canoes, their sailing ships being useless in shallow rivers or through and around rapids. The rhythm of their commerce was determined by the seasons. Their very survival depended upon the bounty and gifts of the land, forests, and waterways. Such a humbly realistic worldview is slowly regaining traction in contemporary thought and among some policy makers.

But many of our leaders, in whose hands our species' destiny rests, are in denial about the environmental crises before them. In my scheme of the four pathways to knowledge, they seem unable to observe. Often they do not reflect, except to construct elaborate arguments rejecting the findings of science, which challenge their blind pursuit of short-term economic gain. In their hermetically sealed urban penthouses and offices, they are beyond the reach of visitations or direct spiritual connections with Mother Earth.

Regrettably, many of those who do see the problems believe we can bioengineer our way out of current environmental crises. They are determined to protect our levels of consumption and are very little concerned about protecting Mother Earth. As a result, the number of environmental refugees, those forced to relocate because of flooding, lack of water, or lack of arable land, is increasing and will most likely increase exponentially in the coming decades.

Suddenly I got it. Kateri, the patron saint of the environment, is also known as the patron saint of refugees. How appropriate to our times, as increasing numbers of refugees and migrants suffer environmental pressures. With this realization, I had a vision of ever increasing numbers of supplicants praying to Kateri for environmental relief—for real miracles, on the order of the parting of the Red Sea and a rescue for human and animal refugees on the order of Noah's Ark.

Kateri Tekakwitha bears an urgent message, a wake-up call: our most profound moral obligation, as Native Americans or as participants in more mainstream society, is to go beyond being good stewards of the environment. Stewardship implies that Mother Earth just needs some tending so that she can continue to service our human needs. In fact, we can only save her and ourselves by recognizing, as Kateri's spiritual traditions, both indigenous and Christian, affirm: the Earth is sacred, and it requires and deserves our utmost devotion. Perhaps we can come more easily to this realization when we have our spiritual feet rooted in two cultures, each one asking the other challenging questions.

I am left with an image of Kateri and her contemporaries worshiping their creator in the forest at Kahnawake. It too was their church, alongside, surrounding, and embracing a small wooden chapel. Kateri's biographers record her hanging small wooden crosses on trees and engaging in rituals in the forest.[21] Actions speak louder than words, or so the expression goes. In the absence of Kateri's own words, such actions speak most eloquently.

9

ASA'S INDIAN SCHOOL STORY

Our entire extended family knows only the bare-bones facts of our ancestral connection with the troubled history of Indian schools in North America. This part of our family story could be written on a matchbook cover or on a small sticky note, like some reminder pasted on the refrigerator.

What do we know? Asa Wall, my Potawatomi grandfather, attended not one, but three of these infamous schools (first, the Chilocco Indian School in Oklahoma, then the Carlisle Indian School in Pennsylvania, and finally the Hampton Institute in Virginia). His involvement with them swallowed up most of his early childhood and continued through his nineteenth year (1895 to 1906). He told us little more than that he had had a feeling of great loneliness. Beyond this, Grandfather's life at the schools presented us with a mystery. Until yesterday.

Yesterday afternoon Carolyn and I attended a musical theater production, *Children of God,* which portrays life in Canadian residential schools in the early to mid-twentieth century. The Canadian boarding schools for First Nations children were very similar to Indian schools in the United States, except that the Canadian schools were active through the end of the twentieth century, decades after most

U.S. schools had closed, and Canadian schools were administered by churches, not by government officials.

On both sides of the border, these institutions were created to force cultural assimilation upon Indian children. Upon arrival, they had their long hair cut, were given military-style uniforms and English names, and were compelled to cease speaking their tribal languages. The goal was to destroy, brutally if need be, the part of the child that threatened to preserve Indian culture for another generation. In U.S. Indian schools, the phrase used to describe this policy was "kill the Indian to save the man," attributed to Richard Pratt, the guiding force behind the schools. In Canada the phrase was "kill the Indian in the child," attributed to Duncan Scott, minister of Indian affairs from 1913 to 1932. Indeed large numbers of Indians actually died at the schools, many from the poor food and severe physical deprivation. Others died from diseases such as tuberculosis, a fatal and common affliction at the crowded institutions.

Typically children were removed from their homes under duress. Parents who refused to let Indian agents take their children were threatened with arrest and/or reduction of any meager services the government might be providing under treaty obligations. For parents such as my grandfather's, living on marginally productive desert land in the Oklahoma territory in the late 1890s, having children taken away may have been both a curse and a relief. We have a letter indicating that Asa's parents encouraged one Indian agent to take their child and place him in a boarding school. But such letters were often part of the coerced separation. It is agonizing to wonder if my grandfather was removed from tearful, loving parents waving from the doorway, or if he was shown the door with a sigh of relief and then left with a final memory of turned parental backs.

Asa was not alone in suffering extreme loneliness and homesickness. His cousin, Jim Thorpe, my first cousin twice removed, was also sent to the Chilocco Indian School. Cousin Jim ran away—running twenty miles to escape and get back to familiar home ground. Sent back to Chilocco, he ran away again and again. Eventually Jim Thorpe would become famous for running—with a football. Difficult circumstances sometimes operate in unpredictable ways to bring out individual strengths, at least for those who survive.

As young adults, both Cousin Jim and Grandfather Asa also attended the Carlisle Indian School, which became a model for other Indian schools across the United States. In theory, Carlisle was to give its students basic competency in reading and writing in addition to manual labor skills. In fact, for many there was little meaningful intellectual education, but a heavy dose of vocational training.

Discipline was harsh at all Indian schools, partly because of the military background of their guiding spirit and designer, Captain Pratt. Uncooperative students were locked in the guardhouse, sometimes for weeks, and given bread and water. Corporal punishment was common. The Carlisle Indian School archive contains numerous detailed records of complaints from students and outside auditors documenting harsh student discipline.[1] Such practices became a national scandal at the time. But as is still a familiar pattern with abuse, offending staff escaped unpunished or were transferred to other Indian schools. The culture of abuse continued even in the daylight of major newspaper stories.[2]

Some students did manage to get a fair amount of formal intellectual education. Our grandfather was well read, and in his later adult life he could often be found sitting in his upholstered rocker in the living room behind the Sunday *New York Times*. Another relative, Aunt Emma, received an education at Chilocco that she described as "splendid training as a disciplinarian, housekeeper, and dressmaker."[3] Eventually graduating as valedictorian from the school's literary department, Emma had an illustrious career as a teacher at Indian schools across the southwest United States.

As I have mentioned, Aunt Emma was a founding member of the Society of American Indians (1911–1923), the first advocacy organization run by and for Native Americans. This pan-Indian movement was a direct outgrowth of the Indian schools, which brought diverse tribes together and provided them with shared experience, opportunities to establish alliances based on common concerns, and skills in cross-cultural communications and organization. Graduates of the Indian schools, particularly Carlisle School, became leading Native American intellectuals. As advocates for minority rights, these Red Progressives were decades ahead of their times, both in Native American communities and in mainstream white culture. In African American communities, the rights and identity movements led by W. E. B. DuBois and Marcus Garvey were expanding at the same time.

This extraordinarily mixed and confusing history left me and my extended family wondering what it was really like for Asa at his schools. What was his psychological and spiritual life during the difficult years away from home, during a shattered childhood and adolescence? *Children of God,* I thought, might answer some of our questions.

As is becoming a familiar pattern in my life, the discovery of *Children of God* was first visited upon me by way of our occasional weekends in Lachine. I heard about the production during a radio interview with the musical's creator, Corey Payette. His message about using the arts for healing was beamed across the St. Lawrence River. It was broadcast by the Kahnawake Mohawk radio station, situated on the same reserve as other recent sources of information and inspiration, such as the Kateri Center, which we can see from our balcony.

Corey explained how his production grew out of and built upon the work of Canada's Truth and Reconciliation Commission (established in 2008) and the 2006 Residential Schools Settlement Agreement. The central idea behind both of these initiatives is to educate the public about the history of Canada's First Nations people, to expose the truth about the harm that was inflicted, and to begin a healing and restorative process.

The idea of using an artistic platform to help accomplish this was intriguing. So Carolyn and I made a snap decision to obtain tickets and managed to get one of two remaining pairs of seats for a Sunday matinee. Front row, far right.

We arrived early at the Segal Performing Arts Centre in Montréal, which is situated adjacent to several Jewish cultural centers, and is surrounded by a primarily Jewish neighborhood. This seemed a highly appropriate venue for a performance about genocide.

What I did not know then, and only discovered by accident the morning after, is that the neighborhood where the theater is located is in the borough of Côte-des-Neiges–Notre-Dame-de-Grâce (the English translation is "Hill of Snows—Our Lady of Grace"). The name seemed appropriate, given the snow and ice on every surface and the temperature, which was far below freezing.

As I repeated the name "Côte des Neiges," it sounded oddly familiar. Then I remembered the name of the birthplace of my great-great-great-great-grandfather, Jacques Vieux, the voyageur who called us back to Lachine a few summers ago. The family history, as told by Jacques' son Andrew, documents: "Father . . . was born in lower Canada in Cour de Neige (or Snow Court) in the suburbs of Montreal, May 5, 1757."[4] A quick search of my family archive confirmed that eighteenth-century Cour de Neige was quite probably the current Côte des Neiges. Any doubt about these two places being one and the same vanished when I discovered that the main industry of the eighteenth-century village of Cour de Neige was producing leather from animal hides. Jacques must have leaned about animal pelts in his home town. This background education would serve him well when he became a voyageur and pelt trader for various North American companies.

Once again I was spiraling homeward.

We arrived early at the theater and found the lobby filled with large posters about Canadian residential schools and the Truth and Reconciliation Commission. Several posted advisories informed those attending that the production touches upon emotionally difficult topics and that viewers could take a break from the presentation if it became overwhelming. An indoor tent was designated as a safe space. From it emanated the gentle aroma of burning sage, which is used in Native American purification rituals. We met a kind and gentle First Nations woman, who explained that she would be available during the performance to counsel people if needed. Her wonderfully understated presence was profoundly welcoming and comforting.

As we browsed the program for *Children of God* and had tea in the cozy lobby, we prepared ourselves. I wondered if anyone would comment on the T-shirt I wore on top of my turtleneck shirt, which had huge lettering stating "Potawatomi" in the form of an eagle. No one approached me or commented. I began to wonder anxiously if we would connect with the performance or the audience.

When we finally found our seats in the far right front row, we realized that the stage was within one meter of us and just barely higher than our knees. The small orchestra was far to the left side. I felt that I might be as much a participant in as an observer of the play. When the lights dimmed and the first characters appeared on stage, it indeed became apparent that we were about to experience theater, not in the distance, but as storytelling literally at arm's length. This was going to be an intimate encounter. I grabbed the arms of my seat as if in a plane about to accelerate down the runway on takeoff.

Then they appeared—gray-suited actors playing the roles of residential school inmates. They scrubbed floors, commiserated, plotted schemes to run away, and repeatedly confronted and then cowered before a priest and nun, who were their tormentors. Talented actors and singers conjured emotions that mere spoken words could not. My sadness and anger were overwhelming at first. If I had had a tomato, I do not know if I could have resisted the temptation to use it to hit the actor playing the priest smack-dab in the middle of his self-righteous face. I had increasing doubts that I could handle this at such close range.

Then something happened, rather suddenly, like the image in a kaleidoscope turned or shaken and unexpectedly coming into focus.

The performance of moving dialogue, song, and dance ceased being an artistic endeavor with an unbearable sense of oppression and became instead the unfolding of a long-awaited and welcome tale: Asa's untold story of his life in the boarding schools. The words and images he could not tell us flowed in musical form, like water slowly and gently released from a stream too long dammed up. The release was not just for us, his descendants. It was also for my grandfather and his spirit, which, until the story unfolded before us, had remained a silent captive of the Indian schools for more than a century.

I began to feel relief instead of anger. And I could feel it for my grandfather, as he at long last allowed himself to weep with all of us in the room. It was cleansing, for him, his spirit. And perhaps also for his French great-grandfather, on whose territory this performance was taking place.* I cannot but believe that Jacques Vieux was there comforting his great-great-grandson.

On rare occasions, when we have assembled four generations of our extended Native American family, we have set a plate at the table for the fifth-generation past: my grandfather Asa's spirit. But never before had we been connected so far back in time. And never before had strangers literally reached out to share our family history in this intimate way. At the close of the performance, the entire production crew came out to take a bow. They linked hands and stepped forward to connect in a chain with the audience. The hands they first connected were those in the two front seats, far right. Carolyn and I made the first link between audience and performers, and unbeknownst to the performers at that moment, between those here and now and many generations of ancestors of at least one family in the room.

The postproduction discussion involved actors and the kindly

---

*Both the theater director and program graciously acknowledged that the venue, the Segal Centre, is on the traditional territory of several First Nations people. It also acknowledged that it had been a diplomatic meeting place for many other First Nations people.

First Nations counselor we had met earlier. I presented the production crew with braided healing sweetgrass and expressed gratitude for giving voice to a part of our family history that no amount of print matter from archives and books could ever accomplish. I explained that as a child, I had sat on my grandfather's lap and he had told me stories of his experience in World War I and the horrors of mustard gas. And then I said, "But he could never speak the story you told today for him. Miigwetch, thank you." The pouches of kinni-kinnick in our pockets must have been on the verge of igniting in such intensity.

10

REFLECTIONS ON WARRIOR CULTURE

Raising questions or expressing skepticism about warrior culture is almost taboo within most mainstream American communities. Hesitation in addressing this matter is even more palpable among Native Americans. For example, in his Ojibwe Word of the Day podcast, James Vukelich notes that the words for warrior, *ogichida* (male) and *ogichidaak* (female), are "so important I am actually intimidated to talk about it."[1]

However, our most widely held cultural assumptions are often the ones most in need of being scrutinized, refined, updated, and ultimately strengthened. Examining and questioning nearly sacred beliefs does not necessarily imply outright or wholesale rejection. In fact, as I am discovering, it may reveal and help to resolve cultural conflicts that others have privately struggled with for a long time.

I take comfort in the fact that questioning a core value of Native American culture finds precedent within Native American traditions, many of which provide for social critics, including those who challenge sacred beliefs and practices. For example, among the Kwakwaka'wakw of the Pacific Northwest, the Raven Dance allows a member of the community to expose and challenge cultural norms. Black Elk periodically assumed a less well-publicized role as *heyoka,* a kind of jester or social commentator who created space for reflection upon cultural norms and practices.[2]

That said, I acknowledge that in this chapter I am questioning deeply embedded values. Being a warrior is a cherished social identity among most Native American peoples. In addition to directly affirming the high social status of a warrior, other indigenous core values also emphasize warriorlike characteristics. For example, bravery, *aakode'ewin,* is one of the "Teachings of the Seven Grandfathers" among the Anishinaabeg. Bravery has various interpretations. Narrowly and historically, it referred to physical bravery before an adversary in war. Other interpretations embraced physical courage in the often dangerous activity of hunting. Young men viewed hunting as practice for war.

Bravery can also refer to leadership in decision making and ceremonial roles. Recent efforts by Native American youth to become role models in environmental protests bear witness to their self-designation as environmental warriors. Protests over transporting oil through the proposed Dakota Access Pipeline at the Standing Rock Indian Reservation, beginning in 2016, put indigenous activists in real physical danger, as police used violent tactics similar to those seen in the southern United States during the civil rights struggles of the 1960s.

Probing even more deeply into Native American culture, we see that among both Plains and Eastern Woodland tribes, traditional practices designed to build tolerance of physical suffering played an important ceremonial role. These activities were seen as displays of bravery in their own right, but also served to harden would-be warriors. Rituals involving mortification of the flesh, as in the Sun Dance, and voluntary exposure to physical hardships such as extreme heat and cold, were means of displaying physical courage for both men and women.

Social norms promoting violence are frequently found in contemporary Native American literature. It routinely portrays, and often implicitly accepts, high levels of violence on the reservation, which is then linked to the persistence of a warrior culture. Ojibwe author David Treuer's books are full of tales of violence on the reservation. This violence might be dismissed as a manifestation of life in any community that has suffered from severe economic deprivation and social afflictions such as alcohol and drug abuse. Nonetheless, readers of contemporary Native American literature cannot ignore recurring themes that point to an independently rooted and matter-of-fact attitude toward, and acceptance of, violence. For example, in *Rez Life*, Treuer quotes a local policeman, who asserts that violence is part of Indian life: "That's why we are here. The only reason there's any Indians at all is because we are fighters. We have a violent attitude. It's helped us, but hurts us too." Treuer then quotes Tom Stillday, who was a spiritual leader from Ponemah: "That's why we have so many Bear Clan and Marten Clan people here at Red Lake. Those were warrior clans. And we had lots of warriors here. This was the last frontier, the final stop before the Sioux and the Great Plains. So there were lots of warriors."[3]

In *The Heartbeat of Wounded Knee*, Treuer begins "Part 3: Fighting Life, 1914–1945" with personal accounts of watching cage fighting at the Northern Lights Casino on his reservation. Cage fighting, or mixed martial arts, involves two adversaries struggling to knock each other out inside a chain-link fence enclosure. It is a no-holds-barred, bare-knuckle version of boxing combined with other forms of martial arts and wrestling. It has few rules. Treuer's cousin Sam, a barroom and street fighter who is in and out of jail, finds social acceptance through his cage fighting. Treuer observes that a "taste for violence runs deep in Sam's veins and throughout Indian Country."[4]

Treuer then shifts his level of analysis to a longer-term cultural issue: the roots of violence and warfare among the Ojibwe. He claims that "our tribe the Ojibwe, are not known for being warlike."[5] He explains that the fur trade with Europeans in the eighteenth and nineteenth centuries set his tribe on the path to being highly aggressive. Traditional life was disrupted; Indians were relocated to reservations, where they were disarmed, and opportunities for practicing warlike aggression were limited. However, World War I provided an outlet for Native American and Canadian First Nations warriors to exhibit their physical bravery and warrior prowess. Treuer describes how famous Native Americans killed dozens, and in one case hundreds, of enemy soldiers in their roles as snipers or combatants.

Native Americans, like African Americans, returned home from World War I, marched in parades, and were initially greeted as returning patriots and heroes. Aspirations of more meaningful participation in white society rose, and Native Americans were granted full citizenship in 1924. Citizenship was a double-edged sword. It was partly a recognition of service during the war, but was also part of a policy of assimilation designed to undercut ties with reservations, which had legal status as separate sovereign nations. African Americans fared far worse. Fears of their post-war social and political aspirations for increased social equality resulted in racial violence during the Red Summer of 1919, when hundreds of black people, and some Indians, were killed in white attacks that occurred in more than two dozen cities. A clear message of white supremacy was delivered brutally.

Military service and sacrifice nevertheless continued to be portrayed as a pathway to social acceptance in communities of color. This argument for military service was made in World War II, and in the Korean, Vietnam, and recent Middle East wars. Historians argue that this strategy of entering the mainstream by way of military service did help to break down racial barriers slowly and to some degree. But these successes raise a more probing question. Since the Korean War, have people of color served in wars that bestow warriorlike honor? Or have recent wars been exposed as human folly steeped in mass deception? To pose the question even more provocatively, as the Canadian First Nations singer-songwriter Buffy Sainte-Marie asks in "Universal Soldier," are those too eager to be warriors actually acting as enablers of avoidable human tragedy?

My answers came to me very far from the culture of violence often found within traditional and modern reservation life. My insights came to me through a family connection with the famous Indian athlete Jim Thorpe.

I want to be very clear about this: I do not claim to have been visited by the spirit of Jim Thorpe. We do share a genealogical connection: his grandmother was my grandfather's grandmother, which makes Jim Thorpe my grandfather's cousin, and so my first cousin twice removed. I may have been fortunate enough to inherit some of the same athletic ability, but that is where the biological and genealogical connection stops.

I do not know if my grandfather, Asa Wall, ever even met Cousin Jim. Family oral history claims that they were at the Carlisle Indian School at the same time. Both attended the Chilocco Indian School, but it appears that they were actually at both institutions at different times. Most likely my grandfather and Jim were ships passing in the night, with missed opportunities to interact. Ultimately, my grandfather's journey took him to the front in World War I. Jim's journey took him to the Olympics and the football field.

I have decided not to let ships once again pass in the night. While the time and space separating me from Cousin Jim are now much greater than they were for my grandfather, I have made the decision to send a bright flare into the darkness between us. I want to reconnect two long-separated family journeys in the hope that one ancestor, now an elder who has walked on, might share some wisdom with a wandering distant cousin.

Making Peace with the Warriors

By questioning the values of the warrior culture, I am undoubtedly acting more in the Sioux role of a heyoka than in the role of an Anishinaabe who is unquestioningly respectful of traditional teachings. This attitude makes it all the more ironic given that I attended a high school whose mascot was a warrior—actually more of an ancient Greek than Native American. We were the Chenango Valley Warriors. When I became president of the student council, I guess I became the chief warrior. Possibly I succeeded in becoming president partly because

I became, ever so briefly, a star athlete, a prominent Chenango Valley Warrior.

Becoming an accomplished athlete was quite an achievement for me. In elementary school I was the epitome of what was then called a "ninety-seven pound weakling," a scrawny, unmuscular kid. In seventh grade, I began to lift weights and exercise like crazy. Eventually, with strength greatly exceeding my weight, I was drawn to wrestling. One of the coaches, a teacher I admired, a former Army Ranger, took me under his wing and taught me to box. He also taught me martial arts moves that could disable or kill another human with one quick, well-targeted move. I never used the martial arts moves, not even when being mugged on a Philadelphia street.

Had I grown up on the rez, I might well have felt obligated to respond as a proud warrior. I might have been embraced by my Native American community and been encouraged to become a fighter, like David Treuer's cousin Sam. Instead I found a more mainstream middle-class outlet for my adolescent aggressiveness. In high school, benefiting from the strength building, I quickly became a good wrestler. As a ninth-grader, I filled in for a varsity team member who was ill or overweight and unexpectedly won my match. From that time on, I was on my way.

Wrestling is a very intimate form of competition. You grapple with an opponent flat out, using all of your strength and energy for three two-minute rounds. In the course of this struggle, you often lift your opponent off the mat, and sometimes over your head. This is civil, rules-constrained, hand-to-hand combat in full intensity. But it is not cage fighting. Striking an opponent would have been penalized by the high school referee as unsportsmanlike. It would have been sanctioned by my coach and probably booed by the audience.

My signature wrestling move was the almost impossibly difficult maneuver called the Crucifix, which requires extreme flexibility, strength, and a lot of practice. I used it once to pin the previous year's state champion. Some decades later, it strikes me as wonderfully ironic that an enrolled Indian tribal member, wrestling as a "warrior," used a move that put his opponents in an excruciating twisted position resembling a tortured body on a crucifix. Might this be some form of role reversal and revenge for my many ancestors who were mistreated at Christian boarding schools? At least it was harmless and bloodless, unlike the Roman punishment for which it was named. I always shook hands with my defeated opponents. And even in high school, I was becoming more interested in promoting peace than engaging in warfare as would soon become evident in college when I was enraptured by Martin Luther King's preaching of nonviolence.

My victories over other white "warriors" were symbolic and unrecognized outside of my small community. By contrast, Cousin Jim's athletic victories made national and international news. His illustrious sports career began when he played on the famous Carlisle Indian School football team in the first decades of the twentieth century. It was coached by the legendary Pop Warner, who transformed the American version of football. At the time players wore minimal protective equipment. Serious injuries were common; deaths were not unheard of. The brutality of the sport in its earliest decades and its role in American culture are documented in Sally Jenkins's *The Real All Americans*. Jenkins reveals how and why the sport grew out of late nineteenth-century American culture, and why it has come to be a near obsession in contemporary American life. It is all about violence and our notions of manhood.

It is paradoxical that this "all-American" sport took root in the soil of the small Carlisle Indian School. Carlisle was only marginally an institution of higher education. It was more of a trade school. Nevertheless, it competed with football teams from the country's best and wealthiest universities, and with the toughest opponents possible. And Carlisle very often came out on top in these competitions. The fact that Jim Thorpe played on the team helped the school considerably. He was, after all, as the king of Sweden commented at the 1912 Olympics, probably the world's greatest athlete of that time.

When Carlisle was scheduled to play the highly rated football team from the United States Military Academy, also known as West Point, in November 1912, the event made national news. It was Carlisle's greatest season. Leading up to the West Point game, Carlisle was scoring an average of nearly fifty points a game, was without a loss, and had one tied game.

> Crack timing and cutting-edge stratagems, as usual, were stock in trade. In the hands of the rapid-fire play caller Welch, the Indians operated a hurry-up offense that kept opponents continually off balance and out of breath. The Indians hardly huddled—they would just line up and run a series of plays at lightning speed as Welch reeled off audible signals or used hand gestures to make adjustments. Some gestures he used were Indian signs.[6]

Newspapers and team members viewed the match with West Point not just in historical terms, but within an epic framework. It was portrayed as a replay of many too many ignominious encounters between the U.S. Army and American Indians. With this in mind, Coach Pop Warner is reported to have given a pregame speech to the team, reminding them that "it was the fathers and grandfathers of these Army players who . . . killed your fathers and grandfathers . . . who destroyed your way of life."[7] He was undoubtedly referring to the massacre at Wounded Knee.

The game was brutal. Carlisle emerged victorious, trouncing West Point 27–6. One player on the West Point team, linebacker Dwight Eisenhower, left the field with the taste of defeat in his mouth. Some reports (later challenged when Eisenhower became president) record him being carried off dazed or unconscious. In any case the great general who would plan and direct the D-Day invasion and liberation of Europe from the Nazis had suffered an ignominious defeat.

Some might dismiss this victory as merely symbolic—small compensation for what the white men's armies inflicted on Native

Americans. But I believe that for Jim Thorpe and his teammates, the victory over West Point was both satisfyingly symbolic and profoundly affirmative. It was an opportunity for the players to express many important Native American values, and more importantly to ground their identities firmly within a constellation of virtues often referred to as those of a warrior culture. This includes physical courage, willingness to make personal sacrifice for the collectivity, face-to-face engagement with the opponent, perseverance, quick thinking, strategizing, and respect for the adversary.

Both at the time of this football battle and since, much has been written about this legendary match. Many competing narratives claim to describe and interpret the game. But I think it still needs and deserves a Native American narrative. After all, don't the victors get to write history?

What I see now is that the Carlisle–West Point game is a story instructing us about what a warrior should actually be.

Modern warfare has become mindless slaughter. Indiscriminate, impersonal nuclear weapons and drones have removed much of the sense of warriorlike courage found in direct engagement with an adversary. After two hideous world wars in the twentieth century, humanity has made some progress in constraining international conflict, writing rules of engagement that take off some of the rougher edges of warfare and its impact on civilians. We have, at least temporarily, succeeded in preventing regional conflict from becoming global conflagration. This has been done by approximating the rules of sport, where competitors, adversaries, agree to be bound by rules that prevent simmering international conflict from disintegrating into utter chaos with limitless destruction. Within this framework we have United Nations peacekeepers, blue-helmet warriors who put their lives on the line to prevent the escalation of conflicts. For me, they are the epitome of courage.

However, viewing Jim Thorpe as a warrior-athlete is even more profoundly paradigm-shifting. The lesson of Carlisle versus

West Point for Native American society is simple yet profound: the fairest, wisest, and most honorable way to engage an adversary is on a *level playing field*, bound by a code of honorable conduct.

For Native Americans, the significance of Jim Thorpe and Carlisle versus West Point is redemptive. When Native Americans have encountered the settler-colonists in the most adversarial of circumstances, and in a fair game where technology does not dominate and where the outcome depends on character and grit, we triumph.

If these are the lessons that Jim Thorpe brings us, I can reconcile myself with having once been a Chenango Valley Warrior.

I have written elsewhere in this book about the outcome of cultural conflict on another kind of level playing field: Indian lifestyles versus white settler lifestyles in the seventeenth century. That outcome was, once again, a victory for the Indians. Many of the whites who were abducted during Indian-settler wars, and who lived both European and Indian lives, chose to remain in indigenous communities when given a chance to return to white society. The explanation of an Indian victory in this case of cultural conflict is that our other Grandfather Teachings emphasizing truth, respect, wisdom, trust, humility, and love overshadowed the teaching of physical bravery exemplified in violent warfare. In such a situation, an entire cultural complex triumphed over blinding single-mindedness and a warrior ethic. It was the former, and not the latter, that won over white settlers. This lesson is almost biblical: the gentle shall inherit the Earth. Is that not the message Mother Earth is desperately sending us in the twenty-first century?

I hope that these reflections will not be misinterpreted as the moralistic rantings of a privileged, off-reservation, white-looking Indian. It is not my intention to juxtapose my privileged life with that of David Treuer, who writes with brutal honesty about the often violent life on the reservation. My purpose is to live up to my newly acquired spirit name, Wshke Nabe, "He Who Sees Things in a New Way." I want to show my fellow Native Americans how they might see things in a new way, to support more Native Americans as environmental warriors, like those at Standing Rock and like the women at the Pokagon Potawatomi reservation in Michigan, who are restoring a river as water warriors. Such a twenty-first-century rethinking of the meaning of being a warrior would, ironically, return the focus of our people to our central core value, living in harmony with Mother Earth.

11

DECOLONIZING POWWOWS

Powwows are typically viewed as celebrations of Native American culture. They even happen in non-Native contexts, such as Germany, where the Native American Association of Germany (NAAoG) once sponsored an annual event, much to the chagrin of many indigenous groups in North America. The NAAoG website explains that the singing, dancing, and wearing of traditional regalia by those who were not Native Americans had created such an outcry over matters of cultural appropriation that it was temporarily suspending its powwow activity, even as other European Native American cultural groups continued the practice.[1]

One assumption behind these European events—and Native American protests about them—is that powwows are aspects of authentic Native American culture. With that assumption in mind, Carolyn and I attended a small powwow near our home in Vermont several years ago. It was my first introduction to such an event. We arrived early and found seats that would allow us an unobstructed view of the opening ceremony, the Grand Entry. In marched an honor guard carrying an American flag, a black MIA (missing in action) flag commemorating war veterans whose remains have never been repatriated, as well as flags for various branches of the U.S. military. All were carried by military veterans in full uniform. Nowhere was there a flag for a Native American tribe.

I felt as if I were at a mainstream Veterans Day or Memorial Day celebration. When the speeches about military service began, we discreetly left the event. We had come to celebrate Native American culture, not to celebrate the army that had conquered our people.

I went home and searched online for information about Grand Entries at powwows. To my relief, I discovered that I was not entirely alone in feeling uncomfortable about celebrations of indigenous cultures and Native sovereignty that prominently feature symbols of the conqueror. For example, my very first online search turned up the following account:

> In the spring of 1980, I went to a pow-wow in Red Lake, Minnesota, with several friends. It was held in a grassy field surrounded with the kind of sparse trees and low bushes typical of the northern regions. The sun was bright and the atmosphere of the pow-wow arena warm and friendly.
>
> As I strolled around the pow-wow perimeter, an old Ojibwa man approached me. His hair was pure white and his face was brown and weathered. Short and slightly bow-legged, he nodded his head and smiled a big, warm smile. I stopped to exchange greetings.
>
> "You know," he said, "We never used to have Grand Entries at our pow-wows." I was surprised he brought the subject up. I always had wondered why pow-wows began with a procession of dancers. "We just sat down at the drum and started singing," he continued, "And the dancers came around and danced whenever they wanted to."
>
> I imagined a sparse arena with one row of benches circling a dance ring. In my mind's eye, I saw a single drum group of old men singing in a patch of bright sunlight. Elderly Ojibwa women danced gracefully through knee-high meadow grass around the drum.
>
> The old man suddenly got a sly look in his eye, turned away from me, and left. I never saw him again at that pow-wow although I kept looking for him so I could ask someone who he was. To this day, I

have never seen that old man again. But his words speak loud and clear to me whenever I witness a Grand Entry at any pow-wow.

I often thought the Grand Entry ought to be abolished from pow-wows because it doesn't have any roots in ancient tribal history. It seemed so contrived, pompous, and superficial, especially when compared to tribal traditional and religious activities. I didn't see anything resembling the Grand Entry at any other type of ceremonial gathering. To me the Grand Entry simply imitated the all-American parade.

At first, I felt relief at finding a like-minded spirit, but the orthodox explanation reappeared quickly. The same author who had expressed skepticism about the Grand Entry then changed his thinking:

As I delved deeper into researching and reflecting upon the Grand Entry for this essay, however, my position changed. Now I think it deserves a respectable place in our history and culture.[2]

As I read this author's account of his change of attitude, I encountered what would soon become a familiar line of argumentation. I read about how veterans honor their country and their country honors them, how military service reflects core Native American values. The more I dug into the matter of powwow Grand Entry origins, the more I encountered exactly the same explanation.

This echo chamber of explanations triggered my skepticism. My intellectual and academic training kicked in once again. When people offer exactly the same explanations and stories, down to minute details, they are often revealing that these stories are being repeated unreflectively and uncritically. Take, for example, the largely unspoken assumption that powwow Grand Entries, with veterans and U.S. flags, are truly rooted in Native American culture.

It turns out that nothing could be further from the truth. The nameless elder (or spirit of an elder) cited earlier got it right. Powwows, as they are known today, are an artifact of early twentieth-century forced assimilation practices and the commercialization and commodification of Indian artifacts and ceremony by settler-colonial cultures. The circumstances surrounding this phenomenon are complex and riddled with paradox.

This part of the tale begins with recognizing that throughout much of the nineteenth century, the Bureau of Indian Affairs was declaring all-out war against Indian dances, songs, and public performances—the extension of a decades-long policy of forced assimilation. Those guilty of Indian dancing or singing often found their already meager government rations suspended. This policy was given new urgency by the appearance of the Ghost Dance in the 1870s and its association with the last dying gasp of Indian insurrections, which were sometimes violent.[3] For Indian agents, missionaries, the media, and decision makers in Washington, the Ghost Dance was a cause of indigenous insurrection rather than a symptom of forced assimilation's harmful effects. Stamping out the dance was seen as an important part of a solution to the "Indian problem."

This perspective changed dramatically, if belatedly, with the publication of the U.S. government's own assessments of its policies toward Indians. Several hard-hitting revelations, such as the 800-page Meriam Report of 1928, officially titled *The Problem of Indian Administration,* documented official abuse of Native Americans and the unnecessary destruction of Indian culture and society. As a result the U.S. government instituted the "Indian New Deal" and then the Indian Reorganization Act of 1934 in an effort to rescue Indian culture from being consigned to the dustbin of history, which many policymakers and ethnographers considered to be nearly inevitable.

Dance and song ceremonies organized by Indians had continued, unofficially and sometimes with a blind eye turned by officials, during the early decades of the twentieth century. Indian pageants with Indian performers, organized by white society for white audiences, were permitted; they had long been a part of late nineteenth-century American culture. Such pageants were exported to Europe with enormous success.[4] Buffalo Bill's Wild West Show is the most famous example of such theatricalization of American Indian life.

The unanticipated consequence of these shows, which involved hundreds of Native American performers, was that the actors learned the skills needed to put on a spectacle that mainstream Americans would love. Thus, when singing and dancing by and for Indians was once again allowed in the 1920s and 1930s, Native Americans possessed the skills needed to commercialize this cultural revival at the very moment when they were suffering from the loss of buffalo and their lands. Two cultural strains—authenticity and commercialization—struggled for dominance; the latter triumphed.

Famous Native Americans, such as Black Elk, became media stars. Pageants became standard summer fare for tourists around sites in the American Midwest. There were daily or even twice-daily events during the height of tourist season near Mount Rushmore. Indian pageants quickly became formulaic. A band of Native Americans, decked out in the kind of regalia that whites expected to see, marched through tourist centers and led crowds to stores that sponsored their pageants. The stores sold Indian souvenirs.

In short order, Native Americans woke up to the commercial opportunities and began to use these processions and parades to gather tourists, much like the Pied Piper, and then bring them to a more intensive and "authentic" experience out of town, at a "genuine Indian powwow," under Native American control. Thus was a tradition born, as was a conspiracy of silence about the origins of modern powwows.

How did the veterans and the U.S. flag get to the head of these processions? Once again, historical context sheds light. When World War I ended, Americans greeted returning soldiers with patriotic parades. Veterans, including Native Americans like my grandfather, marched as heroes behind American flags.

At the same time, American society was struggling to assimilate growing numbers of European immigrants into mainstream life, into the famous melting pot. The explicit cost of admission to being recognized as a full member of American society was to become "American," to surrender foreign language, dress, and customs. This obsession with assimilating foreigners even extended to children's playgrounds, which were consciously used to teach standard American comportment in public.

American cities and towns frequently held parades where ethnic communities marched in their native costumes, but always behind the American flag. In every procession, the order of marchers indicated and reinforced social hierarchy. Native Americans took notice of such public displays.

It is necessary to acknowledge the pervasiveness of place and order in a parade, or in any ceremony. This fact is made obvious at family dinners. Who sits at the head of the table? At a wedding, why is there often a bride's and groom's side in the church? At the bridal reception, it matters who sits at or near the bridal table and who sits in remote corners of the room. Public life is no different. During the Cold War, Western intelligence agencies scrutinized, in fine detail, May Day parades in Moscow's Red Square. Who was seen, and where they stood, shed light on power struggles within the Soviet Communist Party.

Parades in American society also reveal important information to both participants and observers. The lessons taught and the social hierarchy that is being reinforced are rarely stated verbally, but they are embedded all the more deeply in visual memory and even in physical acts of submission.

Think of the prominence of the American flag in a Fourth of July parade. Try to reimagine the same parade with the British flag at the head of the procession. There would be comments, objections, and quite possibly insults and thrown tomatoes.

Imagine a Martin Luther King Day celebration and parade with African American leaders marching behind a Confederate flag. The very thought is outrageous.

Why then do Native Americans march behind the flag of their conquerors?

I can imagine the pushback from my Native American colleagues, friends, and relatives as they begin to see the obvious outcome of this line of reasoning. They may say, "Your analysis is part of white man's culture. It's some kind of university analysis, and does not reflect indigenous cultural values."

Respecting that concern, I now refer to indigenous culture and its long history of established rules about who stands or marches in what order in a sacred procession.

Position, Status, and the Sacred in Native American Pageantry

Fortunately, there is an abundance of well documented information on the topic. One of the earliest and most detailed records is Walter James Hoffman's *The Mide'wiwin, or Grand Medicine Society of the Ojibway*, published in 1891. It documents in remarkable detail, with drawings and information provided by elders, the rituals and ceremonies associated with the Mide'wiwin. Mide'wiwin are traditional knowledge keepers within Ojibwe communities, and within Anishinaabe society generally. They constitute something akin to the confraternities or sodalities that exist in many Christian churches: organizations composed of highly committed worshippers who encourage strict adherence to orthodoxy and ceremonial practice.

There is some reason to believe that postcolonial Mide'wiwin societies reflect an attempt by Native Americans to counteract the assimilationist inroads made by such Christian sodalities, which often played an active role in proselytizing. In any case, Mide'wiwin were prominent in many postcolonial Native American societies of the Great Lakes region and continue to play a role in tribal life today.

Membership in a Mide'wiwin society is hierarchical. Members undergo long and demanding training over decades. They graduate from one level of membership and knowledge to another. The graduation process is the ceremony documented by Hoffman. He describes the precise location of sacred objects in and around the lodge: how, when, and where elders and higher-order Mide'wiwin stand and how they are gifted.[5] The record leaves no doubt about Native American awareness of processional ritual and the positioning of Mide'wiwin authorities through public space.

Similarly, Black Elk displays a well-documented sophistication in creating and performing in processions and rituals for both indigenous and mainstream audiences, reflecting a grasp of social hierarchical demands and theatrical strategy. Like other Indian actors, Black Elk honed his showmanship skills while touring with Buffalo Bill's Wild West Show in Europe and North America. But his talents had been evident long before such appearances in mainstream white society. His astounding performance of the Horse Dance for his own people in 1881, when he was seventeen, involved dozens of performing horses and arrays of singers and dancers.[6] By giving public form to one of his visions, he was establishing his credentials as a knowledge keeper.

It should not be assumed that Black Elk was a mere manipulator of visual reality, a conjurer and trickster, as many whites alleged when describing other Indian medicine men. This erroneous conclusion would lead to the dismissal of his true spiritual nature. As Black Elk's biographer Joe Jackson notes repeatedly, Indian theatrics can be vehicles for expressing nearly ineffable mystical realities.

There is reason to believe that many of Black Elk's ceremonies and performances did involve miraculous events that could not be scripted. The Horse Dance was one such astounding event: the extraordinary animation of horses in the distance and a violent storm stopping in its tracks at the very boundary of the village were not effects that even the best stage manager could carry off.[7]

There is a critical difference between a show and a public revelation. Black Elk knew the difference, as did his tribal audience. His visions invited participation of ancestral spirits and four-legged kin. When horses in distant pastures joined in the ceremony, they confirmed that the membrane separating everyday reality and the spiritual realm had been pierced. So too with signs sent by ancestors in his other ceremonial performances.

Such events raise what is for me the central question about pow-wows and their Grand Entries. It is a question that I have never heard asked by anyone else: Is the powwow's pageantry welcoming to our ancestors? Would the countless thousands who died in massacres by white soldiers feel welcome and gift their presence within the Grand Entry's sacred circle and fire at a powwow, which first and foremost features American soldiers leading the way into the sacred space? Do we need to rethink the implications of our stage sets and celebrations and make them more ancestor-friendly? Might we then experience the spiritual richness that Black Elk so carefully conjured rather than merely witnessing settler-inspired spectacle?

I fear that we Native Americans are manufacturing a terrible confusion with the stories that we tell ourselves about ourselves, and tell others about us and what matters most to us. We claim to affirm our heritage and our sovereignty through reenactments of traditional dance in our own space. But what are the implications of a message that combines elements of celebration and affirmation with contradictory elements of subjugation?

With that pregnant question hanging over us, it is helpful to examine the historical, sociological, and anthropological records of what is called "conquest theater." Its obvious message of subjugation might help us to recognize those same elements in pageants of our own making.

The term *conquest theater* refers to the practice of sixteenth- and seventeenth-century European colonizers, primarily the Spaniards, who integrated theatrical presentations of cultural dominance and submission into their military campaigns of conquest and then into their efforts to maintain control of indigenous people.

Undoubtedly many Indians witnessing and participating in these events understood very clearly what the message was. It is reported that some Native viewers jeered at these performances. However, many others undoubtedly misread the intended and obvious message, and saw what they wished to see: recognition of their identity and acknowledgment of their presence. Unbeknownst to such naive viewers, by lending their presence to these spectacles, they were silently acquiescing to pageantry designed to subjugate them, their families, and community. By analogy, they would be the crowd lining the street in the children's tale of "The Emperor's New Clothes." Except for one child who states the embarrassingly obvious, the public in this fairy tale is collectively indulging and reinforcing a delusion.

The extraordinary lengths to which the conquistadors' pageants blatantly revealed their intentions to overwhelm militarily, and then to subjugate and humiliate, indigenous populations is documented in the work of Ramón Gutiérrez. He describes how the Spanish researched Pueblo culture before invading, and then used their ethnographic knowledge against indigenous people. The leading edge of their invasion was a well-informed and ambitious theatrical production.

From the moment the *españoles* reached the New Mexico banks of the Río Grande in 1598, everything the Pueblo Indians saw and heard was a carefully choreographed political drama intended to teach them the meaning of their own defeat, of Spanish sovereignty, and of the social hierarchies under Christian rule. The European actors in this conquest theater gave dazzling initial performances. The Puebloans watched in attentive shock. At first they were undoubtedly a bit confused, but in time they understood the dramatic messages, for the narrative of this drama was a triumphal history of the conquest of Mexico as the Europeans wanted it remembered.

The Spaniards correctly assumed that New Mexico's native residents had learned of the 1523 Aztec defeat through word of mouth. To make the Pueblo Indians believe that their own conquest and subjugation in 1598 was a continuation of, if not identical to, the Aztecs' submission in 1523, Don Juan de Oñate, the leader of the conquering expedition to New Mexico, and the friars staged for the Pueblo Indians the most vivid episodes of that earlier encounter.

In these initial conquest dramas the Spaniards played themselves as well as the defeated Aztecs while a native audience looked on. In time the actor-audience relationship of the 1598 conquest dramas was reversed; the natives played themselves as the Spaniards looked on. When the Pueblos performed the dances, dramas, and panto-mimes of the conquest, they continually relived their own defeat, humiliation, and dishonor, and openly mocked themselves with the caricatures of "Indians" the conquistadores so fancied. Today, ironi-cally, in many of New Mexico's villages a memory of the Spanish conquest lives on in military dramas still enacted in seventeenth-century attire. How pleased Oñate and the Franciscans would be now if they could only see the spectacle. For what they projected in 1598 as a highly ideological view of history became fixed as an integral and "authentic" part of native ritual.[8]

Other elements of the army's theatrical leading edge showed Indians kneeling before conquistadors and the Christ child, acknowledging the superiority of both foreign warriors and foreign gods. If theatrical intimi-dation did not succeed in triggering voluntary capitulation to the invad-ers, then the soldiers following close behind would use bloody coercion.

The message is clear. The time has come for Native Americans to decolonize our own ceremonies. We need to reclaim our broad defini-tion of *aakode'ewin,* bravery. We need to put our own cultural imprint back on the notion of ogichidaa and odichidaak (male warriors and female warriors) and make these social roles more inclusive. We need to include those who bravely risk their lives as police, firefighters, vol-unteer emergency medical technicians, and UN peacekeepers. We need to include environmental activists and journalists who risk their lives to protect Mother Earth. These warriors deserve to lead the Grand Entry at our powwows. They need not displace veterans. All can march side by side as equals.

Our flags, those of both Native American and mainstream society, can be put on an equal footing as well. When leaders of sovereign nations gather, their flags are displayed equally, not one above the other. As Indian sovereign nations, we should expect the same and model this equality in our powwow Grand Entries, where the U.S. flag and tribal flags can be displayed side by side in recognition of the dual sovereignty and citizenship that so many like me enjoy.

Then our ancestors and kin will return to our powwows, which will become truly spiritual events and places and not mere spectacles.

Who knows? That anonymous elder spirit who questioned the need for Grand Entries may even reappear at our gathering and whisper his gratitude into the ears of those of us quiet enough to listen.

Postscript

Long after I wrote the above passage, something extraordinary happened. Carolyn and I attended the Kahnawake Mohawk powwow, held annually across the lake from our Lachine apartment in Montréal. We took a small ferry across Lac-Saint-Louis and bicycled from the arrival quay down back roads to the Kahnawake reserve just in time to catch lunch. As I stood in line, famished and anxiously awaiting my bison burger, I noticed that the man behind me was wearing a green T-shirt with a familiar face printed on it. There was no name identifying the visage, but it was clear to me who this person was. I asked, "Isn't that Jim Thorpe?" The man smiled and confirmed my identification. I casually mentioned that he was a distant relative. He smiled again and indicated that I was very fortunate to have such an ancestral connection. As we chatted, he mentioned that he was a Mohawk resident of Kahnawake. He was attending his own tribal gathering wearing the image of someone from another tribe and a different country, but a kindred spirit.

Then, hesitating and with considerable trepidation, I decided to watch the Grand Entry and opening ceremony. From afar I could identify the all too familiar flags: Canada, the United States, and the black

MIA flag, but I could not recognize the others. As I approached the open-air arena, I noticed groups of veterans gathering at the front of the honor guard. They were easily identifiable by their jackets displaying names of veterans' groups. I could not read them from a distance. I told myself that I needed to be calm and patient.

Then, as the drumming began and the leading edge of the honor guard entered the sacred circle, I noticed that at the very front, and high above the national and tribal flags, was a tall and beautiful eagle feather staff, a traditional representation of the First Nations and Native American community. Clearly Kahnawake was identifying itself first and foremost as a sovereign First Nation. Behind the staff, the procession of veterans marched with the usual flags seen at powwows—recognition for different branches of the military. After the lengthy Grand Entry came a huge procession of feather- and regalia-decorated dancers, who briefly previewed what the day's dance competition was to bring.

As the opening ceremony participants left the arena nearly an hour later, I noticed that the veterans were both men and women. Nearly all visibly and proudly displayed names and badges indicating the branch of the Canadian military they had served in. Virtually all had served either as UN peacekeepers or as NATO troops during the efforts to stop the ethnic violence in the former Yugoslavia. One woman had a large peace sign sewn on her jacket just beneath her regimental information.

I introduced myself and congratulated them on their service, mentioning that for me, they symbolized the epitome of bravery. At the time I doubted that any of them could grasp the significance that their version of brave warriorship held for me. How could I begin to express that they were the living fulfillment of words I had written as a fanciful dream? Then, as I walked away, I realized that they understood perfectly. After all, Cousin Jim had put in an appearance, presaging what I was to witness.

12
THE RE-CREATION STORY

January 2019, Eve of the Bear Moon's reappearance, first anniversary of the visitation of Coy-Wolf. I am awakened by Coy-Wolf and on the porch I am greeted by Koo-koo-o-koo. So it happens again. I desperately need to write my way to hope. Again I return to fiction.

Grandfather, Mishomis in the Anishinaabe language, sits on a worn and faded blanket spread on the dirt floor of his cabin, by the fireplace, during the dark and cold time of the Bear Moon. His grandchildren gather around him. He holds A Mishomis Book. *It is a collection of stories about their people's teachings. The smooth pages of colored paper contrast with the elder's wrinkled and leathery hands.**

"Come, little ones, it is time that you learn our Creation Story," he calls out as his children's children gather blankets around them and snuggle by the glowing fire.

---

*There are actually two different Mishomis Books, written by Edward Benton-Banai and illustrated by Joe Liles. The children's version consists of five books, each with twenty pages of story, illustrated with line drawings to color in, and including exercises, language lessons, and discussion questions. The adult version of the book is widely referred to as a source of traditional Anishinaabe teachings, or the teachings of the grandfathers and grandmothers.

"Let us first offer kinni-kinnick in gratitude for the knowledge we are about to receive," Grandfather says. Each child takes a pinch of the mix of cedar, tobacco, red dogwood, and mullein from a small leather bag that Grandfather passes around. They had helped him to grow, gather, and dry the mix of sacred herbs and barks. Each child takes some of the mixture and gently places it in the embers.

"Our Creation Story," Grandfather announces, and begins to read from the first Mishomis Book.

I would like to tell you a story about how man* was created on this earth. This story was handed down to me by my Grandfathers. They recorded their stories on rolls of wee-gwas (birchbark).[1]

"Grandfather, the two-legged are flat and do not move. Did Gitchie Manitou make them flat? How could they stand and walk?" Little Red Deer immediately interrupts after first seeing the simple black-and-white illustrations.

"Ah," Grandfather chuckles, "there are two answers to your question. This book's creators made the two-legged flat because images can only be drawn this way in a book, in two dimensions, left and right and up and down on the page, like east and west and north and south, the directions in our medicine wheel garden. But Gitchie Manitou did not draw us flat like paper figures. He gave us form in three dimensions, also with a front and back, like my hand." He holds out his hand, turning it and showing its thickness. "So let us imagine these images in our Mishomis Book taking on form and standing up on the pages." Grandfather flexes his wrist making his hand stand upright at a right angle to his arm. "Now they can be round, and not flat. Can you see them walking now?" he asks as he inverts his hand and makes his fingers into legs that walk across the book.

Grandfather continues with the story.

---

*A Mishomis Book uses male-gendered nouns and pronouns. I use the original language but encourage the reader to consider this linguistic survival to refer to all people.

When *aki* (the earth) was young, it was said that earth had a family. Nee-ba-gee-sis (the moon) is called Grandmother, and gee-sis (the sun) is called Grandfather. The creator of this family is called Gitchi Manito (Great Spirit—Creator).

The Earth is said to be a woman. She is called Mother Earth because from her come all living things. Water is her life blood. On her surface everything is given four sacred directions—north, south, east and west. When she was young, this earth was filled with beauty.

The creator, Gitchie Manito, took four parts of Mother Earth and blew into them using this Megis or sacred shell. From this, man was created."[2]

"But Grandfather, the two-legged are trapped in the book. It is only in the dream time of the book that they exist. How do they know what happened before they were drawn, and stood up, and walked in three dimensions?" Yellow Flower asks.

"Ah, a very important question," Grandfather whispers. "If they have no memories, they will have no stories. Let us give them another dimension: the fourth one, time. Now they can walk not only in the present, but in the past, and they can remember." Then Grandfather continues to read the Creation Story.

It is said that the Great Spirit lowered man to the earth. This man was created in the image of Gitchie Manito. He is natural man. He is part of Mother Earth. He lives in brotherhood with all that is around him.[3]

Grandfather shows the children a drawing from the book. It is a long-haired person paddling a canoe. On the shore there are deer and bear. In the sky an eagle soars.

"But Grandfather, the two-legged looks sad because he cannot talk with the four-legged, the rooted ones, or the winged ones on Turtle Island. He

cannot listen to his ancestors who have walked on. He will be lonely," Red Hawk notes anxiously.

"Ah, yes. Once again we must give the two-legged another dimension, the fifth one, the spirit world. If we add this dimension to the two-leggeds' physical form, they will have the ability to listen to and talk with their kin on Mother Earth and to listen to their ancestors. Not only can they see into the past, but sometimes they can see into the future and travel in dream time and visions. This is the great gift that Gitchie Manitou gave us. Unlike the other changes we have made to the little figures that walk and dance before us, this does not alter the looks of the two-legged. Instead, it changes what is on the inside, in their hearts."

Grandfather's hand, which had been walking on the page, now unfolds, and he shows it to his grandchildren. They see that the deep lines in his leathery palm make the shape of a small heart at the center. It is red, a scar made by a knife injury years ago when he was a child learning to use that tool.

"Can all of the two-legged listen to and talk to their kin in the forest, and their ancestors, grandfather?" Yellow Flower asks.

"No. The settlers who came to Turtle Island long after we began to live here need to be taught how to do this. One time long ago, they too had this ability. But almost all of them have lost it. They mostly live in four dimensions and cannot, or will not, cross the boundary into the fifth dimension, the spirit world. From time to time they fall in and out of the spirit world, but most of the time they walk only in four dimensions."

"Grandfather, how could they lose such a gift?" several little ones ask in amazement.

"They moved out of the forests and into towns, where the noises of their machines distracted them, drowned out the sound of the animals and the voices of the trees and plants. They attended schools like those your parents and grandparents were taken away to. In these schools they were taught to believe only what they could measure with rulers and devices that see in four dimensions. They learned to reject the spirit dimension. When they could not hear the whispers of their ancestors, they lost many of their stories. They also lost the stories that could teach them how to listen to the four-legged and the forest."

Grandfather puts the first volume of A Mishomis Book *aside and picks up the fifth book. "This is the story of the Great Flood," he points to the cover where there is a drawing of a long-haired person with braids, sitting on a log with many animals. In the water are many lake and river creatures swimming.*

Grandfather then reads the long story of how Gitchie Manitou sent a great flood to purify the Earth after the two-legged lost their way, began fighting among themselves, and no longer served as caretakers of the Creation. The story describes how Wanaboozhoo, the giver of knowledge to humans, worked with the four-legged to bring up mud from the deep waters and place it on the back of Mi-zhee-kay (Turtle). The small ball of mud on Turtle grew to become a great island, Turtle Island. Upon this island the rooted ones started life again, as did the two-legged, four-legged, and winged ones. And we on Turtle Island learned that we must be caretakers of their world.

"What about the two-legged who came to Turtle Island later, as settlers? What happened to them?" Little Red Deer asks.

"They have their own creation story. It is like ours. They tell of their Creator sending a great flood. A seer, like Wanaboozhoo, helps the Earth's creatures by building a great boat to save them. Then they too started over.

"This is where our old stories of the creation of Turtle Island end. We must write more of the story. It is not complete."

Grandfather then stands, and puts the Mishomis Books back on a shelf with his collection of other sacred objects—an eagle feather, his pipe, an arrow.

"Where will this new story come from?" Black Squirrel asks.

Grandfather walks slowly to the hearth of the fireplace. He takes more kinni-kinnick from his pouch and places it in the fire, where the small pieces of sacred herbs make the dying embers suddenly blaze in a light so bright that it is like the sun and the children have to look away. Then in the light the children see a wooden box appear on the shelf above the place where the fire burns. Grandfather takes it down and puts it in front of his grandchildren. He says nothing, but sits in silence. After some minutes Little Red Deer opens the lid of the box and takes out a scroll written on birchbark. She asks, "This is more of the story, Grandfather, yes?"

"Yes," Grandfather nods and whispers.

"Where did it come from?" Black Squirrel asks.

"I am writing it down on the bark with this porcupine quill and black ink made from berries," the elder answers as he shows the children his writing tools.

"Can you really write such a story?" asks Yellow Flower.

"We can, and we must. I do not make up the words. I only write down the words. They are given to me in dreams, in whispers in the forest, in the garden, and when the ancestors visit. In these visitations I see the past, the present and the future. So I tell what I see. The story is not mine; it is given."

"How can the story be about what has not yet happened? Who can know this?" Little Red Deer asks.

"Our ancestors, those who walk in the fifth dimension of the spirit world, see these things, because they are not limited to walking straight lines. They are walking spirals, circling round and round, on paths turning in upon themselves, connecting past, present, and future." Grandfather draws a spiral in the sandy floor.

"So our ancestors walk in circles? Don't they get dizzy and lost?" Little Red Deer giggles.

"No. It is those who walk only in straight lines in four dimensions, with their eyes pointed toward the ground and their ears closed, who get lost. Our ancestors see the past, the present, and the future as one. Just as birds do when they migrate and fly around oncoming storms they cannot see with their eyes. They know the future. Just as butterflies do when they return to their ancestral homes long after their ancestors left and walked on. They remember the past of those who came before. Just as trees do when they produce children adapted to dry times yet to come. It is normal for all creatures to see such things, things that will happen and things that happened, if they listen."

"So is the story you are writing about the past, present, and future of our people?" asks Black Squirrel.

"*Yes, and it is a story that is not finished. It is a story about the re-creation of Turtle Island. It is a story I have only begun to write down. A story you will continue to create after I walk on. Then you will write it down for your grandchildren.*"

"*Please tell us how this new story begins,*" the children beg.

Grandfather starts. "*Like our original Creation Story in* A Mishomis Book, *the Re-creation Story begins with a flood. The waters are rising around Turtle Island. The frozen lands of the north are melting, as our brothers and sisters who live there tell us even now. This is a danger for the two-legged and many of the other creatures who live on the shores of Turtle Island, because these parts of where we live will flood and destroy many homes.*"

"*Then is Gitchie Manitou is punishing us, as before in our first Creation Story?*" Black Squirrel asks with some confusion.

"*No. This time it is the two-legged who are punishing themselves, and also the creatures of Turtle Island, including us,*" Grandfather whispers.

"*Why don't they stop?*" Yellow Flower asks.

"*Some of them, and many of us, are trying to stop the foolish things that harm Mother Earth. But just now we are too few. Most of the two-legged, the Zhaaganosh* children of the settlers who came to Turtle Island, and even many of our own people, are like rabbits caught in a trap of their own making. They are unable to escape. They just jump up and down in panic and do not think. Their stories tell them they cannot escape, or tell them that they are too stupid to escape, that they are unable to change, and that others are unwilling to change, that their attempts to walk a new path will fail. The two-legged have scared themselves like children telling ghost stories. Now they are afraid to go not only into the night but into the daylight. They live in fear of one another, in fear of the animals near their houses, in fear of the power of Mother Earth. They have made themselves believe that they are at war with everything, including Nature.*"

"*Will the Zhaaganosh conquer Mother Earth in their war against*

---

*Anishinaabe term for a person of white or European ancestry.

her, just as they conquered our people?" Little Red Deer asks.

"I do not think this will happen. Mother Nature is powerful. And the Zhaaganosh are arrogant. They do not read the seven grandfather teachings. They do not practice or value humility, one of our sacred teachings. This is their great weakness."

"Can't they tell themselves stories about healing medicine instead?" Yellow Flower pleads.

"Yes, that is the story we are beginning. But our story will be difficult, especially for the Zhaaganosh. Our story sees the world in forest change time. There are no instant miracles, no magic potions, no 'pouff—everything is better.'" Grandfather rises and tosses some powder into the fire, and it makes a small sudden burst of flames.

"Such magic as this is a trick. Real change will come, but with pain, and too slowly for many of the two-legged and the four-legged, the winged ones, and the rooted ones.

"Before, as told in A Mishomis Book, it was Muskrat who died to bring Earth from the bottom of the sea so that Turtle Island could support the rooted ones. This time it will be many creatures who will perish bringing gifts. They will bring gifts of wisdom in many forms. They will bring these gifts of wisdom many times. And many times they will not be recognized as gifts."

"Will it always be so?" Black Squirrel asks.

"How will the two-legged begin to see the gifts of Gitchie Manitou and hear the messages of ancestors and Mother Earth?" Yellow Flower asks.

"This time the messages and warnings of ancestors, our natural kin, and Gitchie Manitou will be louder than the stories that the two-legged have been telling themselves."

"Why would they open their ears and eyes now?" Yellow Flower asked.

"Because they can no longer avoid the visitations, which are no longer gentle whispers. They are loud cries of their own bodies, telling them that the food they eat has become poisoned. It is making them and their children sick. Mother Earth will send messenger bees telling a story of the Zhaaganosh medicine that kills the small winged ones. Then Mother Earth will send a *message about the birds, making even the settler tribes' sacred bald eagle nearly extinct. They will begin to understand that the two-legged and the rest of Creation are one. This has begun."*

"But this is not a new story. This is part of our Creation Story. Part of our traditional teachings," said Yellow Flower.

"Yes, but not the Creation Story of the Zhaaganosh settlers on Turtle Island. We, you, the young ones, must find a way of talking with the settlers' great-grandchildren and bringing our stories to them. Then, together you must write a new, Re-creation Story. It will not be easy, as the settlers believe their own stories, but often doubt ours. So you will need to sit and listen. Then quietly show how our stories can be similar. Show how our differences can help the Zhaaganosh to understand, help them to listen, help them with their food and medicine. We must also listen to their stories and learn."

"What can we learn from their stories?" Little Red Deer asks.

"They have ways of understanding how nature works that build on our ideas. They can see parts of the Creation that are both larger and smaller than we can see with our eyes. Their knowledge can add to our understanding and correct our errors."

"There are errors in our teachings?" Black Squirrel asks, shocked.

"Yes. We tell our stories as best we can using our memories and our abilities to see. But sometimes our best efforts are imperfect. We forget the correct story and add mistakes. Sometimes we change the story so that we can feel better about ourselves. Sometimes our knowledge has limits and we can only guess. We are two-legged, not gods. In our humility, we must be open to recognizing our errors. If we struggle with the stories of the other two-legged, and they struggle with our stories, that is good. It means that both peoples are listening to one another. If we sometimes laugh at each others' stories, that is good. It means that we are being open about the strangeness of our stories to the ears of the others. It is not disrespect. It is natural. What matters is that in the end we make a new story going forward together.

"That is the end of my Re-creation Story. It has only just begun. Now

you must write the rest. Respect our traditions, and have the courage to create new ones," Grandfather concludes.

The children sit in silence and watch the fire fade into embers. As darkness envelops them, each takes a pinch of kinni-kinnick and places it in the fire as an expression of gratitude for the gift they have just been given, and in expectation of gifts of wisdom and courage that they now hope their dreams and visitations will bring.

13

KOO-KOO-O-KOO
AND THE BEAR MOON

Asa's Un-Wounding

How do I represent the experience of consciousness and spirit taken on a journey in spiraled time, when I must write in a linear chronological fashion, left to right upon the page? It is difficult enough to compress the long, slow flow of storytelling time from an oral culture and then to jam it into the confines of written text. It is harder still to accurately portray a flash of intuition that connects multiple ancestors' lifetimes stretching back centuries, and to describe such an instantaneous event in the plodding time of written words.

Perhaps it was an effort to avoid the constraints of unidirectional linearity that inspired my ancestors to record some of their most sacred teachings in boustrophedon ideographic texts on birchbark scrolls.[1]

Even more appropriate to the experience presented below are Native American calendars portraying time as a spiral. These calendars represent a yet more complex view of time as circular, returning constantly to the past even as it flows toward and connects with the future. Among the most carefully explored examples of this kind of temporal thinking are Hopi spiral calendars. The extraordinary beauty and cosmological

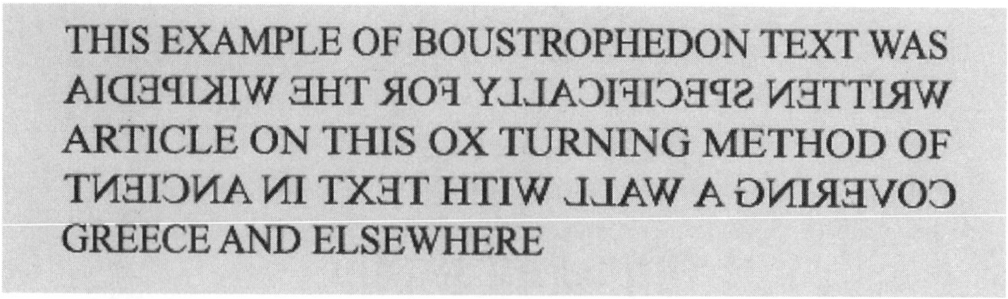

THIS EXAMPLE OF BOUSTROPHEDON TEXT WAS
WRITTEN SPECIFICALLY FOR THE WIKIPEDIA
ARTICLE ON THIS OX TURNING METHOD OF
COVERING A WALL WITH TEXT IN ANCIENT
GREECE AND ELSEWHERE

Fig. 13.1. This example of boustrophedon illustrates the Greek origins of the word, which means ox turning. Words appear in reverse every other line, as if an ox were plowing a field and reversing direction at every other furrow.
Image from Wikipedia, Creative Commons

density of these spiral petroglyphs, and their highly precise sun dagger markings of the solstice, have amazed anthropologists.[2]

The account that follows occurred in such a spiral time sequence (if the notion of sequence can apply). I beg the reader's indulgence as I jump back and forth between events of recent days, those of recent months recorded elsewhere in this text, and events occurring outside of my lifetime. I have struggled to record these personal experiences as if they unfolded in some chronological order, as it is more readable and accessible. But I have resisted the temptation to delve into magical realism to tell this part of my story, even though it might best approximate my subjective experience. I fear that such a device would sacrifice authenticity upon the altar of literary worship and suggest that what I describe did not really happen. As I have learned from Mother Earth, my natural kin, and ancestors, beautiful reality sometimes just does not need to be, and should not be, embellished and turned into fiction.

I can now imagine my journey of recent days, months, and years as a spiral drawn on birchbark, a few points highlighted, like beads in wampum serving as mnemonic tools, reminders of critical elements of a traditional story. As we do not have the luxury of sitting before a fire so that I can show you my scroll and recount my tale face-to-face, I must attempt to use written words and a crude drawing as substitutes.

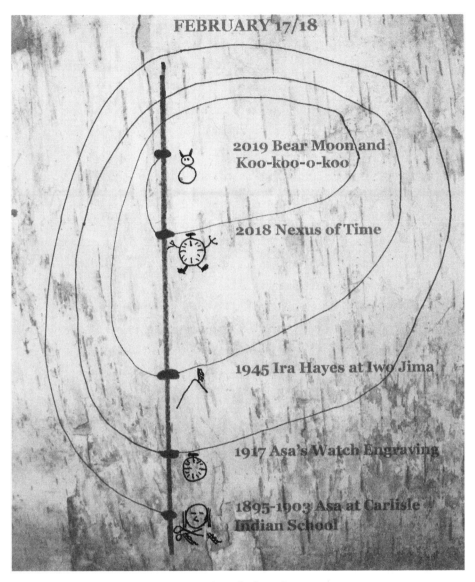

Fig. 13.2. Spiral of synchronicity

Sometimes this journey takes me to places that even my newly expanded awareness, imagination, and openness are barely able to grasp. So it has been these last two nights. And, as is becoming the pattern, my most recent experience has happened on the eve of, or during, a full moon.

It was the Bear Moon. I was just settling in for a night's sleep under a heavy down comforter, reading about the Menominee, who are part of our tribal genealogy. Then I heard Koo-koo-o-koo, barred owl, outside the window, close to the house. Startled by the clarity and proximity of the call, I opened the door into the cold and snowy night and stepped out onto the front porch in my pajamas. Koo-koo-o-koo called again from the forest.

I roused Carolyn, who joined me, shivering on the front porch, where I called, "Koo-koo-o-koo," a bit surprised that I could make the owl's call so well. In reply, "Koo-koo-o-koo" sounded from the forest. I called again, and the reply came through the bright moonlit forest, its floor whitened by today's snowfall and striped by the crisp, dark, moon shadows of trees. Breathtaking beauty.

This was my first experience of consciously interacting, in a reciprocal manner, with a wild animal, an owl no less. After several rounds of call and response, Carolyn and I returned to the warmth of shelter, shivering, partly from the cold and partly because goosebumps appeared in response to a hauntingly spiritual encounter.

In recent years, owls have played a continuing and growing role in my awakening. Our paths keep crossing. The increasing intensity and frequency of these encounters has filled me with wonder and a touch of perplexity. The most recent series of episodes began a few months ago, when I spotted a dead owl by the side of the road while driving through Vermont's largest swamp, a short distance from our house. I stopped and investigated. Other birds of prey had taken their toll on this probable victim of an encounter with a vehicle. But one wing, clean and largely unbroken, lay by the side of the road. I bent and reverently gathered the feathers, half expecting some Vermont game warden to descend on me for taking possession of a raptor or its remains.

Fortunately, my tribal newspaper, *Hownikan,* had recently published articles about Potawatomi efforts to rescue and heal injured eagles. One article explained that enrolled members of Native American tribes are exempt from a federal law, the Migratory Bird Treaty Act of

1918, which resulted from a 1916 international agreement between the United States, Great Britain, and Canada. The treaty protects endangered migratory birds; at the time, the use of feathers in women's hats had driven many birds to or near extinction. The penalty for killing a migratory bird, or even owning a single feather, is $15,000 and/or six months in jail. The exemption for Native Americans who own feathers and use them in ceremonies was introduced informally more than four decades ago. It was only formalized in 2012 by the Justice Department after many well-publicized cases of Native Americans running afoul of the law because of their possession and ceremonial use of eagle feathers.

After checking for my tattered tribal membership enrollment card in my wallet, I gathered the owl's feathers and carefully, reverently, placed them in my car.

Two days ago, at a small family reunion, I presented my cousin Barb with one of the owl feathers. I explained that she had been a messenger bearing cherished traditional knowledge on several occasions, including the extraordinary events surrounding my mother's death. Barb and I had been communicating by email, but decades had passed since any face-to-face meeting. To honor our reunion, it seemed appropriate to present Barb with a feather from kin who are viewed as messengers in Indian lore.

As we discussed naming ceremony possibilities for me and Carolyn, I unexpectedly found myself the bearer of a message as well. I spontaneously asked if Barb might find a name for our grandfather Asa Wall, as well as for Carolyn and me. I don't know who was more surprised by the request—my relatives or me. I have felt a special, deepened, connection with my grandfather since seeing *Children of God,* the play about life in the brutal residential schools. I was still processing the experience when our family gathering occurred.

My request for a Potawatomi name for my grandfather arose from the fact that his Carlisle Indian School records show a blank where "Indian name" was supposed to be recorded. This omission seemed like something that needed to be corrected. And that realization was a message that I needed to deliver, perhaps with the owl feather.

I should be clear: Asa's Indian name quite possibly was not omitted by oversight. We do not know if he was ever given a traditional name. Family letters dating to his lifetime distinguish between traditional family members and those moving into the mainstream white world. Our immediate branch of the family appears to have taken the latter path. So Asa himself may never have been given the choice of affirming his Indian identity with a traditional name.

Carolyn and I were struggling with this confusion and attempting to sort it out by asking, "What would Asa have wanted?" when the owl visitations intensified. The night after our gathering, Koo-koo-o-koo beckoned us to the front porch. It was a wonderful connection, perhaps a confirmation, though of what exactly I did not know. That was two nights ago, before the spiral of time gathered us in once again.

The temporal spiraling and ever-broadening context for these events is more than just a tale of feathers and owls. One year ago, exactly to the day, a Potawatomi elder had visited, and as a result I had written "Nexus of Time" about my grandfather Asa's unwound watch dancing when we were talking about him. The watch is engraved with a dedication dated February 19, 1917, precisely the same month and day that was to arrive in a few hours of our front porch encounter, at the very peak of a full moon.

Perhaps it was bright moonlight that awoke me again tonight. Or perhaps memories of the previous night's owl visitation and conversation. Or memories of events one year ago.

In any case, I was awakened well after midnight and was somehow motivated to go on a moonlight walk down our country roads, which snake through the forest. I have very rarely done such a thing before, and certainly not on a winter's night, with the temperature far below freezing. Bundled in layers of clothing, I took a hike in the lunar glow. I hoped that once again Koo-koo-o-koo would visit as ki did last night. I wanted to, felt a need to, replicate last night's experience of connection with the natural world, and perhaps also with ancestors.

A quarter mile from home I heard the owl's call; its origin was back on our land. So I reversed course, and as I approached our house, the calls became louder and more proximate. Standing alone in the still night and bright full moonlight, I called, "Koo-koo-o-koo." And was answered. Thus the conversation began, and continued for some time. The bitter cold began to force me to consider a cup of hot tea inside. But before my encounter ended, not one, but three owls and I were having a wonderful conversation. I think they were gathering in from a distance and enveloping me. I would first hear "Koo-koo-o-koo" faintly from afar, and then, with a series of calls and responses, the wonderful voices grew louder and closer.

This seemed so miraculous that I wondered about the reality of it all. Were the owls' responses mere coincidence? Without me, would these sounds be filling the forest on a moonlit night, when dark mice and other owl food would be most vulnerable scampering across the illuminated snow-white forest floor?

In a moment of hubris, I decided to test the existence of, the permeability of, perhaps even the reality of, the membrane that so often seems to separate what I once thought of as normal life and what I now experience as a deeply spiritual realm.

I looked up at the sky and saw a few stars. It was not one of those crystal clear winter nights when one can see the Milky Way and countless points of starlight. Only a few stars were visible. Still doubting my own senses, I contrived a test. I thought out loud, perhaps even shouted silently, "Show me a sign that is infinitely less probable than owls this Vermont forest night. Show me a shooting star. I don't know what to believe!" Now that is throwing down the spiritual gauntlet, yes?

No sooner had I released the thought than I began to feel embarrassed at the boldness of my demand. In the Bible, Job is burdened with tortuous doubt and endures. Abraham is pushed beyond reasonable limits in answering his God's demand to take his son's life as an act of faith. And I am demanding proof of the spiritual origins of calls from Koo-koo-o-koo?

Then, in moments, one of the brightest shooting stars I have ever seen slowly and brilliantly streaked from south to north. It was not one of those ephemeral, short, straight, thin-line flashes, like an illuminated dash, as is the norm with shooting stars. This was a wobbly, shaky, thick, extremely long luminescent line that hung in the sky for several seconds. It was like something drawn slowly in the heavens by the trembly hand of an elder.

"Oh my word," I thought. "I think I just saw a sign of our ancestors, more proximate than light-years deep into the heavens. Nearer than the upper atmosphere of the Earth." Nearly frozen and in need of warm tea, I went inside to reflect and to write.

Yes, indeed—my *word, my words.* For this journey of mine has often been about words. I have sought to write myself to deeper understanding with words. More often than not they come to me, unsolicited. Some of us see in visual images. Others hear. For me, words now dominate. I am plagued with wordplay. And I in turn am often a plague of words, of puns. Words routinely for me make the most sense turned upside down and inside out, crucifying clarity upon an unholy spiral of verbal twists and turns.

With this awareness, my thoughts returned to the notion that our ancestors were communicating this particular night, this anniversary, as they did with Asa's watch. I once again thought of this little golden timekeeping treasure, and typed "unwound" in order to memorialize that moment a year ago when Asa's unwound watch had danced and was being celebrated tonight.

Then, as the letters appeared, I realized that *wound* is both a verb, as in the past tense of *to wind*, and a noun, as in physical *wounds* (of war) or psychological and spiritual *wounds* (of Indian boarding school).

Our Potawatomi language, reflecting a culture of animism, is verb-heavy, I recalled. So perhaps I was typing a verb and not a noun?

If so, might Asa's inanimate, then animated, watch *unwound* be a call to healing? My own writings were once again trying to tell me something I had missed right there on the surface: "It is time to *un-wound!*" Koo-koo-o-koo had delivered that message two nights in a row. Another owl had given its life in order to give me the messenger feather.

A patient grandfather spirit, who once had hesitated to tell me of his Indian school days, had now been released by the play *Children of God,* which had been performed almost in my lap, and he was sending a message. The possibility of a healing naming ceremony to fill in that painful blank space on his Carlisle Indian School records was animating his spirit, as it had his watch a year ago. I did not get it then, so he wrote a message across the heavens: Listen to Koo-koo-o-koo. This *is* real.

Time for *un-wounding*—healing. I get it. Sorry you had to tell me so many times in so many ways. I am still learning how to listen.

14

AWAKENINGS ON THE RESERVATION

While I have been developing more intimate connections with my ancestors, my forest kin, and Mother Earth, my connections with fellow Potawatomi living on reservations have been lacking, as my book title suggests and as my narrative has documented. This started to change when Carolyn and I attended a gathering of the Great Lakes Intertribal Food Summit, an annual celebration of Native American food traditions. This year the event was hosted by the Pokagon Band of Potawatomi (Pokégnek Bodéwadmik) on their reservation in Michigan, just northeast of Chicago.

The Pokagon are located on the homeland of my Potawatomi ancestor, Sha Note, who married the voyageur Jacques Vieux and brought Native American roots to my family tree. On the one hand, I eagerly anticipated visiting this reservation as part of my journey homeward. On the other hand, I approached the event with considerable anxiety. I would be a long-lost tribal member returning home and looking very European, more settler-colonial than Native American.

So it was a wonderful surprise when the first hour of the first morning at the summit was an awakening into a beautiful dream. An enticing breakfast buffet consisting of traditional foods such as wild rice, "decolonized eggs," and wild edibles gathered from the local forest made me feel immediately at home. In recent years I have become seriously gluten- and dairy-intolerant and as a result have been forced to eat more and more like my ancestors. In most social situations involving food, I feel like an oddity and a burden for anyone attempting to be a host.

However, as I stood in the breakfast serving line, I had a gut feeling that my visit to the Pokagon reservation was going to be both physically and spiritually welcoming. Meetings and workshops on Native American food growing, gathering, preparation, and ceremonial practices made me feel more at home by the hour. A welcoming sense of peace descended upon both me and Carolyn, who was inspired by hands-on workshops given by Native women on traditional practices associated with handling heritage seeds (seed ancestors).

I went on a guided walk in the forest, where we identified wild edibles and harvested elm bark for basket making. I was surrounded by campfires, where meat was being smoked, dried corn ground or cooked with ash to make it more palatable, and clay pots were being made for cooking directly in the fire.

Then several workshops touching on Native American treaty rights delivered a wake-up call, shifting our attention from hands-on activities within the reservation to conflicts at its boundaries.

We learned that members of tribal communities in the upper Midwest are routinely denied their federally guaranteed treaty rights to carry on millennia-old practices of hunting, fishing, and gathering food. When Native Americans exercised these rights on nontribal lands bordering the reservation, they were often harassed by non-Natives. They were stoned and sometimes shot at. Not infrequently they were arrested by local law enforcement officials, who either did not understand the rights of Native Americans guaranteed in treaties or simply chose to ignore them and instead imposed local or state laws on a federally recognized sovereign nation. In addition to the physical intimidation, tribal members were being denied access to food and income upon which many depended. They were being denied their ability to engage in activities with cultural and spiritual dimensions. Consequently,

Native American treaty rights activists were frequently in court defending their legal rights.

It seemed to me obvious that some considerable part of the misapplication of state law to Native Americans arose from resentment that Indians had unjustifiable "special privileges," such as hunting and fishing outside of permit time frames created for non-Native Americans.

This part of being on a reservation was a new stage of my awakening. It was no longer just ancestors and forest kin who were opening my eyes with gentle prodding; it was my contemporaries, who were forcing me to reflect on conflicts that happen on and around reservations now, and not just in the distant past. An inward journey was awakening a sense of broader social responsibility.

The Lakota (Sioux Indian) Nation's opposition to the Dakota Access oil pipeline linking shale oil fields to distant refineries came to mind. That pipeline poses a threat to water quality on Native American reservations. The environmental impact review for the pipeline did not adequately acknowledge or address Native American claims and rights. The same issues—failing to adequately recognize indigenous people's treaty rights—were playing out in Canada's Trans Mountain Pipeline connecting Alberta to a coastal port in British Columbia. Where I was finding the warm embrace of Mother Earth, reservation Indians were struggling, and often encountering violence, in their frontline efforts to protect Mother Earth.

As with so many other Native American issues about which I previously had only an arm's-length awareness, I was once again being visited with an immediate reality. Indigenous rights issues shifted to the foreground.

I wondered if my spiritual journey was irrelevant to more pressing matters on the reservation. I began to struggle with my conscience for not being at Standing Rock when so many others were putting themselves on the line to stop the mindless march toward more fossil fuel use and climate change. I had spent decades working on environmental issues around the globe and in the United States. For years, I had worked day and night on environmental protection issues—until I burned out and eventually needed to take several years off to physically recover. How could I return to this level of activism?

Once again, connections and a constructive pathway forward appeared, in their usual roundabout but compelling way. It happened during Professor Martin Reinhardt's Pokagon workshop, where he explained his work legally defending Native American treaty rights.

At first hearing, Reinhardt's work sounded like another compelling tale about defending civil rights. But then another abstract concept I had read and heard about came to life before me. Native Americans on and about the reservation were not just interested in protecting mainstream civil rights, which are guaranteed to them as U.S. citizens. They were as much or more concerned about winning consistent recognition for treaty rights they enjoyed as members of *sovereign* nations existing within the boundaries of the United States. This is a mind-boggling reality for many in mainstream society. A legal nation within our national boundaries?

Sovereign is a word that one hears a great deal on the reservation, although it is not heard commonly in everyday conversations in the mainstream. The reason is simple: the United States is a powerful nation, and its citizens rarely if ever have the legitimacy of their constitutional rights challenged at home. Minorities often find that their constitutional rights are not respected, but rarely do law enforcement officials and government leaders deny, outright and boldly, the very reality of applicable laws that protect these rights.

However, when it comes to treaty rights and the sovereign, independent legal status of Indian nations, Native Americans must struggle constantly for acknowledgment of the very existence of their rights, because they must struggle for acknowledgment of their nationhood. Tribal sovereignty is recognized in the U.S. Constitution,* more than

---

*Article I, Section 8 of the U.S. Constitution, which deals with federal powers, refers to Native American nations as separate entities on par with foreign nations. "Congress shall have the power to regulate Commerce with foreign nations and among the several states, and with the Indian tribes."

500 treaties, various declarations of Congress, international agreements applicable to indigenous people,* numerous U.S. court decisions,† and hundreds of federal statutes. Nevertheless, tribal sovereignty is still threatened, and with it Indian societies and culture.

Mining and timber companies with leases on former reservation lands, now held as "trust lands" by the U.S. government, undermine claims of sovereignty and tribal benefits. Seafood companies and hydro-dam operators continually attempt to undermine ancient treaty rights guaranteeing protection of Native American fishing grounds. Petroleum companies wreaking havoc in South American rainforest preserves are being sued in U.S. courts over violations of indigenous nations' rights. Across the United States, the casino industry, resenting competition from gambling on Indian reservations, has mounted massive challenges to the constitutionality of Indian nations' sovereign status, racializing their challenges in order to broaden the base of the attack against their competitors.[1]

Many who challenge the concept of Native American sovereignty claim that Indians benefit from "special privileges" or "unfair competitive advantages" associated with casinos, and that this situation is making tribes wealthy. The absurdity of the claim is refuted by the realities of colonial devastation still evident on the reservations. Native Americans have lost 99 percent of the lands they held when Europeans invaded and colonized. Native Americans on the reservation have statistically high rates of poverty, substance abuse, and suicide. These indicators of extreme social and economic stress go back centuries. Treaty rights were designed to offset this legacy. Nevertheless, the survival of Indian culture and society is still under the same threats that it has faced continually for five hundred years.

Now some in the mainstream are awakening, as I have, to the realization that as indigenous rights are degraded, so too is the qual-

---

*United Nations Declaration on the Rights of Indigenous Peoples, 2007
†Notably the "Marshall Trilogy," three Supreme Court cases between 1823 and 1832 clarifying and reaffirming Native American sovereignty

ity of the environment. The reason is quite simple: Native Americans have a totally different worldview and attitude toward Mother Earth, and frequently put themselves at the leading edge of nature protection efforts.

At Pokagon, I learned that Native American sovereignty, in its broadest sense, lies at the heart of efforts to protect this planet. The kinship I have come to feel toward my forest kin has traditionally been part of Native American culture and consciousness. Although this connection may have been attenuated by the urbanization of many Native Americans, it is alive, well, and beckoning.

A single image leaped off the screen and made this connection for me at Pokagon. As Professor Reinhardt put up a slide of the following drawing, I had the wonderful experience of a picture being worth a thousand words.

Fig. 14.1. Treaty protest pictograph, 1849
Wisconsin Historical Society, WHS-1871

This pictograph was part of an 1849 petition given on behalf of the Ojibwe Indian tribe to the U.S. government protesting violations of the 1842 La Pointe Treaty, which guaranteed hunting and fishing rights as well as land claims. The narrow and conventional explanation of the document is that it pictorially represents the *dodems,* or totems, which are symbols representing tribal clans making the protest. The lines connecting all of the images' hearts and eyes are said to represent the profound interconnectedness and solidarity of the clans involved.

This reading may capture the explicit message contained in the extraordinary document, but it stops far short of acknowledging the deeper significance of what is being portrayed. Totems are not always mere symbols or calling card representations for clans, as are mascots for athletic teams. Indigenous people often have a deeply personal and intimate relationship with their totems,* much as I have described in these pages. The pictograph represents a deeply spiritual and moral grounding that connects the tribal groups involved. It is no mere temporary contract of convenience created for the purposes of a single engagement with the U.S. government. The bonds described are more akin to the fundamental sacred bonds of a "social contract" in the sense used by social philosophers in Europe in the seventeenth and eighteenth centuries. John Locke, Thomas Hobbes, David Hume, and Jean-Jacques Rousseau attempted to ground society, the legitimacy of government, and obedience to the rule of law in a moral imperative that transcends individual and often ephemeral constitutions. Edmund Burke eloquently

---

*The exact nature of Native American relationships with totems is hotly disputed among anthropologists. Theresa Schenck, in "The Algonquian Totem and Totemism: A Distortion of the Semantic Field" argues that totems, or dodems, for Native Americans are merely clan identifiers with no spiritual connotations, and that the deeply spiritual connections attributed to Native American totem relationships are a creation of anthropologists who imported notions of totemism from studies of indigenous Australians (Schenck, "Algonquian Totem," 341–53). Michael Pomedli acknowledges the existence of the argument, but provides abundant evidence throughout his *Living with Animals: Ojibwe Spirit Powers* that Native Americans did indeed have intimate connections with clan totems (Pomedli, *Living with Animals,* 134).

encapsulated the idea of a social contract as inter-generational when he affirmed that society is a contract "between those who are living, those who are dead, and those who are to be born."[2]

There is a startling parallel between the writings of this erudite Anglo-Irishman and the wisdom of the Native American notion of thinking in terms of seven generations—three reaching into our ancestral past and three reaching forward to our descendants.

My new awareness has exposed the limits of Burke's thinking. The lines in the pictograph not only connect totems, they connect the totems to a map in the lower left. The Native American social contract is not only among the humans (two-legged), it is also with their natural kin, embodied as totems. Nonhumans are an essential part of Native American kinship networks and hence Native American society. Most significantly, all of the interconnected creatures are connected by a line to the land, Mother Earth, represented in the pictograph as the lakes where the tribes dwelled. Here Native American thinking is light-years ahead of, millennia behind, and freed from, the mechanistic, presentist mindset of Europe's finest thinkers.

Reinhardt put up another slide that led me to an astounding realization. It showed language from a 2010 U.S. Courts of Appeals decision in the case of *United States v. Confederated Tribes of Colville Indian Reservation*. The court's decision affirms, in several unusually redundant and emphatic instructions, the following message referring to interpreting the meaning of a treaty, which derives from Supreme Court guidance: "The treaty must therefore be construed, not according to the technical meaning of its words to learned lawyers, but in the sense in which they would naturally be understood by the Indians."[3]

The wonderful shock and implications of these words of jurisprudence, presented to me by a Native American treaty rights advocate, rivaled the momentary sense of wonder I experienced when Koo-koo-o-koo, my grandfather's watch, and the midnight shooting star delivered their messages.

If treaties with Native Americans are to be understood and

interpreted as Indians understand them, then the 1849 Treaty of La Pointe petition makes it clear that *when Native Americans signed treaties, their tribes and nations included seven generations of humankind, natural kin of the four-legged, winged, and rooted variety, and Mother Earth.*

If I were to make this argument before the court that handed down the *United States v. Confederated Tribes* decision, I have no doubt that my effort to oblige the U.S. government to protect Mother Earth, Native American ancestors, and natural kin on lands impacted by treaty obligations with Indians would at best be viewed with extreme skepticism and most likely rejected categorically. Cautious judges would immediately sense that I was nudging them toward the slippery slope of recognizing the personhood of nonhuman creatures and also implicitly recognizing the rights of nature.* Notions of Native American sovereignty would expand like protective airbags in an automobile, which inflate in fractions of a second and save lives.

I dream that the day will come when not only our courts, but we as an enlightened population will accept the wisdom of the La Pointe Treaty protest pictograph. It is not too much to dream of a moment when other living creatures will be embraced as "thou" and not manipulated as "it." After all, the Constitution stipulated that each person who was a slave counted as merely three-fifths of a person for the purposes of allocating electoral votes at the nation's founding. The infamous Dred Scott decision of the Supreme Court in 1857 declared that slaves were property, with no right to bring legal actions in federal courts. We have moved beyond such denials of personhood and kinship with our fellow human beings. Might we not be capable of the same breakthrough with our natural kin?

In the meantime, I can hope that this line of argument will seem less incomprehensible to those who have read my book. Perhaps the

---

*The rights of nature is a concept that has achieved legal recognition in courts in New Zealand and Ecuador, among others, used in support of indigenous people's efforts to preserve environmental quality through protection of rivers.

idea that deep connections with our ancestors and natural kin are more than just delightful topics for fiction, and the recognition that they are real and have moral implications, has opened your eyes to wonderful possibilities.

If a middle-class off-the-reservation Indian can help to reestablish the validity of human connections to ancestors and natural kin, maybe there is something out there for others. If a Native American like me with attenuated cultural connections can shed light on how we might rethink our engagement with nature, what more might we learn from Indians living on the reservation if they actually regain all the land, the rights, and the resources they are legally entitled to, so that they might teach us by example?

15

ROOTLESS IN
THE BOTANICAL GARDEN

Is it possible to have a deep, continual, intimate relationship—or for that matter any kind of meaningful relationship—with nature while being rooted in a human-built or highly disturbed environment? Is the answer to this question different for Native Americans and for those who do not have indigenous ancestry and sensitivities? How do we answer if we ask the question from the perspective of other beings: the four-legged, the winged, and the rooted ones?

I am fortunate enough to have lived for two decades in Vermont, one of the more rural places in the eastern United States, and one of the smallest and least populated states in the country. The very name *Vermont* is derived from the French words for *green* and *mountain*: *vert* and *mont*. I look out the window into a forest that is carpeted in the springtime with wildflowers, Dutchman's breeches (*Dicentra cucullaria*). To the west is a wetland and pond where tiny frogs chirp all night and resident geese and ducks call out. North and south is the territory of owls, Koo-koo-o-koo. Coy-Wolf howls come and go in the night from all directions.

When Carolyn and I are not in the forest, we are in our small apartment in Montréal, near where the St. Lawrence River forms Lac-Saint-Louis, the southern boundary of the arrondisement, or district, of

Lachine. Here the dominant sounds are traffic, church bells, and sirens from a nearby fire station. This is an intensely man-made, urban environment. Patches of well-trodden green are to be found mostly in small areas between expanses of concrete and asphalt pavement.

Moving back and forth between these two radically different worlds increases my appreciation for and awareness of the natural world. It also makes me wonder about how we as a species adapt to, or suffer from, urban nature disconnects.

For me, the epitome of this dilemma—being disconnected from nature yet seeking connection—is to be found in the Montreal Botanical Garden, an institution that is, ironically, dedicated to plant and nature preservation. We often bicycle there to enjoy gardens, an arboretum, or greenhouses, which replicate on a small scale the mix of flora to be found in desert, semitropical, and tropical environments.

It is, however, the garden's large bonsai and *penjing** collection of miniaturized trees that continually commands my attention. While standing in the midst of these beautiful, artificially dwarfed trees, I experience many reactions simultaneously: awe at their beauty, admiration for the experts who maintain them, and sadness for these living beings who dwell in containers, their roots one meter above a concrete floor, never to touch Mother Earth. It is the latter fact, real unrootedness, that leaves me struggling to fully understand and overcome my own profound sense of being biologically rootless in Montréal. This experience is all the more perplexing as I have recently reconnected, rather profoundly, with my human ancestral roots in Montréal. Why do I feel so rooted and uprooted at the same time and in the same place? What can this state of consciousness, divided against itself, reveal if I examine it carefully?

All of this muddle has forced me to back up and confront a series of awkward but illuminating possibilities.

---

*Bonsai is the ancient Chinese and later Japanese practice of miniaturizing trees that are grown in containers. *Penjing* is the practice of miniaturizing trees to produce a landscape with multiple plantings and stones or sculptures within the containers.

First, I have been on the verge of uncritically echoing what many naturalists and wilderness advocates implicitly, if not explicitly, affirm: a value judgment that life immersed in "unspoiled" nature is spiritually richer or better than urban life. This notion originates from oversimplification and misreadings of Thoreau's *Walden* and the writings of naturalists such as John Muir, Aldo Leopold, and others.

Second, I was ignoring the obvious fact that many of our most passionate and eloquent advocates of wilderness developed their appreciation of and sensitivity to the natural world partly through their experiences in human settlements. Their enlightenment did not arise spontaneously in a wilderness where they had lived from the beginning of their lives as feral children, in total isolation from human culture. For example, my beloved Henry David Thoreau spent many years of his life working in and managing the family pencil factory.[1] That less-publicized aspect of his life very much contributed to his appreciation of the benefits of living in the wild. Even after he became a celebrated naturalist and Transcendentalist, Thoreau spent years in crowded public places: lecture halls filled with enthralled listeners. Thoreau lived only temporarily in his famous cabin in the woods.

Third, in reflecting upon my own awakening, I have not yet come to terms with the fact that 70 percent of contemporary Native and non-Native Americans now live primarily in human-settled areas, as Thoreau did for most of his life. If I hope for my readers to see the relevance of my writing, I need to explore if and how traditional Native American and mainstream culture and consciousness maintain and cultivate direct connections with the natural world *while being embedded in a primarily human-built and often profoundly disrupted natural world.*

If I do not address and reconcile these issues, I risk setting Native Americans, their culture, and their sensibilities on a pedestal, something akin to the nineteenth-century Romantic notion of noble savages living in a pristine natural world. This mischaracterization, still widely shared as a cultural stereotype, risks turning what should be an admirable model into something more like an exotic, inaccessible, and unattainable uniqueness. This is devastating as it "others" Native Americans, letting mainstream society off the hook from its responsibility to truly understand indigenous perspectives. More seriously, Native exceptionalism does not encourage those in mainstream culture to fulfill their own obligations to protect nature.

Whenever I struggle with these questions, I return to the Montreal Botanical Garden's collection of bonsai and penjing trees in miniature. And I ask, "What do the real experts on living disconnected from nature, the bonsai trees, have to say on this matter?"

To answer that question, let me invite you to join in a tour of their home. I hope that it will be more than just another travel magazine summary of a tourist hot spot. My desire is that this can be a lesson in listening, seeing, and feeling with Native American sensibilities.

Butterflies Go Free

It is March, a grayish and cold month in late winter, when once pristine white snow lies blackened and piled high in the Botanical Garden's parking lots. At this time of year, north of the forty-fifth parallel, long, sunny days seem a distant memory. In order to momentarily escape this gloom, Carolyn and I have decided to visit the botanical garden's annual "Papillons en liberté/Butterflies Go Free" exhibit. The hugely popular event is held in a large, heated greenhouse. Visitors must walk through other greenhouses to reach the exhibition.

The final and smallest greenhouse before reaching the "Butterflies Go Free" exhibition is the bonsai and penjing collection: tiny trees growing in beautiful ceramic containers. They range in age from a decade to nearly a century. Despite their age, each tree is less than a meter tall; most do not even reach half a meter in height. They are living images that appear to have been taken directly from antique paintings of the Sung Dynasty. Nature has been coaxed to conform to human aesthetics, an altered and meticulously curated reality to which we will return after making our way to the butterfly exhibit.

We enter the butterfly exhibition through a double-doored entry lock. This careful effort to secure and contain the butterflies is part of an effort to prevent the beautiful creatures from escaping into other greenhouses, or into the surrounding city, where they and their offspring might become hungry, devastating, invasive caterpillars or spread plant diseases.

Inside, thousands of butterflies and moths of all sizes, colors, and shapes fill the air and cover a wide variety of plants. Some are luminescent and attract the eye. Others practice camouflage and can be located only with great effort. I once asked what happens to the butterflies after the exhibition. I was told that they and any eggs are incinerated.* The information quite literally knocked me off balance for a while. It colored my visit and dulled the luster of the beauty flitting about the room.

My shock and horror resulted in a fantasy which I hold dearly. Perhaps it will become a short story some day. But for now, it is a fragment of newly developed consciousness that I drag about the entire garden, like a ball and chain attached to one leg. Life was so much simpler when I just viewed the world less critically and within a mainstream cultural frame.

After realizing that they are condemned to yearly premature hatching, and then required to hold a carefully choreographed yearly pageant for visitors, the butterflies begin to feel like one of those concentration camp orchestras whose members were allowed to live only so long as they entertained their jailers. The winged ones eventually see the handwriting on the wall, or more appropriately the message written in the dew that accumulates on the inside

---

*One news article, from the *Montreal Gazette,* reports that butterflies alive at this exhibit's end are put in envelopes and shipped to another exhibit.[2] Shipping butterflies is another troubling matter, as many butterflies are crushed while being put inside of envelopes. "The North American Butterfly Association (NABA) points out that 'many wedding planners now avoid butterflies at weddings because they not infrequently arrive dead, or half-dead.'"[3]

of winter-chilled greenhouse window glass. It reads "Escape or submit to a perpetual cycle of doom."

The butterflies plan a prison break. It is in both its mechanics and spirit like the 1973 movie Papillon, *a prison escape film starring Steve McQueen and Dustin Hoffman. In this movie, the central character, a safecracker, is framed for murder, imprisoned, and brutalized in multiple remote locations, from which he continually escapes. Finally he is sent to the infamous Devil's Island prison in the Caribbean, from which no one has ever escaped. The protagonist is nicknamed "Papillon," the French word for* butterfly, *because he has a tattoo of the insect on his chest. But more to the theme of my story, the prisoner's final, successful escape from Devil's Island suggests that he has the freedom of a butterfly within his reach as he floats away on a raft made of coconuts.*

In this spirit, the garden's butterflies slowly plot their escape for generations. They act with the determination of human prisoners who use a spoon or crude metal tool to dig tunnels for countless years through stone walls and under vast distances to the outside world. In my story, some butterflies who scheme to survive the annual postexhibition extermination hide in rafters of the greenhouse and its tiny nooks and crannies. Their next challenge is to escape the effects of cold after the exhibit ends and the heat is turned down. They find steam-heat pipes that are poorly insulated. They then develop a plan to avoid the deadly effect of the "purifying" postexhibition yearly pesticide applications. They manage to transmit this information about the unfolding escape plan and route from generation to generation, much as Monarch butterflies somehow transmit memory of migratory routes and the precise coordinates of their ancestors' birthplaces, to which their descendants will return.

One day, when little children and indulgent parents once again ignore signs about not touching the butterflies, and they pose with smartphones while colorful performers alight on little hands, fingers and clothing, the butterflies do it. They execute the final act of their escape plan. They lay their eggs in the creases of colorful, hand-knit sweaters, and in the machine-crocheted flowers sewn onto them by distant Chinese factory workers. In this pseudonature found on human clothing, the butterflies introduce tiny fragments of real nature. And they give their descendants the gift of freedom, even if they themselves will not see or experience it. Now that is thinking seven generations ahead.

Once these human visitors return to their Montréal homes, the eggs, which were protected inside the human warmed snowsuits, hatch. The resulting caterpillars and butterflies develop a strategy to survive, some living on exotic big box store houseplants that were imported from abroad. These survivor butterflies acclimate. Some reproduce on their own natural schedule. They breathe the outdoor air of summer for the first time in generations. And they find plants and nectar sufficient to nourish them. They establish themselves, eventually making news in local papers as the "latest invasives."

Then, as some of them alight on houseplants around Montréal and rest, they watch humans viewing a French-dubbed version of an old movie, Papillon. The winged ones silently testify to the film's message: while escaped prisoners may pose a threat to society, their liberated spirits are a triumph of the will to survive and ultimately affirm the reason life continues on this planet.

I am eventually overcome by the noise of the crowded exhibit. I return from my reverie to the reality before me: a large greenhouse with butterflies whisking about in great numbers while snow and wind abound outdoors. The sight is certainly breathtaking. And perhaps the event is partially successful, or so I tell myself: after all, it is used to educate busloads of schoolkids about butterflies and other insects. One hopes that some larger sense of appreciating the natural world will take hold, rooting biophilia in young, urbanized minds. The joy on young faces, amazed at the winged ones, is truly wonderful, and I remind myself that I should hesitate to undermine such embrace of the natural world, even if it is rooted in a large measure of naïveté about the destiny of those who charm the young visitors. Perhaps the young children won't notice, can't read, or won't question the rather misleading exhibition title "Butterflies Go Free."*

But I cannot long escape such troubled musings. I have learned to listen to my kin, the winged and rooted ones. The very concepts of rootedness and freedom are being seriously challenged a few steps away in the bonsai hall, and a fated rendezvous with these ideas is beckoning me. With this thought in mind, I reluctantly pass back out of another double door passage and return to the bonsai exhibition. With fanciful images of escaped butterflies still in mind, I stand with agonizing ambivalence before the potted plants.

My thoughts return to rootedness, both in its literal meaning and as metaphor. I struggle; I tell myself that I must be honest and recognize that these tiny, stunted, and heavily pruned trees are forced into perpetual miniaturization for mere human pleasure. Their limbs are forced to conform to human notions of natural perfection by being continually pruned and wrapped with wire that distorts their growth.

The roots of these miniaturized trees, which live in shallow containers fifteen centimeters deep, are also continually pruned. Such actions are painful echoes of foot binding, a practice that made aristocratic women in imperial China have little, "pretty," and broken feet on which they could barely walk.

Between visits to the bonsai, in an attempt to ground my hypersensitive musings about plant suffering, I force myself to reread scientific literature on how trees communicate with one another,[4] how they form communities, and how their roots are connected by vast mycorrhizal networks now called the "woodwide web." Information and nutrients travel along these tiny threads. Although I risk anthropomorphizing,

---

*I am not alone in finding the exhibition's title troublesome. An article published on the North American Butterfly Association website and authored by leading butterfly experts (Jeffrey Glassberg, president of NABA; Paul Opler, author of *Peterson Field Guide to Eastern Butterflies;* Robert M. Pyle, author of *Audubon Society Field Guide to Butterflies;* Robert Robbins, curator of Lepidoptera, Smithsonian Institution; and James Tuttle, president of the Lepidopterists' Society) is titled "There's No Need to Release Butterflies—They're Already Free."

these relations rise to the level of living forms caring for one another.

My delving into science offers little comfort; it merely fuels my concerns. Now I must confront the reality of bonsai trees cut off not only from the Earth, but also from one another.

I try to reconcile myself to the fact that mistreated trees are not about to become an exhibition of "Bonsai Go Free." They cannot hitch a ride to freedom, as the butterflies might.

And then I notice that one of the many beautiful bonsai trees has in fact attempted the seemingly impossible. This plant must have read the sign at the entrance to the butterfly exhibit and decided that the idea of escaping to freedom, of growing real and deep roots, rather than having them perpetually pruned, was worth an attempt. Its ceramic container has been cracked by roots refusing to recognize the limits of their imprisonment. I momentarily wonder if this effort will set off some kind of alarm, if pruners will soon arrive in an electric golf cart with a flashing light, prepared to end a budding insurrection. I even imagine a plants rights advocacy group making a documentary about the Great Bonsai Escape attempt, and that it might have a soundtrack of Montréal's own Leonard Cohen singing "There is a crack in everything."[5]

As a result of this fanciful encounter, I write to a Chinese colleague, Liu Yang, about my reactions. She has just written a Ph.D. dissertation on urban and rooftop gardening in China.*[6] A fan of bonsai, she has recently written to me explaining how much pleasure she finds in a small bonsai-like plant in the window of her urban room. When contemplating it, she imagines herself as an ant-sized being in the mossy forest. It was an idea inspired by Kimmerer's *Gathering Moss,* which I had previously sent to her because of its possible connections to her research.

I hesitate at first to undermine Yang's wonderful fantasy, concerned that she might view my questions about the botanical garden's bonsai as an implicit criticism of her thesis. After all, its premise is that urban

---

*The theme of a disconnection from nature in an urban context is explored in "Analysis of Urban Farming Practice through the Lens of Metabolic Rift: Case Studies at the City of Chengdu in China and at the City of Freiberg in Germany."

dwellers do indeed reconnect to nature with their tiny balcony plantings, rooftop gardens, and urban gardening plots. She was even suggesting that urban gardeners were maintaining some deep, even spiritual, connections with nature.

I am surprised by Yang's response. She directs me to a nineteenth-century Chinese poem, "Sick Plum Blossom." In the poem the author, Gong Zizhen, reflects on his encounter with a collection of heavily pruned bonsai plum trees and laments their fate. He buys them, releases them from their confining containers, which he shatters, and plants them in the ground. Chairman Mao purportedly liked this poem; he saw it as a portrayal of the decadence of aristocratic life.

Encouraged, I wonder if Gong Zizhen, or I, might have a protest exhibition featuring liberated plants. It would be called "Bonsai Plants Go Free." It is an inviting fantasy, but I doubt that the Montreal Botanical Garden would entertain such a suggestion. My previous experience with the institution indicated that they are not receptive to suggestions challenging fundamental assumptions about eighteenth- and nineteenth-century horticultural traditions, "conservatories," and collections of specimens. Even less comforting for them is raising fundamental questions about human engagement with the natural world and the ethics and spirituality surrounding these efforts.

I discovered that botanical gardens are rooted rather narrowly in a scientific model of botanical knowledge. They are laudably committed to scientific inquiry, and the rigor that such a scientific mindset entails. Consequently, they often challenge and correct public misconceptions about plants. There are wonderful little signs to this effect throughout greenhouses and gardens at the Montreal Botanical Garden. But on matters of human culture rather than horticulture, they are more than a little stuck in the mud.

This became obvious to me when the Montreal Botanical Garden hosted a wonderful international exhibition of mosaiculture in 2013. Dozens of giant floral images, both flat and three-dimensional, filled acres of the garden. The images and sculptures were composed of plants that were used like living pointillist dots in Impressionist paintings or like fragments of glass and ceramic in mosaics—hence the notion of mosaiculture, which might better be thought of as mosaisculpture. We visited the display multiple times and brought many friends. It provided memories for a lifetime.

But, once again my rational, historical awareness combined with my budding Native American consciousness to complicate what could have been an unmediated aesthetic experience. This occurred as I stood before a humongous, three-dimensional, fifteen-meter-tall mosiaculture creation titled *Mother Earth*. One of the most popular and awe-inspiring installations, it was intended to celebrate Canada's First Nations peoples and their teachings. As the event catalog notes:

> Montreal International Mosaiculture 2013 could have no better ambassador than *Mother Earth*, the exhibition's second masterpiece, to set the tone for the event's key theme, "Land of Hope", and to illustrate its first subtheme, the interdependence of man and nature.
>
> Taking its cues from North American Aboriginal culture, *Mother Earth* was inspired by a speech reportedly delivered in 1854 by Chief Seattle during his meeting with then President of the United States Franklin Pierce on the occasion of the sale of Native land to white settlers. His words capture the essence of the privileged relationship our continent's first inhabitants maintain with nature.
>
> From that speech, the following excerpts served as the basis for *Mother Earth*:
>
> "We are part of the earth and it is part of us. The perfumed flowers are our sisters, the deer, the horse, and the great eagle are our brothers. The rocky crests, the juices in the meadows, the body heat of the pony, and man, all belong to the same family. . . .
>
> What is man without the beasts? If all the beasts were gone, man would die from great loneliness of the spirit. For what ever happens to the beasts, soon happens to man. . . .

Preserve the memory of this Earth as [we] deliver it. And with all your strength, your spirit and your heart, preserve it for your children and love it as God loves us all."[7]

These thoughts about the relationship of humans to nature are noble. The real author of these words, however, is a professor who taught at a college where I once was a research scholar in environmental studies. I interviewed the author decades ago and wrote about the true origins of the speech for the ECOLOGIA Newsletter.[8]

The revelations collided with the claims of some of my ecologically passionate colleagues, who asserted that they had the original version of Chief Seattle's speech in its Native American language. Their dismay was probably increased when I exposed numerous settler-colonial misconceptions and embarrassing historical distortions in the speech. In fact the speech was re-created for a television movie, and was taken from a minister's highly imaginative reinvention, made thirty years after the fact, of what Chief Seattle might have said.

When I wrote to the Botanical Garden about their error and misattribution, I was ignored. I offered to have a small seminar explaining that although the origins of the speech were confusing, its lesson was affirmative and valid, perhaps even more so: we can reinvent ourselves. We can reimagine ourselves within the frame of Native American sensibilities, even if we are not descended from indigenous ancestors.

Had I written to the administration with a botanical fact check, I think there would have been a rapid response and correction. But cultural matters, even in the context of Canada's enlightened reconciliation efforts with First Nations, do not easily resonate with botanists and the public relations staff who act as promoters of popular exhibitions. So the plaque with quotes from "Chief Seattle's speech" remained in place, prominently in front of the mosaiculture monument, for the duration of the summer and autumn. No corrections or errata were noted at the exhibition site or in the catalog. A white man's words building on another white man's words, which attempted to put unspoken words into the mouth of Chief Seattle, remained standing as a tribute to the wisdom of indigenous people.

More troubling was the possibility that this was yet another manifestation of the disconnected-from-nature consciousness that I was struggling to understand: white settlers living in an urban environment pretending to be more Native than Native Americans, and preaching to other urbanites about the virtue of the deeply interconnected natural world. Talk about cultural appropriation.

With the bitter taste of this experience still lingering, I reconciled myself to not raising questions about the bonsai exhibit. I even let go of my more practical fallback fantasy of leaving tiny cards with lines from "Sick Plum Blossom" in the bonsai exhibition hall. Such surrender was difficult, because I could easily anticipate the vibes of disappointment I would get from the bonsai that had cracked ki's ceramic prison. Ki had sent a message to those who looked carefully. It was the bonsai hall's equivalent of a message in a bottle. Had I picked up and tossed this desperate plea back into an ocean of misunderstanding?

You see, once you begin to imagine how plants and other natural kin feel and once you open yourself to what they actually have to say, both wonderful and deeply troubling awareness descends.

Then it occurred to me: Perhaps the message was not about one plant's escape dream. Maybe what I saw was a wake-up call about breaking out of the boundaries of our thinking about human relationships with nature.

I was forced to step back yet again to rethink my dilemma about how and when to act upon my emerging Native American consciousness. I returned to personal connections that informed me of other forms of rootedness in Montréal. I returned to the fact that my French Canadian ancestor had left Montréal in the late eighteenth century for the wilderness, where he married into the Potawatomi. His indigenous relatives were later uprooted and marched off their forested ancestral lands in what is now the Chicago area and the Michigan peninsula and violently and temporarily transplanted in the Kansas prairie, only to be uprooted again and retransplanted into the Oklahoma desert, each time having to adapt to radically different physical surroundings.

And if my spiritual imagination serves me, the spirits of some of those ancestors returned northward, disguised as coyotes, to our ancestral lands. They then bred with wolves and now inhabit the forests and meadows around our house in Vermont, where they are known as Coy-Wolves. They mingle with the soaring hawks, owls, and plants, who have all been patiently struggling to collectively enlighten me about what we need to attempt together.

The spiral of these ruminations embraced and captured me, looping past, present, and future into one thread leading back to the same haunting questions: What is the human potential for engaging directly with nature? What does this capacity actually amount to in the twenty-first century? What are the possibilities for Native American sensibilities to inform such capacity?

At this juncture, I encountered another complication: a provocative book, Gavin Van Horn's *The Way of Coyote: Shared Journeys in the Urban Wilds*. The book forced me to examine my assumptions about spiritual connections with nature in urban settings. I learned, once again, that examining our least tested assumptions can be demanding and emotionally exhausting. But often it is also where something akin to enlightenment begins. The path to enlightenment is zigzaggy.

Van Horn writes about his personal spiritual experiences with coyotes and a wide range of flora and fauna in and around Chicago. Many of these encounters occur in very small urban green spaces, which the author calls "urban wilds." In one account, he extols the merits of hiking on a greenway path built upon an abandoned elevated train track high above street level.

My initial reaction was to recoil and see this as the tragedy of the bonsai writ large. Miles of greenery, with their roots suspended high above the earth below, which itself is paved and so disturbed as to no longer resemble a complex, living woodland ecosystem. "Wild? Really?" I asked.

The fact that Van Horn is writing about industrial society built on
the forest homeland of my Potawatomi ancestors made his claims to
spiritual connections with nature all the more troubling. White settler
descendants extolling their spiritual connections to a paved-over and
dug-up version of the natural world where my ancestors lived? At first
glance, this was nearly impossible to accept.

When Van Horn wrote about his sense of kinship with urban coyotes, once again my initial reaction was to cringe. How could he possibly use language, and even playful fictitious stories that were so similar
to mine, to describe his encounters with coyotes who live on pesticide-
and herbicide-saturated golf courses jammed in between superhighways
and shopping malls? My relationship with Coy-Wolf happens in the
Vermont forest and meadowlands surrounding my house, in a rural setting where Coy-Wolves enjoy something approximating unlimited free
range. Not only are the species we describe different, but might not
their spiritual well-being and psychological states be unbridgeably dis-
similar? How could I compare my experience of being welcomed to the
neighborhood by Coy-Wolves roaming free to Van Horn's encounters
with coyotes dodging cars on superhighways and scrounging garbage in
backyards? Grrr! Coy-Wolf howls of protest.

When Van Horn described how well peregrine falcons manage
in an urban landscape whose skyscrapers vaguely resemble the cliffs
where these raptors traditionally dwell, I nearly lost it. He enthusiasti-
cally describes their remarkable adaptability. But looking at this from
a peregrine's perspective, I questioned whether mere survival could
even be vaguely connected with any possible concept of thriving. So
I researched how peregrines and other migratory birds fare in urban
areas. It turns out that these same "welcoming urban habitats," where
well-intentioned urbanites build nesting boxes on building ledges,
along with the light they emit in major migratory paths, are responsible for an estimated one hundred million to one billion bird deaths
yearly across the country.[9] Birds collide with windows, and their dead
bodies accumulate on the sidewalks below. Does this not undermine

the claim that densely settled humans and wildlife can comfortably inhabit the same space?

While reading Van Horn's book I encountered an article in a science magazine about chimpanzees losing their own cultural and adaptive practices, such as using sticks and stones as tools, when they come into contact with humans.[10] This depressing news raised questions beyond those of the mere physical survival of species. It raised questions about the well-being of our kin of the meadowlands, forests, waterways, and sky, and the preservation of their knowledge.

I apologize, dear reader, for this short journey into the now familiar territory of depressing daily news about the degradation of the Earth's ecosystem. Unlike the media, which have learned that such stories attract readers' eyes for would-be advertisers, I am not attempting to exploit emotional environmental news to capture and hold attention. I hope to show that there is currently a small but potentially huge and hopeful silver lining in these dark clouds.

The sword needed to cut the Gordian knot of concerns I had wrapped around myself appeared when I finally allowed myself to identify with the *sensibilities* that Gavin Van Horn so wonderfully records in his book. Van Horn reveals a genuine and profound sense of joy and celebration at feeling connected to the natural world, if only sporadically and in small, green wild pockets in an otherwise desolate urban wilderness.

Then as I read and reread parts of his text, I sensed hope, sometimes desperate hope, hope against the odds, that reason and science place like tripping stones in our path. Van Horn's defiance of reasonable evidence that the glass is three-quarters empty rather than one-quarter full reminded me of my college readings of the existentialist philosophers whose worldview grew in large part out of the devastation of World War II. Witnessing so much of human indecency and so much basic morality upended, they argued that it is humanity's destiny and responsibility to affirm meaning, even in the face of overwhelming evil and absurdity. Even in the face of what they saw as a godless universe.

I see Van Horn, living and working with the Center for Humans and Nature in Chicago, as a similar affirmation of the urgent need to keep our sensibilities about and with the natural world alive, against all odds and in the face of daily challenges. Even in the rubble of postmodern urban society. I finally came to see *The Way of Coyote* as an ethical affirmation rather than an empirically grounded perspective.

My overzealous rural elitism and the mindset of a new convert to Native American spirituality were finally brought within bounds as I read Liu Yang's interviews with urban gardeners in Chengdu.[11] Here I found a much-needed dose of evidence suggesting that I think with more humility. In page after page of rich transcripts buried in a Ph.D. dissertation, speaking in their own words, young and old, highly educated and less formally educated former denizens of the Chinese countryside describe their heroic efforts to cling to and revitalize connections with the natural world. They seamlessly combine practical objectives, such as a desire to have safe and affordable food, with spiritual objectives, such as a desire to feel intimately connected with a part of the world of nature and the world of their ancestors. Often they conduct their activity in tiny plots of disturbed land tucked between apartment buildings or near railroad tracks, on rooftops, or on balconies. Some of the passages I read could have been written by contemporary Native Americans, or even by my ancestors, who lived centuries ago on what is now Van Horn's home turf.

Van Horn and Liu Yang's findings all point to a similar conclusion: there is quite possibly something innate in humans that compels us to seek connection with nature, even if it is with a bonsai plant, an above-street urban greenway on a former railway bed, or in a rooftop vegetable garden ten floors above street level in the polluted air of a Chinese city. This allowed me to answer the question of whether or not it is possible to cultivate a *personally* meaningful connection with nature in a disturbed and human-built environment. I can now say that my answer is yes.

However, I still believe that prolonged immersed contact in the natural world, as my ancestors enjoyed, and as I enjoy to a degree in

Vermont, is more nourishing to the human soul than struggling to overcome material and spiritual obstacles in order to occasionally connect with nature in an urban environment. I believe that there is a qualitative difference between a relationship with some slice of the natural world and an intimate and ongoing daily reciprocal relationship with an enveloping nature. That difference is of great significance not only for us, the two-legged, but also for the four-legged, winged ones, and rooted creatures that share the planet with us.

The distinction between focusing on nature-derived benefits solely for humans, as opposed to a reciprocal, mutually caring relationship between humans and nature, is critical. This distinction is thrown into relief by two high-profile perspectives in mainstream society.

First is the now fashionable academic habit of referring to the benefits of nature to human society as "ecosystem services." Part of the motivation behind this approach to economically valuing nature is to arm environmentalists, who have long been disadvantaged by having economic cost arguments used against their efforts. By monetizing the benefits of a healthy ecosystem (or so the argument goes), policy makers can argue that expenditures for nature protection yield measurable economic benefits; therefore they are an investment and not an expense. For example, cleaner air reduces medical expenses for asthma treatment. While there is truth in this argument, it is extremely anthropocentric. It also opens the door to a perilous line of reasoning implying that nature with no demonstrable economic "service" is less important, or even unimportant.

Second, and equally anthropocentric, is another fashionable perspective that superficially appears to be nature-friendly, but actually leaves Mother Nature and our natural kin as subservient to our needs. I refer to the growing host of activities surrounding *biophilia.* The term was popularized by Edward O. Wilson's 1984 book *Biophilia,* although the concept had been introduced decades earlier by Erich Fromm, a pioneering psychologist who used the idea to refer to the innate human need for intimate connection with nature.

Many seek to capitalize on this need. The Montreal Botanical Garden's annual butterfly exhibition is one example. This urge also accounts in part for the global ecotourism industry. Ecotours routinely offer opportunities to commune with nature, spend time with wild animals, or meditate in wild places. Japan, one of the world's most densely populated countries, has made "forest bathing" part of its health care culture. Millions of people go to the forest or urban gardens and parks to get their nature fix. A book by Florence Williams with that title, *The Nature Fix,* discusses how humans benefit from immersion in nature and suffer from "nature-deficit disorder."

I find much of this line of reasoning to be well grounded in science. It also resonates with my own personal experience. However, I am concerned with the term *fix.* It refers to an unhealthy drug dependency and invokes an overmedicated culture that seeks immediate solutions from a bottle when social and cultural remedies are called for. In fact much of Williams's book focuses on quick-fix solutions to our societal disconnect from the world of nature. This is not just the author's perspective. The notion is deeply embedded in a centuries-old assumption that nature is there for our benefit and for our taking. If such a variation on *biophilia* wedded to a "nature fix" translates as *love of nature* in contemporary society, then it is a possessive, narcissistic form of infatuation, not a mutually respectful and caring relationship.

For this reason, I am concerned about quick-fix, urban, service-oriented views of nature engagement.

Uprooted Indigenous Culture

Recognizing the distinction between *some* meaningful connection with nature and an *ongoing* intimate connection with nature returns me to the question of how contemporary Native Americans are coping with the postcolonial legacy of being uprooted from ancestral homelands. In fact, they confront not only a dilemma but a trilemma.

This is more than a semantic distinction. It acknowledges a complexity that adds more than just one additional option to the proverbial two horns of a dilemma. A trilemma creates complexity more akin to an order of magnitude. It introduces the potential of debilitating confusion.

This becomes evident if we examine the Native American dilemma of two paths to connecting with the natural world: (1) a heroic, against-all-odds struggle to recapture intimate, continual connections with nature, and (2) some less demanding form of occasional, personally meaningful engagement. But there is a third option: to abandon any pretense of placing a high moral value on human-nature spiritual connectivity in our daily lives. I fear that this option is far more inviting and widespread than most of us in the Native American community wish to acknowledge.

Assuming a posture of indifference to disconnects from the natural world is seductive, because it allows us to escape our discomfort over the damage we have done and are doing to Mother Earth. This is not just some "liberal" hypersensitivity found only in educated urban elites. It is the existential guilt most of us, Native and mainstream, feel because in our heart of hearts, and perhaps in our genes, we know that the Earth is our mother. Mother Earth is being raped and much of the time we are nonparticipating but nonintervening witnesses. We are complicit, like frat-house brats who know what is happening upstairs during a drunken party that is out of control. We turn a blind eye and a deaf ear to the calls for help.

As social critics often claim, this posture of indifference to the fate of nature is not the sole province of anthropocentric capitalist exploiters. The posture lies buried deep within the core of most Western, and many modern, worldviews. I am not referring only to economic systems, but also to our dominant philosophies and religions. Humans are widely considered to be superior to the realm of nature, which is viewed as some "thing" placed here to serve our needs, so that we should not hesitate to maintain our hegemony over, and separation from, nature. Challenging this largely unexamined position is deeply threatening.

I am not exempt from the desire to escape from what often feels like a burdensome responsibility for protecting Mother Earth. That is the whole point behind my attempt to be honest about the extreme ambivalence

I feel when I stand before the bonsai tree or have a butterfly from the "Butterflies Go Free" exhibition alight on my arm. I too struggle with the tendency, after being seized by remorse, to seek refuge from guilt and to avoid committing to a solution, which I know is going to put me in a very awkward position with my own interests and my social standing as a "reasonable person."

Although it may come as a surprise, the notion of near irrelevancy of human-nature connections, particularly for urban residents, even has currency in the contemporary Native American world. This is nowhere more evident than in the highly reviewed novel *There There* by Tommy Orange. To be fair, the author is attempting to address the neglected topic of contemporary urban life of Native Americans. In Orange's example, this is Oakland, California, about as far from natural wilderness as one can get.

As Orange explains, many of these urban Indians, or their parents, were forcibly transplanted to cities under the Indian Relocation Act of 1956. At this time, in an effort to reduce the financial burden of honoring treaty obligations to tribes, the federal government discontinued recognition and decreased funding for some tribes. Indians were encouraged to relocate to urban areas. Incentives such as relocation cost grants and job training programs were promised but not always provided. With or without relocation assistance, the cultural shock was devastating. Many Indians were turned into the equivalent of human bonsai plants, their roots pruned and their outward forms cruelly altered.

In this context Tommy Orange's words assume particular poignancy. In his novel's prologue, he asserts, in words echoing and perhaps mocking those of the reimagined Chief Seattle, previously discussed:

Urban Indians were the generation born of the city. We've been moving for a long time, but the land moves with you like memory. An Urban Indian belongs to the city, and the cities belong to the earth. Everything here is formed in relation to every other living thing and non-living thing from the earth, all our relations. The process that brings anything to its current form—chemical, synthetic, technological, or otherwise—doesn't make the product not a product of the living earth. Buildings, freeways, cars—are these not of the earth? . . . Urban Indians feel at home walking in the shadow of a downtown building. We came to know the Oakland skyline better than we did any sacred mountain range, the redwoods in Oakland hills better than any deep forest. We know the sound of the freeway better than we do rivers, the howl of distant trains better than wolf howls, we know the smell of gas and freshly wet concrete and burned rubber better than we do the smell of cedar or sage or even fry bread—which isn't traditional, like reservations aren't traditional, but nothing is original, everything comes from something that came before, which was once nothing. Everything is new and doomed. We ride buses, trains, and cars across, over, and under concrete plains. Being an Indian has never been about returning to the land. The land is everywhere or nowhere.[12]

Orange buys into the notion that indigenous culture and identity are portable, hovering, disembodied abstractions. This is apparent when he states that "the land moves with you like memory." Orange is denying the importance of rootedness in nature for Native Americans, while paradoxically affirming the importance of place. For him, Oakland, California, is home, the place. Indian culture is a powwow in a giant coliseum, the place where his novel ends in tragedy.

It is ironic that Orange echoes so much of the destructive misunderstanding of Native American culture from the late nineteenth and early twentieth centuries. For anthropologists and ethnographers of that era, the essence of pan-Indianness, and the uniqueness of individual Indian tribes, could be captured and reduced to placeless qualities. For example, before Franz Boas helped to establish modern anthropology, Indianness was reduced to race, and Indians could be identified by skull shape and size. Boas, a nineteenth-century German Jew, presciently saw the dangers and scientific fallacies involved in this kind of thinking, and then abandoned and openly challenged it.*

However, the very anthropology and ethnography that Boas helped to found sought to capture the essence of "vanishing Indians" in large part by gathering up material aspects of Indian life, their artifacts. For Boas it was masks that fascinated him. Anthropologists acquired such items, removing them from their cultural context, and put them into museum collections. How many of us have visited natural history museums with dioramas displaying the habitats of extinct and exotic animals? Then we walk into an adjoining wing and see more dioramas, with mannequins dressed in authentic Indian clothing, surrounded by Indian artifacts, doing authentic Indian things. The not-so-hidden message of these displays is that Indian people have become or are about to become extinct, just like the showcase animals.

This premature declaration of the extinction of Native peoples became a self-fulfilling prophecy that facilitated government efforts to break many remaining Native American peoples' connection with their land. After all, as policy thinking went, indigenous people had virtually ceased to exist as sustainable tribes anyway. Ethnographers were dispatched to capture the final remaining traces of Indian stories and ceremonial practices.†

In her essay unmasking the assumptions of salvage anthropology

---

*Boas's transformation and awakening are analyzed with great sensitivity in *Indigenous Visions: Rediscovering the World of Franz Boas,* edited by Ned Blackhawk and Isaiah Lorado Wilner.

†John Neihardt's *Black Elk Speaks* was conceived in this context. Neihardt, an ethnographer, poet, and author, collaborated with Black Elk to rescue remaining traces of his tribe's Indian culture. Both shared an understanding that with the land gone, only Indian teachings and stories remained. They believed, to different degrees, that the culture could be preserved if it were written down. For Black Elk, performing dances in pageants, famously Buffalo Bill Cody's Wild West Show, was another opportunity to preserve his culture. However, Black Elk struggled to his dying days with a sense of failure because he had not been able to restore his people to their glory on *their* ancestral lands. Similar echoes of ethnographic preservation of Native American culture are to be found in James Walter Hoffman's *The Mide'wiwin or Grand Medicine Society of the Ojibwa.* This extraordinarily detailed ethnographic study of Ojibwe traditional knowledge keepers, published in 1891, was a collaboration between a white settler and indigenous people who also believed that Indian culture could be written down, captured, and preserved.

("Why White People Love Franz Boas; or The Grammar of Indigenous Dispossession"), Audra Simpson documents why mainstream culture was fascinated by late nineteenth- and early twentieth-century anthropology: it confirmed and legitimized the belief that indigenous cultures could be preserved in disembodied form, uprooted, and removed from ancestral lands.[13] Anthropology saw Indians as trees that could be preserved in bonsai containers and fenced-in arboretums, without the nurturing threads of mycorrhizal networks connecting the web of plant life. Perhaps a more apt analogy would be eighteenth- and nineteenth-century botanists' practice of tearing leaves and flowers from rooted plants and then pressing them flat and lifeless in specimen books to be "preserved."

Where do Native Americans stand in this discussion? It would be a mistake to use Tommy Orange's prologue to draw sweeping conclusions about contemporary Native American perspectives on spiritual attachment to specific lands and ancestral places. Passionate proclamations about the importance of such connections are to be found widely in the writings and utterances of many prominent Native Americans. Authors like Winona La Duke articulately advocate a Native American spirituality that is rooted in an intimate connection with nature. The writings of Kimmerer have confirmed the ability of Native Americans to combine science and connectedness with nature in a manner that resonates with a broad readership both mainstream and Native.

The importance of connectedness to land and nature is evident in highly publicized public struggles between Native Americans and resource extraction companies, which erupt frequently and often focus on land rights. Sometimes the disputes involve explicit treaty obligations that are being abrogated. More often disputes involve treaty rights involving public lands beyond the boundaries of a reservation as with disputes over hunting and fishing rights "off the rez" in the Great Lakes region. Indians there are still arrested, shot at, and physically attacked for exercising treaty rights that guarantee their traditional sources of food, not to mention the maintenance of their cultures.

Clearly many Native Americans remain deeply connected to the natural world even as they live with one foot planted in contemporary society. Meanwhile, other off-the-reservation Indians, like me, are rediscovering diminished or nearly extinguished connections with the land and are struggling to rekindle direct engagement with the natural world.

So many of us in the twenty-first century are in the same boat. We have much to learn from indigenous people who have struggled, against all odds, to preserve their traditional spirituality and connections with Mother Earth. It is at this interface of indigenous and mainstream cultures that the potential for cultural transformation is greatest precisely because the differences are so great and the creative tensions so wonderfully provocative. It is here that the embers of a new kind of environmentalism, rooted in an understanding of intimate connections with Mother Earth, may be rekindled.

I found support for this notion in Naomi Klein's *This Changes Everything: Capitalism vs. The Climate*. She dedicates an entire chapter, titled "You Want an Army? Indigenous Rights and the Power of Keeping Our Word," to examining the implications of indigenous peoples' legal and spiritual claims to ancestral lands. It is appropriately one of the more optimistic episodes in the book. She draws heavily upon her Canadian roots, and the comparatively stronger legal, social, and cultural status of Canada's First Nations people. Unlike Native Americans, Canada's indigenous people have control over, or at least significant influence within, vast tracks of resource-rich territory.

Much to her credit, Klein does not view indigenous land claims merely as opportunities for temporary issue-based protest movement alliances. She makes it clear that the most important contribution of indigenous people to environmental protection is their spiritual connection to the land and the wisdom of their cultures, which view a reciprocal relationship with Mother Earth as paramount. She paints a scenario in which indigenous land claims buy time by stalling rapacious resource extraction projects driven by short-term thinking and capitalist greed; and with this time, a new land ethic and a spiritual relationship with nature takes root beyond the confines of indigenous society. How wonderfully ironic it would be if settler-colonial society were rescued from its own self-destructive impulses by the very culture it sought to destroy.

I don't see this cultural transformation merely as a moderate adjustment in personal spiritual connections, or as delivering intermittent doses of daily escape from the nature alienation of urban life, as is sought in forest bathing. I believe that Klein is describing, and prescribing, a deeper and more radical shift in North American society. If her vision comes true, Sick Plum Blossom bonsai may yet be replanted on a sacred mountain and tended by future generations as well as by the spirits of nurturing ancestors and our forest kin.

Such an aspiration can be kept alive in part by urban residents, be they descendants of white settlers or indigenous tribal members, who find refuge and spiritual strength in a plant on the windowsill, a walk on an abandoned elevated railroad track greenway, or a rooftop garden.

We, Native Americans, mainstream European settler descendants, Mother Earth, and our natural kin need all the allies we can muster.

That leaves one remaining question concerning the welfare of the rooted ones, the four-legged ones, and the winged ones. My musings have focused mostly on the spiritual well-being of humans in various wild and human built environments. With the exceptions of noting peregrine and migratory bird deaths, a struggle in a bonsai container, and the contradictions in a butterfly exhibit, I have taken a rather anthropocentric approach to the concept of intimate connections with nature.

I want to address the issue of our natural kins' spiritual lives and connections, their well-being, their expressed desire for more connectivity with real nature, and their rights. However, to do this adequately I would need more than a few additional paragraphs, or even a few more chapters. I would need an entire book.

At this point in my journey of rediscovery, I simply wish to acknowledge that the field of studying plant and animal communications, culture, and even feelings is a rapidly developing area of study. Scientific evidence is confirming the central assumption of Traditional Ecological

Knowledge (TEK): our kin are alive and conscious. We, the two-legged ones, are not alone in suffering from rootlessness. We are not alone in desperately seeking meaningful and intimate continual (re)connections with Mother Earth.

Consequently, for the coming critical decades, those of us rerooting ourselves and our spirits will be hearing and feeling the beckoning call of Mother Earth and her creatures as they reach out to us, guide us, seek our assistance, and show gratitude for our caring.

Like my bonsai friend in the Botanical Garden cracking a ceramic container, none of us needs to accept rootlessness as a permanent condition. We can begin pushing beyond current boundaries regardless of our location. We can hold on to our dream and use our instincts to reconnect with the Earth.

16

TOWARD A NEWLY RE-SPIRITED ENVIRONMENTALISM

For many readers, a spiritual awakening of the sort I have described may be interesting in its own right or perhaps as a window into some deeper cultural dynamics. Others may see this spiritual journey as occurring on a path that is parallel to, but rarely intersects with, practical life. In this chapter I hope to show that my spiritual journey has brought, and continues to bring, new perspectives to my local and international environmental work. I hope that these reflections will be relevant and useful to the increasing number of people concerned about the future of our planet.

Trapped in the Stories We Tell Ourselves

As part of their 1971 Earth Day celebration, the Keep America Beautiful organization released a television advertisement with what was intended to be a simple antilittering message. It features an American Indian* paddling his canoe in a junk-infested river full of

---

*The actor, who called himself "Iron Eyes Cody," famously played American Indians in Hollywood Western movies and television programs. His claims to being Native American were unmasked when it was proved that he was actually a second-generation Italian-American.

garbage, past factories belching smoke. When he steps ashore, it is littered with more waste. As he approaches a traffic-clogged highway, a vehicle tosses out a bag of garbage that breaks open at his feet. The camera then moves to a close-up of the Indian's face. A tear trails down his cheek. This one-minute video, which became famous as the "Crying Indian," is considered one of the most successful advertisements ever shown in the United States.

For a generation of activists, this advertisement captured the tone and spirit of the awakening environmentalism of the time. Though not explicitly stated, here was visual recognition of a mindset that assumed that to be truly environmentally aware and "fully conscious" (to use the terminology of those times) was to live with moment-to-moment awareness of being in a once pristine world now despoiled by human action and moral failure.

That theme has an obvious parallel in the biblical tale of the expulsion of Adam and Eve from the Garden of Eden, as told in Genesis. Some postcolonial Native American creation stories, probably reflecting colonial influences, echo this theme of an angry creator punishing the two-legged. Such parallels suggest that the darker aspects of our modern ecoconsciousness may be partly rooted in Judeo-Christian attitudes of original sin. Only this time the sin is not just tasting forbidden fruit—it is mindlessly despoiling the entire garden into which we were born. The forbidden fruit reenters our modern narrative, the tale we tell ourselves about ourselves in order to understand ourselves.

Have not those of us born into late twentieth-century affluence enjoyed our material riches knowing that they were illicitly taken and harmfully extracted from the great garden? And that the day of reckoning would eventually come and there would be hell to pay? Perhaps not hell in the form of a sudden descent into the bowels of the Earth, Dante's Inferno, but more in the style of a slow elevation of temperature, along the lines of the urban myth about the frog that does not notice the heat rising in a pan of water in time to escape.

Recognition of the magnitude of our harm inflicted on nature, buried within our subconsciousness, condemns us to a state of being deeply, possibly permanently, distraught. Understanding this dynamic may help us to realize how a mere antilitter advertisement tapped into other threads of the late 1960's zeitgeist to become an icon for a generation struggling with issues of existential threat, such as nuclear war. The power of this advert comes not only from its reflection of a growing sense of unease, but from an intuition that Native Americans might provide an alternative cultural narrative of a forgiving and embracing Mother Earth. I will return to that more hopeful theme shortly. But first we need to dig deeper into our contemporary culture and explore the pitfalls we have dug and placed in our own path.

I will begin by admitting that I can understand the entire range of sentiments surrounding the Crying Indian, who appeared in the years of my political awakening as a college student in the 1960s. The United States had not yet ended its disastrous war in Vietnam; in fact it was mired in its most deadly phase as peace negotiations dragged on. The country had lost its innocent belief that government and industry would provide for the general welfare. Some of our finest leaders had been assassinated. The gloomy message of Rachel Carson's *Silent Spring* and the recognition of how massively humans were poisoning the environment were taking root in mainstream consciousness.

With the benefit of my awakening, I can now empathize with the fictitious Crying Indian, caught between ancestral memories of an unspoiled, embracing world of nature and an everyday life tainted with human-built ugliness. But I also know that the intimate and powerful sense of connectedness with Mother Earth implied in the famous ad can be a *daily* source of profound comfort, strength, and inspiration. I believe that is the message that my kin, both ancestral and natural, have been delivering day and night to my doorstep and to the sky above my house in the forest.

The Limits of Reason

The heart has its reasons which reason knows nothing of. . . . We know the truth not only by the reason, but by the heart.

Blaise Pascal

Nearly five decades after the Crying Indian appeared, melancholia is settling upon environmentalism. Once it was just a faint hint, a barely detectable scent in the scintillating atmosphere of inspiring mass activism, but more and more often it is coloring the atmosphere of environmentalism. It has become something more like a temperature inversion that traps pollutants, leaving the sky gray and causing us to gasp for fresh air.

I use the term *melancholia* because it captures a mood and state of mind beyond depression. Depression can be rationally grounded, passing, and manageable. Melancholia is a profoundly depressed state of mind in which the sufferer embraces guilt and torment as self-inflicted punishment, perhaps expiation, for sins real or imagined.[1]

Many of us are desperately attempting to reason our way out of such a funk. We collect ever larger stacks of books and expert reports about environmental degradation, many of which we can barely tolerate reading. We then give up, unable to continue plowing through the discouraging data. We attend to the latest news stories about yet another vanishing species or yet another indicator that global warming is increasing more rapidly and will be more devastating than previously thought. Almost daily, we read fundraising appeals with the same themes. We do all of this in the belief that being more fully informed will somehow empower us. Although we know that lack of evidence of environmental problems is not the issue, we become hoarders of gloomy facts, stuffing them into the last unoccupied recesses of our offices, heaped on bedside nightstands, and filed away in our consciousness.

The problem is that we are seeking a much needed spiritual transformation of our society with the tools of reason. Sometimes I worry that the spirits of my ancestors despair and see this effort as silly voyageurs trying to fix a leaky canoe by pounding on it with an ax.

Nowhere is this futility more evident than in environmental education. I realized this when I had the opportunity to sit in on an end-of-year faculty meeting for a college environmental studies program. As student evaluations were examined, a disturbing reality emerged. After an initial boost in knowledge and sense of efficacy during the first two years of undergraduate education, more advanced study seemed to cultivate a sense of inefficacy, disappointment with education, and declining hope about environmental problem solving by the fourth year. It was as if students were becoming cognitively impaired, not by having their abilities to reason diminished, but by having their self-worth ever more dependent upon fragile intellectual constructs, many of which were routinely and matter-of-factly "debunked" and shown to be solutions that are of limited efficacy or not effective at all.

Knowing this, I was not surprised when, years later, I met with a group of students from the same program and they lamented that "something is missing." Participants explained that an overemphasis on policy abstractions and science left them feeling personally empty. They were eager to ground their work and worldview in something more spiritual. Although they had majored in environmental studies to learn how to make a difference, they felt increasingly distanced from the world of nature that they studied.

The students were not seeking a spiritual escape from the demands of real-world problem solving. They did not want to distance themselves from the frustrating world of politics; nor did they secretly hope for a cabin in the mountains where they could detach themselves from human turmoil. They wanted to feel more intimately connected with nature, physically and emotionally, *while* engaging in positive change.

I have belatedly arrived at a realization that my younger student colleagues have attained at the starting point of their careers. This convergence of intergenerational thinking suggests two wonderful possibilities. First, we humans are collectively awakening to a shared realization about the importance of spiritual connections with the natural world and the need to work more intimately with our natural kin. Second, the living, conscious system that some call Gaia and Native Americans call Mother Earth may at last be succeeding in delivering to an increasing number of us her messages and guidance about traveling down a healing spiritual path.

So what are her messages? Hesitate to jettison all that you have created in the vain conviction that you can save the world by instantly remaking the human enterprise and the reengineering of nature itself, upending centuries-old social institutions and millennia-old ecosystems. While your scientific, economic, political, and social models may have defects, they are not solely attributable to structural features. They are often failures caused by the *spirit in which these systems are operated and managed.*

Spirit is a word that has fallen out of use in contemporary culture. It is even tainted with disapprobation in many modern intellectual circles, and certainly within most secular institutions of higher learning. Such a reality is perplexing, given that many of the wisest social philosophers and theorists of the nineteenth century, those who witnessed the emergence of the modern world order, often invoked the concept of spirit as a critical ingredient in their analyses.

Max Weber laid bare the roots of modern capitalism in his book *The Protestant Ethic and the Spirit of Capitalism.* Weber believed that it was not possible to understand capitalism without grasping the animus, the driving spirit, at its core. The same notion was presented to me decades after reading Weber, when I once wondered aloud how the Soviet system of communism managed to work despite gross inefficiencies and corruption. A Soviet colleague patiently informed me that the system worked because a small, caring, highly competent set of individuals *really* believed that the state should raise the living standards of all and worked tirelessly in that spirit. They made cumbersome structures function despite almost impossible odds and delivered some financial and social security to the great masses of the population in the spirit of the lofty promise of communism. To make this abstract point real, he introduced me to many such individuals. Some were parliamentarians; others were scientists; many were idealistic students. One was a humble potato farmer and manager of a Soviet collective farm. All were dedicated, selfless individuals who found ways of doing good even in the most difficult circumstances.

Later, in China, Carolyn and I would meet the Rabbit King and Queen,[2] who worked in the spirit of that country's new "socialism with Chinese characteristics" proclaimed by Deng Xiaoping. They combined their rural animal husbandry skills with a culturally sensitive form of entrepreneurialism to form a considerable regional and then international business empire.

Deng told the young Rabbit King, who would eventually become quite wealthy, that he should share his wealth widely as if it were a gift to be regiven rather than his personal entitlement. The Rabbit King did just that, using his business to develop a training center and poverty alleviation program that helped tens of thousands of people. China's new economic spirit, which lies beneath the great economic miracle of the late twentieth century, initially sent a clear message: it is acceptable to become wealthy if the benefits are distributed in a *spirit* of sharing.*

So it was in China that we found confirmation of Max Weber's assertion that capitalism could only be understood by considering the unique context of its animating spirit in a particular historical setting. But it was another insight of Weber's that connected my academic training with my spiritual awakening. Weber wrote about "the disenchantment of the modern world." Like many social theorists in the nineteenth century and early twentieth centuries, he reflected on the growing

---

*The notion of wealth sharing is not antithetical to the spirit of capitalism. Adam Smith, author of *The Wealth of Nations,* is often portrayed as the spiritual godfather of laissez-faire economics. However, in his 1759 book, *The Theory of Moral Sentiments,* Smith notes that the very entrepreneurs who are driven by the pursuit of self-interest "are led by an invisible hand to make nearly the same distribution of the necessaries of life, which would have been made, had the earth been divided into equal portions among all its inhabitants, and thus without intending it, without knowing it, advance the interest of society, and afford the multiplication of the species."[3]

secularization of society and culture. He applauded the replacement of ignorance and superstition with empirically grounded knowledge. But Weber also recognized that the modern world was growing impersonal; people were becoming disconnected from the organic ties that connected them to one another and to nature. So too, Karl Marx, known today for his materialist view and explanations of history, wrote earlier in his life with enormous insight about the implications of the urban resettlement that was breaking farmers' organic connections with nature. He emphasized gritty, earthy connections, as basic as knowing that food and human and animal waste were recycled. Breaking that cycle was an early manifestation of alienation in the evolution of human societies, appearing as rural farmers migrated to urban factories where, as wage workers, they would experience a shattering spiritual disconnect from life in the countryside. Marx called this the "metabolic rift," in which the workers' once organically productive farming efforts were replaced with the monotonous making of inanimate things.[4]

So is it not appropriate for us to consider regrounding our work to save this planet in a more nurturing *spirit,* that which Native Americans have held at the center of their cultures for millennia? Perhaps it is time for a reality check of our scientific assumptions and to reexamine core cultural assumptions through the lens of Native American spirituality and its closely connected, very long-term survival strategies. Such an exercise can be accomplished most easily by boiling down a complex of indigenous teachings to a single core value: the humble recognition that Mother Earth is the dominant force on the planet, our gracious benefactor, and has not abandoned us to our own devices.

As with so many efforts to examine deeply rooted assumptions, bringing contemporary culture to this understanding is more easily said than done. For mainstream thinkers, to engage in such an exploration of their values requires either a spiritual awakening and shift in mindset, or at least assuming a temporary empathic imagination that admits the legitimacy of an animist worldview.

Committing to Animism

The implications of shifting to an animist worldview and language, including the significance of using animate pronouns such as *ki* and *kin*, have been explored by Kimmerer.[5] The origins of the term *animism* and recognition of its import is traceable to the work of anthropologist Edward Tylor and his 1871 book *Primitive Culture*. Tylor understood the significance of a worldview shift from viewing the natural world as one dominated by relationships of "thou" to one dominated by relationships of "it."

Anthropocene, Ecocene, and the Unseen

In order to make such a spiritual adjustment, we will need to first pull ourselves out of a cultural tailspin, much like pilots who have lost control of their aircraft because of some mechanical failure. In order to accomplish this, we need to firmly grasp the control wheel. We need to readjust our directional guidance systems, which are overly dependent on purely mechanical instrument readings. We need to allow those holding the control wheel to trust and utilize their experience and intuition. We need to refocus our landing approach by keeping an eye on Mother Earth as our primary navigational beacon.

The first navigational obstacle we confront is the spiritual equivalent of a false GPS signal telling us where we are headed. For contemporary environmentalists, such an image is more and more rooted in a geological time frame. We have learned to think big and in the long term. We religiously quote Native American wisdom indicating that we should think seven generations out into the future. Unfortunately, this notion has been detached from a broader body of teachings about Mother Earth and her embrace. Consequently, at this point in our history, we are thinking in the longer term, but more negatively. We are cutting ourselves off from imagining a livable future.

The stark implications of this thinking are evident in a proposal that we retitle our geologic time frames. I refer to a groundswell of sentiment suggesting that we rename the present geologic era in which we find ourselves. Much of mainstream environmentalism embraces the notion that we are now navigating our way in the "Anthropocene."[6]

Geologic eras, very long and enduring epochs in the earth's history, are designated with Greek-derived names, which summarize their identifying feature. We are currently living in an epoch that the International Commission on Stratigraphy and other authoritative bodies refer to as the Holocene, or postglacial era, which began about 12,000 years ago. The age of dinosaurs, or Mesozoic era, lasted from 252 million years ago to 66 million years ago. Other geologic eras come to mind, such as the Pleistocene era, or time of glaciations (multiple ice ages) beginning about two and a half million years ago.

Those arguing for the Anthropocene designation claim that sometime in relatively recent human history, perhaps during the agricultural revolution, or more recently, with the Industrial Revolution, or even more recently, with nuclear weapons testing in the 1960s, the human footprint on the planet became so dominant that it marks a dramatic new beginning. Proponents of the Anthropocence concept argue that future archaeologists, or those visiting from other planets after the human species has extinguished itself, will be able to detect a change in the earth's geologic strata, much as we see traces of the impacts of glaciers, massive volcanic eruptions, or the Chicxulub asteroid that contributed to the extinction of dinosaurs.

Many advocates of the new geologic designation argue that human dominance over nature is already an accomplished fact. Others, a bit more moderate, claim that human impacts on the planet have become enormously disruptive, so much so that they may be forever visible in the geologic record, but that we are not yet condemned to live on the wrong and cataclysmic side of geologic history. Still more circumspect advocates argue that human impacts of the Anthropocene are merely potentially transformative and that we have adequate time, however little, to reverse much of the potential damage. For these more moderate proponents of the Anthropocene designation, the concept is more of a provocative wake-up call than an announcement of a fait accompli.

Despite their differences, all of these arguments affirm that human activities, and not Mother Earth's natural systems, have become the distinguishing feature of our times—the boldest signature written on the surface of the planet. It is, then, ironic to hear the same geologists and stratigraphers describe how aluminum, plastics, atomic fallout, and fragments or imprints of urban centers will appear millions of years from now as fossils trapped in layers of geologic sediment left behind after Mother Nature has ground up our most enduring physical monuments into small particles or even reduced them to their original chemical constituents.

It seems that even panic-struck stratigraphers recognize that during the later Anthropocene and subsequent eras, signs of human activity will be swallowed up by the older and more powerful natural processes of re-creation and erosion. This image belies that notion that human and not natural forces now have or will have the upper hand on the face of our planet.

When I hear these claims, I cannot help comparing the destruction story of the Anthropocene with the Anishinaabe Creation Story. For my Native American ancestors, Turtle Island was created as an enduring place for nurturing us, the two-legged, and equally for the four-legged, the rooted ones, and the winged ones. All forms of life are seen as interdependent. None are to assume a role as lords of the dominion. This was not a mere moral perspective; it was and is an empirical perspective. Native Americans understood that no life form is capable of becoming so powerful that it can, by itself, determine the course of a system of interconnected natural processes as complex as Mother Earth.

So in the spirit of decolonizing our thinking, perhaps it is worth examining the assumptions behind the notion of an Anthropocene era from a Native American perspective. We can begin with a sound, skeptical, scientific question: Is the fact that we may leave signs of having been here, or that we can in theory even make ourselves and many other species extinct, adequate justification for jumping to the conclusion that we have become dominant on the planet, that we have deposed Mother Nature as top dog? When we ask such questions, the implicit assumptions and overstatements associated with the Anthropocene become clear.

For example, in my lifetime I have repeatedly encountered the same impending doomsday assertion made by Anthropocene advocates. At the base of such thinking is the claim that *Homo sapiens* as a species is having more impact on the planet than any other creatures to have inhabited its surface. This assertion flies in the face of the findings of stratigraphers, who have documented how primitive fungi, bacteria, and algae radically altered the Earth's once barren rocky surface, released oxygen and minerals as they worked together in lichenlike symbiosis, and transformed a dead, rocky sphere into a global garden, unrecognizable to any who might have visited before life forms appeared. That is an example of life forms altering, permanently, the planet's basic physical systems.

Such a reality check on hyperbolic assertions does not diminish the sobering reality and sense of urgency that Anthropocene designation advocates seek to bring to our attention. *Homo sapiens* are indeed having an accelerating and devastating impact on the planet. Recognizing that, we still have to ask why we dwell so incessantly on our destructive capacity and why we feel compelled to overestimate our species' import, thereby underestimating the resiliency of Mother Earth and her capacity to be a healing partner, *supporting all forms of life, including the two-legged, far into the future of the planet.*

To pull ourselves out of our tailspin, we need to critically reflect on our propensity to sound the alarm bells of imminent doom. I remember my first encounter with an authoritative claim that human history was about to come to an end and that we could and must alter our course immediately, or else. It was a book titled *Peace Is Possible*, published in 1966, the year I graduated from high school. As a college student, I latched on to the book like a life raft appearing miraculously in a stormy sea. Struggling with the threat of nuclear war (the Cuban missile crisis, which brought us close to nuclear Armageddon, had already occurred), and facing the real possibility of a draft for a war I could not support, I read and reread this book, looking for hope and answers. However, where I sought consolation and hope, I also confronted troubling signs of despair. On the cover of *Peace Is Possible* is a disturbing quotation from Kenneth Boulding, a seminal systems thinker, economist, and peace advocate. It read, in tall, bold, black letters, "If the human race is to survive, it will have to change its ways of thinking more in the next 25 years than it has in the last 25,000."

Inside the book, the table of contents signals even greater urgency. Boulding's chapter titled "Population and Poverty" is followed by the following byline: "This crisis will reach a point of no return within 10 to 20 years." Between the cover quotation and the table of contents, in the brief time it took to turn five pages, the human race had lost five precious years needed to save itself.

Despite such confusing messages combining hope and despair, I devoured more such books, seeking answers. Then in 1968 *The Population Bomb* by Alvin Toffler was published. It predicted massive global famine in the coming decades. China had experienced horrific famines just a few years before the book's publication. Few if any soothsayers envisioned the miraculous economic, agronomic, and social changes that would transform China in the coming decades. Consequently, the extreme claims of the book quickly seized the public's imagination.

One of my most recent encounters with predictions of impending global disaster came from James Martin's 2006 book, *The Meaning of the 21st Century*. Martin had anticipated the advent of the Internet, which he described in a prescient book titled *The Wired Society* in 1977, predicting such then-unimaginable developments as doctors diagnosing patients long-distance using telecommunications. So when Martin wrote on the second page of his new book that "a drastic change is needed in the first half of the twenty-first century to set the stage for the rest of the century,"[7] he was echoing Kenneth Boulding's sense of urgency. Of course, if Boulding's required time frame for change had been correct, Martin's hoped-for "transition generation" that would transform the world would be two generations too late to make any difference.

Jim Martin and I actually outlined a book on how the transition generation might come about, and we worked together for a time on his visionary projects to accomplish this at Oxford University. Jim was optimistic about the potential of human technology to solve environmental, security, and health problems. But like his futurist predecessors, he clearly believed that massive and transformative change must come within no more than a few decades or else.

Given the constant drumbeat of impending apocalypse, it is not surprising that I am often asked the same question. It comes from surprising sources: educated and affluent individuals who have no reason to be concerned about their personal security and comfort. But they apparently have grave concerns about the security of future generations, and even for our great commons, Mother Earth. Late at an evening gathering or dinner party, after wine has unleashed inhibitions and people often speak what is really on their minds, I am asked, out of the blue, "So, Randy, are we going to make it?" The first few times the question was asked, I tried to put the question in some context. I thought, "What are you trying to make?" or "Is the house in imminent danger of falling down?" or "Is someone seriously ill?" Or perhaps the question referred to the vicissitudes of elections and global processes of economic or political disintegration. Then something in the questioners' eyes signals a deeper concern. Often a brief explanation or clarifying questions follow. "Is it too late?" "Can we save this planet?"

All of this occurs in the defining context of the Doomsday Clock, which the *Bulletin of the Atomic Scientists* began employing in 1947 as a tool of awareness concerning the threat of nuclear warfare. It was a highly effective messaging strategy, like the Crying Indian. An image of a ticking clock progressing toward the midnight of doom was simple to grasp; it reduced mind-boggling complexity to a comprehensible metric.

However, in the intervening seven decades, humanity has never succeeded in getting to a point more than nine minutes from doom, within
a twelve-hour window of potential self-rescue activity. For example,

A new abnormal: It is *still* 2 minutes to midnight
2019 Doomsday Clock Announcement
Washington, D.C. • January 24, 2019[8]

> Humanity now faces two simultaneous existential threats: nuclear
> weapons and climate change. These were exacerbated this past year
> by the increased use of information warfare to undermine democracy
> around the world, amplifying the risk from these and other threats
> and putting the future of civilization in extraordinary danger.[9]

I greatly admire those whose lifelong work is limiting the prolif-
eration of nuclear weapons. I believe that nuclear war is *the* existential
threat of our time. I understand why those who keep the Doomsday
Clock so tightly wound have also embraced the cause of climate change.
Nevertheless, on countless days I resent the emotional calibration
involved in warning us that there are just two minutes left to fix the
problems. In the privacy of my dark humor defenses, I imagine respond-
ing to that recurring question, "Are we going to make it?" with an
answer reflecting the absurdity of our self-inflicted disempowerment:
"Well, if the Doomsday Clock is any indication, we are very close to
solving the issue of global warming with a dose of nuclear winter."

How do we, then, both in our private moments and our public discourse, address the numerous interconnected environmental problems
and the spiritual challenges they pose?

In such moments, I return to the contrast between the Crying
Indian and my recent journey homeward. I ask my elders, those still
among us and those who have walked on, what light do these experiences shed on the question, "Are we going to make it?" Their answer is
not, "Well, you are aboard the Anthropocene. The airlock doors in your

compartment are now closed behind and before you. Sorry, but you're going down with the ship."

Nor is the answer that we are about to enter the Ecocene Era, a radical transformation whereby a natural balance of ecosystems will suddenly be restored to the planet by human intervention. I thought for a few fleeting hours that I had come up with the concept and term as an antidote to apocalyptic thinking. Then I was initially pleased to discover that numerous visionaries and environmentalists had already proposed the designation of an Ecocene as a hopeful alternative to the Anthropocene. But as I read the literature associated with this notion, I quickly realized that the theme of utter urgency—"or else"—was once again omnipresent. In many instances, advocates of the Ecocene even argue that if short-sighted humans cannot make this transition of their own free will, the dysfunctional *Homo sapiens* species will be made extinct and the planet will heal without our disturbing presence.

This is not my vision of a hopeful future, or even of a probable one. My people have known unbelievable dislocation, and we know the possibilities of resilience. Sometimes I want to shout, "So, Zhaaganosh, just stop your self-victimizing disempowering negativity and get on with the healing!"

Neither the Anthropocene nor the Ecocene are informative or helpful visions of our future. Instead I am convinced that imagining and embracing an era of the Unseen, when we pay closer attention to what is too often unseen and unnoticed, is how we will find enduring solutions. This is problematic for stratigraphers, as spiritual awakenings and renewals will not leave direct physical evidence in the Earth's geologic strata. It will be a challenge for those dedicated to examining physical evidence to begin thinking about cultural eras and how they may be just as, or even more important than, material culture, which leaves traces in rock. Our most precious and important experiences do not leave fossils. How wonderful it would be if they did! What a treasure it would be if such records could be found and opened from the distant past of human history!

But in another way we do have memories of our spiritual past. Indigenous people have stories and other mnemonic devices that encode and preserve wisdom. Most likely, important memories and wisdom are embedded in our genetic material. We need only learn how to access them.

To do so we need to take down the gates that Western culture has put in our path as we wander seeking spiritual reconnections. We can begin by rejecting a dismissive hyperrationality and deadening empiricism that instructs us to only believe in what we can measure with our current configuration of science. We can awaken to the unseen and listen, in a process that Stephen Harrod Buhner describes as "de-gating."[10]

This message was delivered to me this very morning. Unlike two years ago, when I began writing this book, today it was not the lightning bug that awakened me in darkness. It was not Koo-koo-o-koo, who brings a message in the bitter cold dark of winter. It was not the lonely howls of Coy-Wolves at 2 a.m. It was not even Grandfather patiently affirming the reality of the presence of our ancestors by writing across the heavens in meteoric script. These spirits have been silent for many days, making way for the chorus of hope. That came this dawn as a strawberry moon came into its fullness and the longest gift of daylight, the summer solstice, approached.

This morning, just before the sun rose, I listened to a symphony of bird calls, their voices too numerous to disentangle and identify separately. And, why, I asked myself, would I want to give these instruments of divine creation individual names? It is the message of their togetherness that is this dawn's gift. And their message is an ode to joy. It is the same message that is being delivered proudly and defiantly by Native Americans in song, dance, art, and literature: "We are still here." Do *not* dismiss us, do *not* write us off as vanishing or vanished. We are *not* tearful artifacts to be turned into advertisements, nor are we subject matter for museum displays and salvage ethnography.* We are resilient survivors. Listen to the unseen.

---

*The terms *salvage ethnography* and *salvage anthropology* refer to the efforts of late nineteenth- and early twentieth-century scholars, such as Franz Boas, which attempted to capture and record what were assumed to be the last remaining material fragments of disappearing Native American culture.

If I could give you this morning the ability to experience the unseen as I have these past two years, you too could then step through the looking glass and participate in the experience captured in a sculpture that appears in the first pages of this book (see page 3). You too could live with a wonderfully divided dual consciousness, more aware, ever questioning, joyous.

If I have succeeded in my writing, then perhaps for some I have opened the gates, or created a passageway in the fence that has kept you out of the wonderful unseen world I hear. Are you considering enveloping yourself in a posture of empathic imagination, allowing yourself to imagine entering an animate world where there is more "thou" and less "it"?

Fig. 16.1. États de choc (States of shock)
Sculpture by André Fournelle, 1985. On the shore of Lac-Saint-Louis, Lachine, Montréal.
Photo by Carolyn Schmidt.

Partnering with Mother Earth

Waxing spiritual will not be sufficiently persuasive for many of my readers immersed in gloom. So I end this plea to join in the making of a new era of the Unseen with the culturally required dose of empiricism. If you need proof that Mother Earth is not mortally wounded and instead is present and partnering with us in the great healing, please consider these examples.

I offer these brief summaries to serve primarily as inspiration, and in order to encourage new thinking; I am not producing a scientific treatise. Nevertheless, these examples are not novel deviations from accepted practice. They actually reflect what has been standard practice and wisdom for millennia of human development and problem solving. In that sense I am presenting reminders, not awakenings.

The first example involves some of the most inhospitable and damaged agricultural lands on the face of the Earth, the arid near desert grasslands of Australia. They are being healed and turned into productive green farmland that produces food while undoing centuries of damage inflicted by white settler culture. The beautiful tale is told in *Call of the Reed Warbler: A New Agriculture, A New Earth* by Charles Massey. I am deeply grateful to my friends at the Danthonia Bruderhof in New South Wales, Australia, for bringing this story to my attention. They have appeared again and again in their gentle way and shed light into what can be dark corners of mainstream life. Not surprisingly, the members of this intentional Christian community live communally, in many ways like my Native American ancestors, for example by sharing wealth. I recommend their account of healing the land, as told in their own words and within their spiritual frame of reference, in an article called "Beating the Big Dry."[11]

These stories involve the combined application of three sources of problem solving knowledge. The first is the Traditional Ecological Knowledge of the original human inhabitants of Australia, the Aborigines who listen to the song of the land and understand it intimately and animately. Second is a body of agricultural wisdom created by innovators who were willing to step outside of and challenge standard agricultural teaching and practice about arid grassland farming. Third, the essential methods of science, empirical observation, and continual experimentation were employed to open minds to the need for entirely new methods and/ or reviving old and ancient methods of land stewardship.

Call of the Reed Warbler and "Beating the Big Dry" epitomize, on many levels, the notion of a positive new era of the Unseen. Both accounts profile pioneers in Australia's regenerative agricultural movement, many of whom insist that working effectively with natural systems requires doing so from a spiritual as well as scientifically informed posture. Part of this dynamic is respect for the complexity and wisdom inherent in living systems that are millennia old. A corollary of the spiritual mandate is a moral imperative calling for extraordinary patience and resilience, including a willingness to engage in lengthy trial and error, with the conviction that doing so can solve highly complex problems.

On yet another level, the Massey book directs our attention to the unseen. Many of the living systems of soils he discusses are microscopic, unseen to the human eye. Like currently emerging scientific understanding of the critical role that the gut biome plays in human health, soils have their own interdependent ecosystems of fungi, bacteria, organic materials, water, and minerals. Not only are these systems mutually supportive, they are to a high degree self-organizing and self-regulating, for example, by increasing numbers of critical organisms or nutrients in response to environmental conditions.

Unlike Peter Wohlleben, who argues for an approach to healing nature that is virtually hands-off, Massey makes the case that humans can and should intervene to partner with and assist Mother Nature. Like Wohlleben, he warns that this intervention should be done with humility and great care. Both ultimately assert that we are not alone and should not be limited to scientific and mechanical strategies in the healing process.

My second example of healing comes from Kimmerer's essay "Tallgrass,"[12] about efforts to recover the prairie ecosystem that once constituted much of the midwestern United States. It weaves together both her scientific and Native American perspectives in the spirit of *Braiding Sweetgrass*. Rather than focusing on what has been lost since the advent of settler-colonial culture and technology, Kimmerer illustrates how an intimate and loving embrace of the natural world can both inform and energize a difficult task.

The beauty of this tale is the compelling and gentle affirmation of a critical fact: new solutions to critical environmental problems require a humbler and more spiritually informed mindset. In this sense Kimmerer's work echoes and affirms a subtext of Massey's book. The difference is a Native American's willingness to let her love of nature lead her to discovery.[13] Most relevantly to the argument being made here, "Tallgrass" reminds us that embracing nature is both an act of nature healing and self-healing.

For the third example, I draw upon my own experience working in the desert of western China's provinces of Inner Mongolia and Ningxia. Our nonprofit, ECOLOGIA, conducted a desert reclamation project there for several years.[14] Our work was completed well before we knew of the grassland recovery efforts described in Massey's *Call of the Reed Warbler*. It also predated our awareness of Kimmerer's approach combining indigenous perspectives and science in prairie restoration. Nevertheless, we managed to slowly realize some of the wisdom more fully developed by these healers of Mother Earth. I present this example, not to tout our work, but to illustrate a theme that cannot be overstated: many of us are independently awakening to the same realizations about the wisdom and resilience of natural systems. In our case, we were trained social scientists muddling our way through the new territory of botany and environmental restoration.

This realization came slowly to us, in part because the problem placed before us by our project funder was formidable: extreme and advanced desertification in China. Desertification had become so severe that the 2008 Olympics were at one point jeopardized by predictions of dust storms that could have made air in Beijing unhealthy to breathe under normal circumstances, not to mention the exertion of athletics. Sand dunes were known to advance several kilometers in a matter of years and bury entire villages in the deserts of Ningxia Province, where we worked.

As we read background papers on desertification, one perspective, rigidly adhered to by many Chinese and foreign NGO experts, as well as Chinese government officials, emerged as commonly accepted wisdom: overgrazing by goat herders was primarily to blame. The solution offered was simple, or overly simplistic, as we were to discover: get rid of the herders and their animals. The strategy was supported by compelling documentation: color photos of grasslands and deserts before and after herders and their animals were fenced out.

The results were immediate and dramatic. Biomass increased, and the desert became green on the side of the fence with no animals and no nomads. At least for a few years. However, shortly after policy makers, NGOs, journalists, donors eager for quick results, and scientists all had left, another reality appeared. Topheavy ungrazed desert plants, many of them nonnative invasives introduced by centuries of travel along the Silk Road, died when serious droughts came. The plants had not been pruned by grazing animals and thus had not been encouraged to develop deep and strong root structures. They died. The previously green success stories quickly became brown vistas of dead grass and shrubs.

The herders in Alashan (the westernmost region of Inner Mongolia) showed us another possibility. If they were allowed to practice their traditional nomadic lifestyle, they could achieve an ecological balance by allowing both camels and goats to graze, but not overgraze. In tandem, these animals grazed different plants, or in some cases grazed the same plants differently, promoting both root growth and biodiversity.

Sadly, policy and market incentives to produce more cashmere, thought of as "white gold" in the early days of China's ventures into foreign markets, incentivized poor grazing practices. The result was too

many goats, who have sharp hooves, and too few camels, who have flatter and softer padded feet that move more gently on the fragile desert
soils. We slowly awakened to the fact that Inner Mongolia's desert and
grasslands had long ago ceased to be a pristine, self-regulating ecosystem,
functioning in balance without human presence. Humans now played
a huge role, for good or bad. But before the advent of market pressures
to overproduce cashmere, Mongolian nomads had not made the desert
their dominion. They had entered into an intimate partnership with
the landscape and their animals. *Together* they were the ecosystem.

These examples all deliver the same message: humans are not inher-
ently destroyers of the Earth's ecosystems. We two-legged are certainly
capable of disruption, but humans working with Mother Earth are also
capable of healing. The key to unlocking this solution is the willingness
to listen to and see what the land has to teach.

This lesson is made clear in the fourth example, which features
Native Americans as owners, entrepreneurs, caretakers, and scientists.
This example involves forestry, which many in the environmental community see as harming ecosystems and climate change. However, the
Menominee Nation of Wisconsin in the upper Midwest practiced sustainable forestry long before the term appeared in forestry curricula.
They are now preparing for climate change, not suffering a failure of
nerve before warnings of the Anthropocene or viewing this threat as
the coup de grace by the settler-colonial culture.

Despite a century of unusually intense struggle over their tribe's
legal status and sovereignty, the Menominee have remained faithful to
their culture's ethic of viewing the surrounding forests as a living system
for which they are responsible. Since the mid-nineteenth century, they
have cut more than two billion board feet of timber, while increasing
the quality and quantity of trees in their care. They have done this in
part by operating their own sawmill and subordinating its production
and profitability to the needs of the forest. This is an inversion of the
region's prevailing business model, which is to view local forests as a service provider subordinate to a sawmill's need to maximize output. The

Menominee have also deviated from standard forestry practice when they felt that their stewardship role and culture called for more care for the living system.

Facing the threat of climate change, the Menominee are creating a plan that looks more than a century into the future. They are asking what kinds of trees will be most adaptable to an altered climate. They are envisioning how their timber industry will need to change. These questions are being asked within the context of a larger question: How can the tribe make this adaptation while maintaining its core values and traditions? The answer is being shaped by a combination of state-of-the-art science, TEK, data from sophisticated mapping and monitoring, on-the-ground observations tapping an intimate understanding of localized variations, and most importantly, tribal culture.

In order to provide future generations of the tribe with both the continuity and the expertise to adapt to climate change, the tribal College of Menominee Nation Sustainable Development Institute[15] created a curriculum to educate the young on the reservation. When the climate change curriculum committee created a graphic representation of how and where their tribal values and mainstream science overlapped, they concluded that there was no consistency.[16] The finding stands in stark contrast to the actual methods of decision making of the tribal government. On its surface, the conclusion also contrasts with the case studies presented here. After all, I have been arguing that TEK and modern science can proceed in partnership and point to healing solutions.

However, the Menominee curriculum committee revealed the fact that there are creative tensions between and contradictions within decision making systems attempting to bridge the gap between objective scientific understanding and values. And they are wise to hold on to the fact that this creative tension must be recognized and maintained if both science and tribal culture are to benefit.

If we are to reap the benefits of combining modern science and TEK, we need to adopt a spiritual mindset of trust and love of our natural kin. Then we can act with a loving embrace and patience, rather than rushing into desperate short-term measures, which often precipitate more unintended negative consequences.

If we were to remake the famous ad of the Crying Indian, perhaps now we could allow him to announce, "We are still here." The "we" would include the four-legged, the rooted ones, and the winged ones.

This is not to suggest that our sad Indian is going to show all seven billion of us how to return to the land and live more gently and sustainably in a fantasylike fulfillment of a decolonizing vision whereby the white settlers would just disappear. But those of us in the mainstream can recognize two sobering lessons of Native American history: resiliency and humility.

First, resiliency. *Homo sapiens* is an adaptive and resilient species. Among the larger creatures upon the Earth, we occupy the widest range of habitats, and we can adapt to sudden and radical changes in our living conditions. Many Native Americans have already lived through the harsh realities of socially induced climate change. My Potawatomi ancestors were driven out of the lush forests and lake regions of the upper Midwest and forced at gunpoint to march first to the prairies of Kansas and then into the desert of Oklahoma, all within a single generation. As a consequence of this tragedy, we are certainly not accepting the inevitability of seeing much of the world's population being force-marched down a similar path by our leaders' inaction in regard to climate change. But our history does show that, if a less than optimal scenario for reversing climate change fails to materialize, and if some of the worst predicted damage occurs, and if it becomes irreversible, we can and will adjust. We will do this, not simply by surrendering or holing up in gated communities or protected compounds, but by partnering with the genius of Mother Nature's resilient systems and by holding on to as much of the natural world as we can.

The second lesson, perhaps the more difficult, is to assume a posture of humility and engage in a reality check on our sense of power. Much of the melancholia that afflicts us is due to our enormous overestimation of our importance in the natural scheme of things. But we are not in control. We are not omnipotent, even with our best science and engineering

The daunting environmental problems that confront us have been centuries in the making, and it is human folly to imagine that we are smart enough to fix them in a few short decades. More than folly, our conviction of omnipotence is a self-victimizing delusion. Perhaps this is why so many climate scientists suffer from symptoms of clinical depression.[17] They, and we, are like young medical students who are still learning the limits of their profession and coming to terms with the fact that even the best medicine does not cure all ills.

What lies before us is an era of environmental destruction of yet to be determined proportions. But we also face the possibility of engaging in a time of healing, recovery, and spiritual rediscovery. These need not be mutually exclusive realities.

We will be most effective in our healing and recovery if we act from a newly re-spirited perspective and allow ourselves to feel daily the embrace of Mother Earth.

Such a possibility brings me to my final example of healing Mother Earth. It stands in stark contrast with earlier examples, which are large-scale projects covering expanses of geography that can be captured with satellite imagery.

Fam Jam Café

As with so many sources of inspiration and enlightenment about which I have written, this discovery emerged unexpectedly, when we found the Fam Jam Café just a few blocks from our apartment in Lachine, Montréal. Once again the wonderful spiraling confluences of this city swirled around and enveloped us.

The Fam Jam Café is just a few blocks from the Lachine Fur Museum where my ancestral connections blossomed. Across the street from that museum is the church where a Sunday concert awakened us to the cultural offerings of Québec society, where access to the arts is often free or at a very affordable cost. That discovery contributed to our decision to take up part-time residence nearby. From that residence and its balcony, we can see the shrine of the Native American Catholic saint Kateri Tekakwitha. Need I mention our easy access to a bike route to Vieux Montréal? If you are this far into my tale, these are now familiar stories and you know that Native Americans repeat important stories. We do so to reinforce cultural themes, to repeat lessons, and to encourage the listener or reader to make new connections.

Our encounter with a wonderfully accessible and replicable example of nature healing began when we peered in the window of a new café on Rue Notre Dame. This street intrigued us as it suddenly came alive after years of neglect and stagnation. Once abandoned store fronts became a book store, used clothing and household items store, a variety of ethnic restaurants, and a health food store. Among these new businesses was the Fam Jam Café, offering a most unusual family friendly environment.

Intrigued, we entered its welcoming environment. The first thing we noticed was the newness and simplicity of the café's natural wood furniture. Then we saw the kids playing joyfully and quietly among toys on soft foam block floors. Parents participated, or quietly sipped coffee or tea, sometimes enjoying a snack. Carolyn and I did not hesitate to be seated; our grandparent consciousness projects a desire to be near young children, their laughter and joy.

As we had coffee, tea, and chili, I overheard two young women at the next table speaking a language we had once been constantly exposed to, but which had faded into memory. "Is it Russian?" I asked myself. The question arose because we had worked for two decades in the Soviet Union and in various countries with a Soviet history. Those decades, part of our global environmental awakening, had long seemed remote in time and space.

However, an overheard language called us back to more complicated times in our lives and more tumultuous times in twentieth century history. This semiconscious connection ignited when the café's co-owner,

Iryna, spoke to the women at the next table in the same language. My curiosity got the better of me. I asked her, "Is that Russian, Ukrainian, or Belarusian?" The answer came back, "Russian. Belarusian is rarely spoken and is nearly a lost language." To which I responded, "We have a friend from Minsk, had an office and staff in Minsk, and know at least one family where Belarusian is spoken."

Iryna then disclosed that she was born in Minsk and our distantly entangled histories began to reveal uncanny connections. We mentioned that our connection with Minsk was environmental, including work related to the Chernobyl Nuclear Power Plant accident in 1986. Iryna shared remembrances of Chernobyl and being given iodine tablets as a child.

In response to our comment that our life journeys were now converging in Montréal, Iryna revealed her own circuitous and serendipitous migratory route to Toronto and then to Lachine. We reciprocated with tales of our adventures in Belarus. Like the characters in my Re-creation Story who begin as two-dimensional flat images drawn on a page, and then slowly become three dimensional beings, we were all progressing from surface first impressions to complex multidimensional beings. We then found ourselves continuing this journey in the fourth dimension, time, as we connected our pasts, presents, and futures. And that journey, in the spirit of my fictional story, ultimately assumed aspects of a fifth dimension, one profoundly spiritual and on the topic of partnering with Mother Earth.

As we put on our coats and prepared to leave, we lingered in front of an aquarium that attracts the café's small children with its brightly colored fish, plants, and coral. Iryna pointed out a colorful urchin and several tiny hermit crabs, and then showed us how it all looked under black light. "Wait a minute," she requested and disappeared. Shortly she returned with a food cube, which she floated on the aquarium surface. It attracted colorful shrimp that had been invisible and a small eel. She pointed out a living coral and noted, "I am trying to demonstrate the possibility of coral reef restoration."

It was some hours later that I began to connect the dots. Here was a refugee/immigrant from a Chernobyl-impacted society setting up a new life in Canada, creating a space affirming family friendly values, and in her own small way, using an aquarium to model a healing planet. How like our Chinese friend Yang and her imaginary walks as an ant in the moss forest that grew in her German apartment's window.

Curious, we soon returned to the café to learn more about its owners and about its customers. We learned that Iryna and her husband Anton offered their own brand of Costa Rican coffee from a plantation that they had visited and carefully observed. A quiet gesture of affirming the need to strive toward environmental sustainability sat on the café's shelves in small bags and appeared in its coffee cups. There were no blaring signs about "our coffee is certified by . . ." displaying the logo of some large international verification body. Supply chain attestation work was being done quietly, and quite credibly, by the owners.

Slowly we began to see other aspects of the work being done in the café. Iryna mentioned, in a very understated manner, that she and Anton were seeking to educate their customers about healthy food, responsibly sourced products, and a low-key, less technologically overwhelmed lifestyle. This was being done by example rather than preachy slogans and banners. "Taste the atmosphere and see if you like it; taste the coffee and see if you like it," were thoughts made all the more powerful for being unsaid.

We returned to the topic of the aquarium. I needed to confirm that its intent was instructive and not just aesthetic. Iryna nodded in agreement. She then explained that in their home there was no television. Entertainment was to be found by observing life in an aquarium and looking out the home's window where the world of Mother Nature offered a living panorama in place of a prerecorded video or some nature documentary. I looped back to the aquarium. Iryna mentioned that one customer came and practiced yoga in front of this miniature calming seascape.

So many spirals swirling. Not the least of which was Iryna's connection with the chapter of my book, "What Coy-Wolf Taught Me," that I had sent by way of introduction and in hope that she might allow an interview. Iryna's response was understated, but knocked me over. We connected on the wolf dimension too. Iryna has a wolf tattoo on her back.

I feel blessed. So many of us in the twenty-first century seem involved in desperate searches for hope and inspiration. But these stories seem to find me and beg to be passed along, like proverbial "pay it forward" gifts.

What did I learn from this encounter? Some of us, even when faced with the century's greatest dislocations (such as the Chernobyl nuclear power plant accident and rural-urban migration in China) simply refuse to surrender to despair and give up on our dreams of one day, somehow, reconnecting with a healed Earth. Big dreams are often kept alive in the human imagination and in small pots or aquariums. Hope sinks its roots even when everything around it conspires to limit growth.

Some will caution me that I should not invest too much emotional energy in tiny examples of planetary healing, that I should not make mountains out of mole hills. Fantasy bonsai mini-forests on a windowsill in Germany are not solutions to the burning Amazon. One muffin-sized piece of coral transplanted to a reef regeneration experiment in an aquarium in Montréal is not a solution to climate-induced coral bleaching in the Great Barrier Reef. One small café on a Lachine street that sells sustainably grown and fairly traded coffee is not a solution to global supply chain problems for a major commodity.

But, what if these grassroots efforts are in fact how change will come? Taken individually they do not amount to the "scale" that economists, policy makers, and foundations invariably require before they will pay attention. But perhaps we are missing something more significant than scale. A new consciousness, increasing commitment, and hope are spreading like a benevolent virus. They represent a life-giving process of self-replication that cannot be stopped.

17

MICROBES
AND BLACK SWANS

Occasionally we live in moments that we know will always be remembered, events and times that are going to have an enduring impact on our individual and collective lives and consciousness. Such was the moment in March 2020, which began with a message delivered to me on a super-full-moonlit night of Ziinzbaakwatokewin Giizis, Maple Sugarbush Moon. This time, unlike other midwinter full moon nights when visitations abound and the muses awaken me to give dictation, it was not Koo-koo-o-koo, nor hawk, nor the whisperings of ancestral spirits who spoke. It was the tiniest of messengers that the natural world is capable of dispatching into the human realm: microbes. Actually, it was two different messenger microbes, one from afar, and one from the forest in which I live.

It can be difficult for us two-leggeds to come to terms with the fact that a tiny, brainless living organism has something noteworthy to say. After all, many of us are only at the very beginning of a steep learning curve with respect to the lessons that nature offers and the wisdom of creatures who were, until very recently, widely believed to be inferior to us.

But now, our minds are slowly being opened to the wisdom of plants and animals. We experience amazement and wonder at tales about trees in the forest sharing information through their roots and mycorrhizal networks. Smaller plants and ecosystems also have wisdom to offer, as Kimmerer illustrates in *Gathering Moss* when she introduces us to the wonders of some of the more diminutive flora on the planet. But I am asking my readers to think even smaller, orders of magnitude smaller, and to journey with me to the outer limits on the scale of what is living, into the microscopic world of nature.

The key to making sense of this microrealm's lessons is to see and to listen with the sensitivities of indigenous people and, simultaneously, to apply the rigor of a scientific mind. I know too well that this is a demanding and tricky balancing act as I have spent the last month literally knocked off my feet by the enormity of this intellectual-spiritual challenge, made more daunting because it was combined with the physically debilitating power of a microbe.

This chapter in my awakening journey began innocently enough, during a January thaw, when atypical temperatures momentarily approached springtime levels. I waded into our snowy Vermont forest to see if the maple trees were letting their sap run. This normally happens in March. But sometimes we can capture an early sap run in January or February. And indeed for two sunny days, I gathered sap in buckets and made the most remarkable honey colored and delicately flavored maple syrup.

In my eagerness to gather sap I forgot to use the insect repellent that I have used for years to avoid tick bites. My antitick clothing and spraying protocol was made necessary by the fact that we have an epidemic of Lyme disease (*Lyme borreliosis*) in Vermont. A tiny, tick-borne bacterium can inflict devastating harm; the disease can become a lifelong chronic condition if not quickly diagnosed and treated. I thought that I had learned to take vigilant precautionary measures. But I was mistakenly lulled into the idea that such protective measures were irrelevant because of deep snow on the ground. Ticks are typically dormant in extreme cold. However, as I was soon to discover, hungry ticks awakened by warm weather were hanging out on low-lying tree limbs and stalks of grass. They had a biting commentary to make on my carelessness.

This lesson came as a very painful reminder of the need to be eternally on-guard and to never underestimate the persistent efforts that our natural kin must make to find nourishment at every possible opportunity. If my ancestors had made such a miscalculation by under-estimating bears thought to be in winter hibernation, they might have been mauled or killed. Being mauled by a tick is not immediately life threatening, nor is it the stuff of which family legends are made and then told to spellbound grandchildren gathered around winter fires. But I did wake up several weeks later with back and neck pain so intense that I could barely get out of bed.

On my first Lyme morning I settled my aching body into a chair in front of a laptop computer and confronted the now daunting task of a morning ritual cup of coffee. I discovered that it was nearly impossible to move my jaw enough to eat or drink. Seeking a distraction from pain and having little energy for more ambitious activity, I read the news online. Headlining was a story from China. Another microbe, a corona-virus, had crossed over from the wilds there and ventured into an open air food market in the city of Wuhan. It was wreaking havoc.

I dragged myself to the doctor; actually Carolyn drove me as I did not have the energy. And another assault was unleashed on my body, a thirty day antibiotic treatment, supplemented with powerful medicinal herbs. The necessary but disruptive cure came with its own additional physical costs.

Then the parallels began to emerge. The world's most populous society was struggling to contain a potential epidemic. Echoing my fate, it was implementing a solution with an enormous cost for its body poli-tic. In the case of China, these costs were immensely greater than my minuscule personal disruptions. An entire society was shutting down its economic engine, the second largest in the world. More than a hundred million people were isolated by a quarantine. Streets, which I knew from my travels to China to normally be crowded, were eerily empty. Beijing looked like a ghost town or a scene from a science fiction film about some end-of-the-world cataclysm. One of the most tightly controlled and regimented societies on Earth was employing all of its intellectual and societal resources to contain a tiny living invader from within its own boundaries. And for weeks and weeks it was losing the battle. Even when China finally began to contain the coronavirus microbe, Chinese citizens and observers across the world wondered about the social dislocation costs of the cure. The global economy experienced shock as the virus spread beyond China and virtually every society was forced to take extreme and disruptive measures.

This was a classic case of "the black swan," a concept made famous by Nassim Nicholas Taleb's book of the same name. Taleb uses the rare appearance of a black swan mutation among its normally white kin as a metaphor for the massively disruptive and unanticipated events that occasionally upend human societies.

Clearly, for the Chinese, and then quite suddenly for the rest of the world, a tiny microbe had risen from obscurity and invisibility to the status of a giant black swan. My own experience with a microbial black swan did not make the news. But it struck home for me in the very same weeks that China's leaders were first struggling with their mighty microbe, COVID-19. That coincidence suggested connections for me that I might have missed under other circumstances. However, my local forest was once again acting as a teacher.

What was the mighty microbe telling me, and us? The first lesson is one of humility. It is one of the seven "Grandfather/Grandmother Teachings" representing core values of the Anishinaabe people, of which my Potawatomi tribe is one constituent sub-group. The teachings are: Respect (*Mnaadendimowin*), Love (*Zaagidwin*), Honesty (*Gwekwaadziwin*), Bravery (*Aakode'ewin*), Truth (*Debwewin*), Wisdom (*Nbwaakawin*), and Humility (*Dbaadendiziwin*). These teachings are painted on small stones that sit on a dish in our main living room. An Ojibwe artist friend, appropriately named Patricia Le Bon Herb, who played an important guiding role in my spiritual awakening and healing, gifted us with these stones, which are intended to act as a reminder. The teaching stones sit upside down in a dish with their one word messages on the underside. I blindly touch and turn over a stone at least once daily, seeking their guidance. The Humility stone has been turning up a lot lately.

My painful instruction in the practice of humility is more than a mere personal reminder of the power of nature's littlest creatures. There is a much broader cultural lesson being offered here: we humans continually overestimate our significance and our power within the realm of nature.

Evidence of such hubris is, ironically, often to be found even among those who study nature. Increasing numbers of scientists and environmental activists promote the notion that *Homo sapiens,* as a single species, have come to dominate nature. This notion is explicit in the idea of the Anthropocene, the assertion that humans and our activity have become more forceful than other natural processes or species on the planet. The underlying assumption is that science and technology have become so powerful in magnifying human impacts that natural forces are no match for our onslaught. With dire and scientifically grounded predictions of the effects of climate change staring us in the face, it is not surprising that the notion of a dominant human footprint on the Earth has become deeply, almost unquestioningly, rooted in our thinking. But isn't there a critical difference between a large and environmentally disruptive human footprint on the Earth and total ecological collapse caused by a Godzilla-like crushing foot? That question is more than a philosophical query or systems modeling problem for biology and environmental science. It is *the* question for our time.

I have come to understand that our answer can be informed by the smallest of creatures who are presenting another series of provocative queries of their own in the spirit of a Socratic dialogue. Enveloped in the tiniest of Greek togas and perched sagely on limbs and rocks they ask, "So, Kritkausky, if human technology and science are so powerful, if the economic institutions and systems of *Homo sapiens* are so overwhelmingly dominating as to constitute virtually irresistible forces, why do they collapse suddenly with the appearance of a tiny microbe? Why are the best of human science and pharmacology unable to triumph easily over little viruses?"

Answers began to appear for me at the personal level when I explored online medical information to inform my healing. I soon learned that my microbial adversary was better equipped than I in the struggle enveloping me. The bacteria that cause Lyme, *Borrelia burgdorferi*, have the ability to very quickly adapt to our bodies' defenses. They change shape so as to be unrecognizable to the immune system and in order to defend themselves against attacking pharmaceuticals. They can go into something like protective hibernation within our cells as they await the subsidence of an antibiotic inundation. After antibiotic treatment ends, the bacteria may then reemerge and proliferate. This method of adaptation is just one tool in their microbial arsenal.

Viruses, such as those causing the flu diseases occurring yearly across the globe, are continually evolving, intentionally mutating, working around human efforts to eliminate them with vaccines. They leave their DNA in our cells where it is picked up and used by other microbes.

Microbes not only outsmart us, their numbers, dwelling in our gut biome and on our skin surface, rival the total number of human cells in our body. Without these microbes we could not extract life-giving nutritional content from the food we ingest and digest. Like bears in the forests of my ancestors, they can give us life, or they can take it from us.

Microbes of various forms are by far the most numerous life forms on the planet. However, we rarely think of them as fellow living creatures worthy of our respect. Consequently they don't appear as charismatic nature protection images, like polar bears on postage stamps. Celebrities in the world of nature protection don't build careers posing and interacting with cuddly microbes.

Our unwillingness to acknowledge the power of microbes distorts our understanding of history. For example, we learn about the human devastation inflicted during the American Civil War (1861–65). However, less well known is the fact that two-thirds of that war's 660,000 combatant deaths were attributable to disease and infection, known at the time as "the third army." While the percentage of soldier deaths attributed to disease and infection declined dramatically after World War I, the Spanish Flu that followed inflicted mortality rates on the civilian population greater than did warfare. Ongoing regional wars continue the trend, as civilian populations are impacted by opportunistic microbial attacks following in their wake.

However, these testimonies pale before the power of the mighty microbe revealed within the narrative of the Western Hemisphere's colonization. Much of mainstream society still accepts a centuries-old story of conquest that credits European explorers and settlers with military triumph based on superior technology. Slowly an alternative explanation and truth are emerging; it was diseases Europeans introduced to an indigenous population lacking immunity, sometimes by accident but often by design, that laid waste and rapidly killed 90 percent of Native Americans. This fact refutes the settler-colonist narrative of their more advanced culture, religion, and social institutions triumphing over less robust and less worthy societies. It also makes Native Americans wonder at the lack of historical understanding and memory of mainstream society when we hear daily news reports proclaiming an "unprecedented" coronavirus pandemic victimizing helpless people.

This historical reminder points to the second lesson that our microbe and black swan visitors offer: prepare for unanticipated events. They are not only probable, they are likely. To be more accurate, they are certain to happen. We just don't know when they will happen, what they will be, or where they will occur. Nassim Nicholas Taleb's book was applauded for this wisdom. It is a sobering reminder to modern society about the need to build resilient institutions and systems that can withstand events that fall at the outer edges of the normal curve of probabilities.

The lesson is nothing new for indigenous people, and Native Americans in particular. In addition to Traditional Ecological

Knowledge, my ancestors had something akin to traditional historical wisdom, THW. Front and center in our culture, our stories, and
our agricultural and food-gathering practices was the recognition that
nature takes its own course and we, the two-legged, are subject to its
whims and fancies. Harvests were understood to be alternately bounti-
ful and meager. Calendar time was marked by events such as "the year
of the great wild rice harvest," but also as "the year of no elk" or "the
year of early snow that killed corn." Hunting was highly unpredictable.
It was also dangerous. The hunter often became prey.

Indigenous technology made humans susceptible to the powers of
Mother Earth. Nature is occasionally mean, nasty, and brutal, red in
tooth and claw. It is therefore not surprising that some ask if Native
American society's vulnerability to this reality was a failing or weakness. But if we are to ask and answer such a provocative question, then
we must also ask if modern industrial society and technological culture
have insulated us all too well from the vicissitudes of nature, saddling
us with the delusion that we dominate our planet and that we need not
prepare for her surprises.

The power that mainstream society occasionally wields over
Mother Nature should be viewed within a Native American perspective, as very "strong medicine," to be used judiciously. We should know
that something bad happens when we overuse or overdose on strong
medicine. The tiny print that comes with our prescription medication
contains a long list of physical side effects. It also contains important warnings about cognitive impairment, if we take the time to read
them. But we too rarely have had the time or patience for reading
or reflecting on this. With an economy overheated by huge doses of
nearly free money and affluence abounding for much of the upper
middle class, many have been lulled into thinking that good times
and security are here for all time. We paid no heed to the warning:
"Do not continue to operate the machinery of national government if
delusions of grandeur or dizziness occur." And that may explain why
our leaders in Washington began defunding our public health care

system a decade before the current pandemic. And it might shed light on why they abolished institutions designed to plan for health care emergencies two years before COVID-19 appeared. Who needs a medicine man or woman, or a shaman, to divine the future when it is already known, certain, and entirely within our control?

I sometimes feel that I am caught in a societally scaled Greek tragedy where pride goes before the fall. As I look around, it is clear that the warning signs of a pandemic-type crisis were everywhere. They were clear for any audience watching from the slightest distance, observing us caught in an unfolding tragedy not yet revealed to the players.

The extraordinary degree of our delusion and hubris was made evident when I reflected on the fact that not only have many of us come to believe that it is no longer necessary to prepare for surprises from the realm of the microbes, but people who are touted as the most innovative and gifted with forethought entertain the idea that we can conquer and entirely end disease. Billionaire entrepreneur Mark Zuckerberg and pediatrician Priscilla Chan, his wife, have pledged three billion dollars to end disease, not to end a single disease or group of specific diseases as with the Gates Foundation, but to end virtually all disease.

And it is not just biological disease that we seek to eradicate but alien ideologies, which can be viewed as plagues and which we believe can be eliminated with meager doses of economic development nutrients, occasional strong doses of nature eradicating pesticidal chemotherapy, and surgical strikes with drones. In recent decades the United States has spent more than a trillion dollars on wars to eliminate insurrections around the world. They are no more successful than our efforts to "conquer" COVID-19. Centuries of bitter lessons about the cost of colonization and empire building and the uncertainties of decolonization, so familiar to indigenous people, seem lost on the mainstream.

Is it not time to turn over and ponder the Humility stone again? And perhaps the Love and Wisdom stones as well? The time has come for traditional, less ego-inflated views of power wielding, more gentle nurturing models of collaboration, and even a dose of matriarchy in appointing and deposing chiefs, as was the practice among the Haudenosaunee. Native American women who planted and harvested crops in Native American communities knew how to plan for the unexpected, and knew the consequences of not anticipating infrequent but devastating events.

Native Americans know how to cope with a more powerful adversary while maintaining our dignity. We make necessary accommodations as best we can, and we hold on to what is dearest. Negotiating with human adversaries, or adversaries from the natural world, is messy. The disappointments and humiliations are many.

Crisis can be time to dig into our alternative and neglected historical narratives and to gather their wisdom. The isolation and time-outs imposed on us in the form of quarantines may be a hidden gift, a pause button encouraging such reflection. Imagine our families and communities gathered in small groups around a fire, exchanging stories of ancestral wisdom and reimagining our future. Imagine the cultural enrichment that might come if this became routine.

That possibility brings me to the third lesson I see buried within our current microbial event. It is possible to discover hope and inspiration in how *Homo sapiens* have responded to massive societal disruptions of the past. Without ignoring the human cost of catastrophes, we can learn from the creative responses that came out of previous pandemics.

The Black Death, bubonic plague, that struck Europe in 1348 and in recurring waves thereafter provided the impetus for massive social and culture change. Peasants who had been victimized by feudal social and economic inequality discovered that their depleted numbers made their labor a scarce and more valued commodity. They rose up in England and across the continent and began a long process that eventually shifted the balance of power in society. So too with urban residents and merchants who saw opportunity and a potential for power shift as royals suffered from depleted coffers. Cities and towns demanded and succeeded in getting new charters and new freedoms. A centuries-old monopoly on power by aristocrats was weakened.

Even the power of the Roman Catholic clergy was eroded. They were on the front line in the battle against the plague. Ministering to the sick and dying, they were most vulnerable, as are today's health professionals. With their numbers seriously depleted, they were often not available to perform routine religious ceremonies. As a result, ordinary members of church parishes formed self-help and self-ministering bodies, religious confraternities or sodalities. We see echoes of this in the life of Kateri Tekakwitha when she and other Native American women attempted to form their own religious order. Kateri's effort was discouraged. But the groundswell and need in medieval Europe could not be so easily turned back. Empowered and independent, the faithful sowed seeds of the Protestant Reformation.

Similarly, with labor in short supply, economic demand for labor-saving devices and machines became a priority. New technologies were welcome. A period of technological innovation began and new sources of wealth materialized. The Renaissance followed.

The story of demographic collapse following pandemics for Native Americans is more grim, and the upside less immediately evident. This is due in large part to the fact that pandemic was followed by intensive efforts at forced cultural assimilation. Consequently the recovery timeframe was also longer. But in time, including recent decades, indigenous people have borrowed elements of European culture, combined them with traditional values, and are now creating new and more sustainable economic models that are being used successfully to heal the Earth.

I see a glimmer of hope in the painful message sent from my forest and from around the globe. This may be the first global epiphany. Many had expected that the threat of climate change would bring a new awakening and collective response. But decades of scientific debate and discussion have not dislodged enough of us from our daily life–focused mindsets. Then, suddenly a small microbe accomplished what political discourse could not—binding us together in a shared moment of consciousness in which all of humanity confronted the dire necessity of putting aside differences and rising to the challenge of survival.

My epiphany is more humble and small scale. I began this book with an image of stepping through the looking glass and being caught halfway. When I commented on this to tribal elders, they alerted me to the fact that it is exhausting to be living in two spiritual worlds simultaneously, and that I should prepare myself. But now, I am discovering that if I can step entirely through the glass, I can abandon and repurpose it. Its glass can be recast as a lens, a Native American lens through which I can reexamine contemporary society and nature. Looking through that lens I now see things, both large black swans and the smallest microbes, much more clearly. I am grateful.

CONCLUSION

UNTANGLING THREADS
OF HISTORICAL NARRATIVE

I began this book, and my journey, by standing before a mirror and asking, "Am I really an Indian after all?" My question has been answered in a resounding affirmation by ancestral spirits, Coy-Wolf, Koo-koo-o-koo, a multitude of other natural kin, a shooting star, historical data, and a Potawatomi ceremony giving me an Indian name.

What I did not anticipate is that in, around, and through my personal reflections, another, more complex image would emerge and come into focus—that of Indianness writ large. I now see unfolding before me something like a five-dimensional hologram of my collective tribal history through time, and even beyond that, an emerging image of our continent's human history.

Longue durée

Natives of North America began our journey, like all of humanity, hundreds of thousands of years ago, as hominids migrated out of Africa northward into Europe, the Middle East, and across Asia. Over the eons they encountered Neanderthals, Denisovans, and other beings. We interbred and shared our DNA with them, and they with us. In this process of evolution, hominids evolved new branches, only to have them diverge and later reconnect, blending and reblending our histories. Our species' various strains were spun into a common thread of humanity that modern paleoanthropologists now envisage more as a process of crisscrossed or braided journeys than as an evolutionary tree with totally distinct and diverging limbs, as was once simplistically diagrammed in anthropology textbooks.[1]

For indigenous peoples of North America, our history probably begins with migrations across Asia. Genetic evidence suggests that our ancestors migrated to North America at least 19,000 years ago. It is now understood that we arrived in multiple waves of migration across land bridges in a frozen Bering Strait, by sea across the Pacific, and possibly over a land bridge from Europe through Greenland. Maps with arrows showing one-time unidirectional human migrations out of Asia and into North America are being replaced with a more complex tale of braided histories. For example, those who settled North America sometimes migrated back to Asia and reblended DNA in a confusing mixture that may have then been transferred back to North America by additional later migrations. Then the Europeans arrived, and things got even more genetically complicated.

The complication arose partly from the blending of new races with the Indians: whites from Europe, blacks from Africa, and, later, migrants from Asia. Cultures also melded. During the first stages of cultural and racial blending, the "New World" became a melting pot where cross-cultural influences often resulted in conflict, but also produced rich new mixes. This positive outcome occurred at the level of highly individualized relations in which European traders, like my French Canadian ancestor, married into and lived among the Indians. Africans, held in bondage or freed, married Indians and shared stories and music as well as DNA.

Following on this multiplicity of unique biographical journeys came the Great Complication, and it began to lay waste to the land. I am not referring to the physical diseases that Europeans brought to the New World, and which they spread both unwittingly and intentionally, reducing the indigenous population by 90 percent. I am referring to a culturally toxic pathogen that slowly infected the land, lay dormant like the flu for short periods, and would then break out again and again in epidemic proportions. The process continues to this day.

I refer to a standardized social narrative steeped in Aristotelian logic. Unlike a physical disease, which destroys the body, constraining logic attacks the soul. Like tiny viruses, logic remains invisible, working its way into host communities and taking over its very thought DNA, seriously weakening if not killing the organism.

Let me explain. The very foundation of Western logic and thought is the law of identity. It quite simply states that "A is A." Or more familiarly, "a rose is a rose is a rose." Corollary principles are those of noncontradiction and the excluded middle. A rose cannot be a rose and not a rose at the same time. It cannot be somewhat of a rose and somewhat of something else in between. Thus philosophers, scientists, and schoolteachers reprimand us when we "contradict" ourselves. The notion that contradiction is an intellectual sin is so ingrained in us that we can barely see our way to questioning the idea or its implications.

Such was not the case among Native Americans, who embraced ambiguity. Indigenous cultures have no difficulty asserting that sometimes "boy is boy" does not hold. For example, when boy is bear spirit, or actually bear, he is both boy and not boy, all at the same time. Sometimes boy and bear are both something in the middle, boy-bear.[2] This is the essence of Native American spirituality and our intimate connections with nature. For us, there is no "we" on the one hand and "it" (Nature or Mother Earth) on the other, without a meeting ground in the middle. We are individuals and also simultaneously part of, or even momentarily subsumed in, the natural world or by our natural kin.

The social implications of this are enormous, and become obvious when we examine how social categories, such as gender, work in society. For example, the principle of identity once pointed to a rigid binary for gender identity: one was either a male or female. By Western logic, it was not possible to simultaneously be male and not male, or to simultaneously be both male and female. Being both male and female, being male-female, was the excluded middle; it was not allowed by logic and by extension was not culturally allowed. Unless you lived in many Native American cultures where "two spirited" gender identity was understood and often embraced.[3]

In recent decades, mainstream society across the globe has made enormous progress toward recognizing the harm inflicted by a rigid gender binary, and toward tolerating gender ambiguity. This breakthrough occurred, not through logical argumentation, but because courageous individuals told compelling tales of their spiritual lives and how they were harmed by exclusionary logic.

Paradoxically, at the same time, largely because of cultural contacts resulting from mass migrations, we have seen factions within nation after nation taking steps backward toward what was thought to be a discredited racial and cultural binary. People in North America and Europe are being relegated to mutually exclusive categories such as "one of us" or "one of them." How often do we hear or read statements along the lines of "if *they* want to live here, *they* must become just like us and abandon *their* language, dress, and religion"? The implication is that you can't be "one of us" and partly something else at the same time. Native Americans have suffered from this binary categorization from the beginning of European contact, and we continue to suffer from it, frequently in ways that we do not fully grasp.

Like many discoveries in this book, this recognition came to me, partly through reacquaintance with my own ancestors and partly by wonderfully serendipitous encounters, such as with Prince Dr. Sar Amiel. I met Prince at the Great Lakes Intertribal Food Summit at the Pokagon reservation. He introduced himself as an African American interested in the Potawatomi. The idea intrigued me, as a connection between African American and Native communities seemed remote. Then I learned that Prince had lived a tale of diaspora and forced but failed cultural assimilation that was uncannily similar to the people of my tribe. His people, the African Hebrew Israelites, emigrated from the United States in 1967, first to Liberia and several years later to Israel, where they have established the African Hebrew Israelite Nation of Jerusalem. It has proved no easy feat being a Black Hebrew anywhere in the world.

The abstract parallels of minorities caught in history were intriguing, but grew more personal as Prince explained exactly why he was at the Pokagon gathering. While in the United States, he lives in Chicago, near the DuSable Museum of African American History. It is named for Jean Baptiste Point du Sable (c. 1750–1818), a black man of Caribbean descent and the first nonindigenous resident of Chicago. Du Sable is considered by many to be the city's founder. He married Kitihawa, a Potawatomi woman. Prince was at the Pokagon Food Summit hoping to build on these historical links between Indian and African American communities and to enlist the Pokagons' support in lobbying to have a new wing of the DuSable Museum named for Kitihawa.

As I soon learned, getting Indians and Blacks to work together in Chicago has been a challenge for centuries, despite the founder's obvious affinity for Indians. But I did not know that the Chicago story of mixed race relations between Indians and African Americans was the tip of a continental iceberg. Prince patiently began to walk me through a new perspective on race in America about which privileged northeastern white guys like me know too little. He helped me to explore more deeply the extraordinary role that racism has played in the founding of the United States, the settling of the New World, and in both uniting and separating Indians and African Americans.

Like so much of my awakening, this tale developed an intimate family connection. Once again I found myself on a spiraling journey, sometimes beautiful and enlightening, and at other times disturbingly and almost unbelievably horrifying. In both instances, I am grateful for a new friend joining in my journey.

The White Man's Imaginary

I have now come to understand that the Western Hemisphere was settled by, and continues to be ruled by, people whose thinking is dominated by a distorted historical narrative and a sociocultural delusion based on a white-nonwhite binary.

Social philosophers refer to an intricately constructed social narrative of group identity as "the social imaginary." An *imaginary* can be an inspiring image of where we could be, as in the case of Martin Luther King's famous "I Have a Dream" speech where he imagines a society in which justice and equality have triumphed over gross inequality and hatred. But it can also be a construct seeking to establish a brutal and restricting social order in which a group that feels threatened can imagine being securely dominant over "others," as in Nazi Germany's imaginary of a purely Aryan society where imaginary non-Aryans have been extinguished.

The power of an insidious imaginary that bends the trajectory of history came into focus as I once again acted as a historian in order to better understand my own origins in events that unfolded shortly after Columbus set foot in what was then called the New World.

In 1493 Pope Alexander VI issued a papal bull titled *Inter caetera,* which translates into the innocuous words "Among Other Works." As a reward for their service to the Catholic faith and as recognition for having just, the year before, finished their reconquest of long held Muslim territory in Spain, Pope Alexander bestowed unusual power upon the Spanish monarchs who had financed Columbus's voyage. Ferdinand and Isabella were given exclusive claim to the vast majority of the entire New World. The Pope declared, in the spirit of *terra nullius* (that is, territory belonging to no one), that the entire New World was unoccupied, because those who lived there were barbarous heathens not living in a civilized, Christianized state. Therefore their lands as well as "all their dominions, cities, camps, places, and villages, and all rights, jurisdictions, and appurtenances" were conveyed to Ferdinand and Isabella.[4]

Inter caetera eventually became known in English as the "Doctrine of Discovery."

I would have been happy to dismiss the Doctrine of Discovery as a strange and outdated fossil of long-extinct European thought. But that hope vanished when I learned that it had been cited by Supreme Court Chief Justice John Marshall in 1823 as part of the *Johnson v. M'Intosh* decision, which established important precedents concerning who could own and transfer Native American lands. That ruling stated that Indian land titles predating independence of the United States were invalid. Further, the Doctrine of Discovery was cited to assert the right of the discoverer to withdraw the "right of occupancy" to Native Americans. The right of occupancy concept stipulates that people are allowed to live on territory only by virtue of conditional grants made by a "discoverer." Even though indigenous people had lived in the Americas for millennia, their land rights were now in the hands of the conquerors. In addition, the court ruled, Native American sovereignty was not an inalienable right; it too was granted and could be withdrawn, as was the case with rights to occupy land. As Native American history illustrates, the right of occupancy, even when granted by treaty, was continually withdrawn, and the boundaries of reservations were redrawn again and again. The Doctrine of Discovery was subsequently cited numerous times by the U.S. Supreme Court, as recently as 2005, and always in decisions related to limiting the sovereignty granted Native Americans by treaty.

Ultimately, it is not just the metalegal implications of the Doctrine of Discovery and its diminution of Native American rights that matters. Greater damage has been done by the underlying attitudes and values revealed by continued application of the doctrine. These social and cultural assumptions are so ingrained in our national imaginary that they are not challengeable in any legal forum. They are the assumptions that shape life in the New World to this day for Native Americans and "others" in every sense of that word. At the base of these assumptions is a profound and inadequately examined assumption of white, European racial superiority and entitled ownership.

Until I dug into my own family's Native American history, I thought that egregious racial stereotyping and discrimination happened to other people of color but fortunately had not touched my family so deeply and directly. I was proven wrong, as Aunt Emma's biography would reveal.

We have just one handwritten note from Emma, which outlines her academic biography. She proudly states that she has acquired skills as a "disciplinarian." That phrase sent chills down my spine when I read it, as people in this role in Indian schools were those who sentenced recalcitrant kids to the guardhouse and meager rations at the Carlisle Indian School. But as it turned out, I misjudged Emma. She was not, as I feared, a capo in the Indian stalag, nor was she an unreflective advocate of total assimilation.

Who Aunt Emma really was and what she had to reveal to me about American culture remained a mystery until I began to dig into the Chicago-Indian connection that Prince Sar Amiel had intriguingly laid before me. The complex and fraught history of Indians in Chicago became apparent when I read *City Indian: Native American Activism in Chicago, 1893–1894,* by Rosalyn Lapier and David Beck. There I encountered the 1893 World's Columbian Exposition, intended to celebrate four hundred years of progress since the settling of North America. Advances in technology and the arts were on display. To throw these accomplishments into relief, Indians were featured at various venues. They were the living picture of the "before," or primitive stage of human development, in a spectacular before and after comparison. Unstated but hanging over the exposition were four-hundred-year-old assumptions about the inferiority and unworthiness of indigenous cultures that were embedded in the Doctrine of Discovery. If the New World had not actually been *terra nullius* in 1492, by 1893 it was generally agreed, even among Indian advocates, that doomed New World "primitives" were about to vanish. As the popular media noted, people should come to the exposition to see them before they totally disappeared. So it was that Indian villages were erected and populated with real live "Injuns" who were allowed to showcase their arts and artifacts, such as totem poles and dancing.

Anthropologists from Harvard and other major institutions argued about whether Indians should be portrayed as mere primitives beyond the reach of civilizing influence or as worthy of efforts to educate and raise them to the general level of technical and cultural accomplishment on display at the Exposition. Both images appeared side by side and were often muddled.[5]

One showcase of Indian potential at the exposition was a model Indian boarding school. Aunt Emma, age seventeen, a model boarding school student, was on display, as were other Indian kids brought to the exposition for several weeks at a time. They dutifully displayed their sewing and carpentry skills. It is impossible to read accounts of these displays without imagining them as living dioramas of indigenous life similar to the inanimate ones found in natural history museums, typically in the same wing as glassed cases displaying stuffed extinct animals.

In addition to the horrific images, I also found glimpses of inspiring resistance among Indians who objected to demeaning racist portrayals at the exposition. During its opening ceremonies Simon Pokagon, son of the founder of the nearby Pokagon band of Potawatomi, made a passionate and excoriating speech to a crowd of thousands. "The Redman's Rebuke" was printed on faux birchbark at Pokagon's expense and distributed.[6] (It was later reissued and distributed as "The Redman's Greeting." Although the new title was a euphemism, the text itself was unaltered.) Indians also brought and displayed cultural artifacts they valued, often to the displeasure of exposition organizers, who did not want any suggestion of the continued vibrancy of Indian culture, since this challenged their narrative of a disappearing people.

While Aunt Emma was used at the Chicago Exposition, some

inkling of her mixed feelings emerged a decade later when, now a schoolteacher, she was asked to bring her own delegation of Indian kindergarten students to the 1904 Louisiana Purchase Exposition in St. Louis. The following excerpt from *Anthropology Goes to the Fair: The 1904 Louisiana Purchase Exposition,* by Nancy Parezo and Don Fowler, describes her reaction.

> A special Kindergarten class came as a compelling example of the boarding school system's success. It was under the direction of Emma Johnson, a Pottawatomie who as a student had demonstrated at the 1893 Chicago Exposition. Johnson was not enthusiastic about the assignment. "From my experiences at the Chicago fair I know that the work in St. Louis will be no picnic." She thought six year olds were too young for the trip. But McCowan repeatedly suggested she would have light duties, caring for the class, singing occasional solos, and chaperoning field trips around the exposition. He also agreed to pay her mother's expenses from Shawnee, Oklahoma to help with the scarf drill.[7]

This story is a crack in the dominant narrative of successful forced cultural assimilation that the U.S. and Canadian governments promoted for centuries. It also challenges defeatist narratives of Native Americans who sometimes overestimate the negative impacts of assimilationist policies and boarding schools. It illustrates the degree to which Native Americans struggled against the negative cultural and racial stereotypes they had internalized. I began to see hints of the hidden spiritual struggles that Aunt Emma must have worked through and my grandfather probably lived with his entire life. Emma's resilience is evident in the fact that she became one of the founders of the Society of American Indians in 1911, which marks the beginning of pan-Indian movements in the United States.

Other efforts of self-healing, communal healing, and seeking cultural validation within Chicago's Native American society emerged

at the 1933–1934 Century of Progress Exposition. At the behest
of Indians, it contained a Hall of Fame displaying photos and brief
biographies of prominent Native Americans. In addition an annual
Indian Achievement Award was given to an individual who achieved
professional success in mainstream society. However, this victory
unraveled as the white-dominated Chicago organization granting the
award refused to consider nominations for anyone of mixed Indian
and African heritage. A few Indians saw this for what it was—
racism—and protested. In the same spirit, one non-Indian Chicago
professor resigned from the award-granting organization. However,
the majority of Indians capitulated to mainstream society's requirement to exclude black people. In a prescient and revealing commentary, Elaine Eastman, the white wife of the award winner, Charles
Eastman, noted:

> There is some reason to sympathize with the ambitious individual
> of mixed ancestry who hopes, by passing as Indian, to gain social
> recognition denied one of African origin. This has been done a good
> many times, though resented by educated red men, doubtless rather
> in self-protection and imitation of white intolerance than from
> innate race prejudice.[8]

Our society has only made a dent in the 1493 doctrine that rele-
gates nonwhites or non-Christians to something less than second-class
citizens. In the twenty-first-century United States, people of color and
of foreign origin continue to hold on to a very tenuous "right of occupancy" that may be suddenly revoked, as thousands of expelled Latin
American workers and families, who are of mixed Spanish and Indian
ancestry, can attest.

Elaine Eastman's observations about why Indians seek to distinguish themselves from African Americans are unfortunately not
outdated. In the twenty-first century several Indian tribes are removing once-enrolled biracial black people from their rolls.[9] In part this

is to reduce the numbers who can share in lucrative proceeds from reservation casinos. But this is also a signal that Indians have internalized the superiority of whiteness and desire to distinguish themselves from African Americans.[10] Native Americans acting in this manner do not see themselves and their black brothers and sisters, who are often literal relatives, as victims of the same overarching racist imaginary. As is regrettably the case in much of human history, one marginalized minority group seeks to climb one rung above another in order to claim some marginal social and economic advantage.

But it is not just African and Native American people who suffer under this imaginary of white supremacy. It infects mainstream white culture. In Canada and the United States I constantly meet white-looking people like me, and they tell me, often sadly, "My family oral history is that we too have Indian ancestry, but we can't prove it." I tell them that this connection was often lost because being Indian was a social disadvantage, and families hid their Indianness. The problem was not just social ostracism or difficulty getting a job with a label of "Indian." It was a deeply threatening status with severe consequences, as my family is reminded when we drive to the neighboring town of Brandon, Vermont, to attend a music concert or visit a restaurant. We pass a sprawling brick campus known in the early decades of the twentieth century as the Vermont State School for Feeble Minded Children. Now it is a converted office and residential complex, but in the 1930s it was a center for forced sterilization of Abenaki Native American and French Canadian women who were declared "defectives" because of their ancestral heritage. The Vermont state legislature, faced with a declining population of colonial descendants, saw French Canadian and Abenaki, who often intermarried, as a threat to their racial purity and dominance.[11]

The long legacy of stigmatizing Indianness does not only afflict marginal people. When Senator Elizabeth Warren announced that she was seeking the Democratic nomination to challenge President Trump, he began calling her "Pocahontas," as if being a nonwhite and a woman were enough to doubly disqualify her from high office. After explaining that her family oral history included a story of Indian ancestry, she took a DNA ancestral test. The results came back with a minimal trace of Indian ancestry, as such tests often do with Native Americans.[12] Rather than doubling down and proudly affirming her attenuated Indian ancestry, she apologized to Native Americans and distanced herself from her mixed ancestral claims. She became a white person again.

Senator Warren missed an opportunity to seize her own life history and affirm that being American typically means being of multiple cultural and racial ancestries. That would have been a healing message for a nation racked by a rising tide of white supremacist organizations. Why did she take this path? Perhaps Elaine Eastman provided the answer when she wrote that many individuals act "doubtless rather in self-protection and imitation of white intolerance than from innate race prejudice." Boldly affirming pluralism and thereby rejecting cultural and racial binaries such as that of white and nonwhite is a difficult political path to walk, even in the twenty-first century.

However, there is a path forward out of this cultural quagmire. It can be found in the culture that has most suffered from the notion of a white-nonwhite binary and the imaginary of America as a white Christian society. This path is to be found in the Native American practice of braiding sweetgrass.[13] This aromatic herbal grass is woven into baskets and used in ceremonies. But it is braiding that offers us a road map. Especially if we combine it with another Native American healing practice: the medicine wheel.

The medicine wheel is a sacred space where herbs, including sweetgrass, are grown. It is divided into four quadrants oriented to the four directions. It is also associated with the colors connected with these directions: white, red, black and yellow. These are the same colors that we associate with racial groups.

So it is that I envision different strands of sweetgrass dyed the colors of the medicine wheel. I then return to the image of journeys braided together, as in human evolution. My imaginary—one that is profoundly Native American—is of a future in which we at last triumph over the legacy of the Doctrine of Discovery, as we gently rebraid our dominant historical narrative, respectfully intertwining colorful strands of sweet-grass, thereby creating a strong new social contract of inclusiveness.

It would be a just and inclusive society that we can all live in. And I can say this without reservation.

GLOSSARY OF INDIAN WORDS

NOTE: Potawatomi, along with Ojibwe and Odawa, belongs to the Anishinaabe language family. There are also different dialects and different linguistic conventions used to transcribe the various spoken languages into Latin characters. In *Without Reservation,* the author has used the words most available to him in their context—Potawatomi or Anishinaabe. This glossary is provided as an aid to the reader; for anyone seriously interested in the derivations and variations of the Anishinaabe languages, an increasing number of nations and bands are developing their own bilingual dictionaries and posting them online.

Aakode'ewin: Bravery (one of the Seven Grandfather/Grandmother Teachings)

Bozho: Potawatomi greeting

Chimookmaan: "big knives"; whites

Debwewin: Truth (one of the Seven Grandfather/Grandmother Teachings)

Dbaadendiziwin: Humility (one of the Seven Grandfather/Grandmother Teachings)

getsijig: elders

Giiwedinang: the North Star; literally "the going-home star"

Gikendasswin: Knowledge

Gitchie Manitou or Gitchie Manito: the Creator

Gwekwaadziwin: Honesty (one of the Seven Grandfather/Grandmother Teachings)

heyoka: a sacred jester and social commentator in Sioux culture

ki (plural kin): third-person pronoun applied to animate beings

kinni-kinnick: a fragrant blend of tobacco, sage, cedar, and sweetgrass

Koo-koo-o-koo: Owl

Ma'iingan: Wolf

Manidoo Giizis: Spirit Moon

Mide'wiwin: keepers of traditional knowledge in Anishinaabe society

Mishomis (plural Mishomisag): Grandfather

Mi-zhee-kay: Turtle

Mnaadendimowin: Respect (one of the Seven Grandfather/ Grandmother Teachings)

mnomen: wild rice

Nanim'ewé: Coyote

Nbwaakawin: Wisdom (one of the Seven Grandfather/Grandmother Teachings)

Nibiseh manidoosag: little water spirits

Nitaawes: cousin

Nokmis (plural Nokmisag): Moon; grandmother moon

Nokmis Pwaagan: Grandmother pipe

ogichida: male warrior

ogichidaak: female warrior

semaa: ceremonial tobacco

Waabanong: the eastern direction

Wanaboozhoo or **Nanaboozhoo:** the giver of knowledge to humans

wee-gwas: birchbark

Zaagidwin: Love (one of the Seven Grandfather/Grandmother Teachings)

Zhaaganosh: a person of white or European ancestry

Ziinzbaakwatokewin Giizis: Maple Sugarbush Moon

NOTES

Introduction

1. "The American Indian and Alaska Native Population: 2010 Census Briefs."
2. "Aboriginal Peoples in Canada."

1. Bozho, Bonjour, Hello, Dear Reader

1. Jones, "Etymology of the Anishinaabe."
2. Horton, "Where Does the Word Boozhoo Come From?"

5. What Coy-Wolf Taught Me

1. "Killing Wolves."
2. Cobb, *Native Peoples of North America.*
3. Kimmerer, "Speaking of Nature."
4. "Neanderthal Mother, Denisovan Father!"
5. Takemura, "Wolf Species."
6. Miller, "DNA Barcoding."
7. Takemura, "Wolf Species."
8. Lind-Riehl et al., "Hybridization."

6. The Nexus of Time

1. Personal email communication, June 14, 2017.

7. Roots Connect in Vieux Montréal

1. Wohlleben, *Hidden Life of Trees*, 7–8, 51.

8. Encounters with Kateri Tekakwitha

1. "St. Kateri Tekakwitha," Our Lady of Martyrs Shrine.
2. Axtell, *Invasion Within*, 105.
3. Axtell, *Invasion Within*, 302.
4. Chauchetière, *Narrative*.
5. "St. Kateri Tekakwitha, Mohawk Saint," *Encyclopedia Britannica*.
6. "Tekakwitha, Kateri," *Dictionary of Canadian Biography*.
7. Shoemaker, ed, *Negotiators of Change*.
8. McCaa, "Peopling of Mexico," 246–47; and Martin, "Anthropology Alum."
9. Shoemaker, "Kateri Tekakwitha's Tortuous Path," 54–57.
10. Shoemaker, "Kateri Tekakwitha's Tortuous Path," 57.
11. The work of Natalie Zemon Davis on confraternities as mechanisms for both subverting and reinforcing power relationships is most relevant here. See especially *Society and Culture in Early Modern France*.
12. Shoemaker, "Kateri Tekakwitha's Tortuous Path," 67. This refers to Pierre Cholenec's 1696 biography of Kateri, cited in the Vatican's Positio, or documents prepared for the consideration of canonization.
13. Shoemaker, "Kateri Tekakwitha's Tortuous Path," 51.
14. Shoemaker, "Kateri Tekakwitha's Tortuous Path," 66.
15. Shoemaker, "Kateri Tekakwitha's Tortuous Path," 67, note 1.
16. "Saint Kateri Tekakwitha," Canadian Conference of Catholic Bishops; and Gadoua, "Native Americans Divided."
17. "Relics," Kateri Center. The Kateri Center lists one hundred documents pertaining to Kateri relics and requests for such items.
18. "Lily of the Mohawks," Saint Francis Xavier Mission.
19. The following sites and organizations have played a role: Kahnawake Quebec Shrine of St. Kateri, Saint Kateri Interpretative Center in Kahnawake, Saint Kateri Conservation Center, and Catholic Ecology.
20. Holmes, "St. Lawrence Seaway Expropriations."
21. Chauchetière, *Narrative*, 103–5.

9. Asa's Indian School Story

1. Carlisle Indian School Digital Resource Center.
2. "The Hampton Indian School."
3. Family correspondence, undated letter.
4. "Narrative of Andrew J. Vieau Jr."

10. Reflections on Warrior Culture

1. Vukelich, "Ojibwe Word of the Day."
2. Jackson, *Black Elk*, 211–12.
3. Treuer, *Rez Life*, 186–87.
4. Treuer, *Heartbeat*, 183.
5. Treuer, *Heartbeat*, 185.
6. Jenkins, *The Real All Americans*, 277.
7. Anderson, *Carlisle vs. Army*, 4–5.

11. Decolonizing Powwows

1. "Powwows in Europe," NAAoG.
2. Benton, "Grand Entry."
3. Jackson, *Black Elk,* 279–315. Jackson's account of the rise and suppression of the Ghost Dance documents this phenomenon with great respect and historical insight. See chapter 18, "The Messiah Will Come Again," and chapter 19, "Dances with Ghosts."
4. Jackson, *Black Elk,* 267–78.
5. Hoffman, *The Mide'wiwin,* 176–77.
6. Jackson, *Black Elk,* 184–89.
7. Jackson, *Black Elk,* 187–89.
8. Gutiérrez, "Politics of Theater."

12. The Re-Creation Story

1. Benton-Banai, *A Mishomis Book,* 1:4.
2. Benton-Banai, *A Mishomis Book,* 1:5–7.
3. Benton-Banai, *A Mishomis Book,* 1, 9–10.

13. Koo-koo-o-koo and the Bear Moon

1. Hoffman, *The Midewiwin,* contains examples of scroll text used by Native Americans.
2. "Chaco Canyon."

14. Awakenings on the Reservation

1. Barker, "Recognition," 133–61.
2. Burke, *Reflections,* 110.
3. *United States v. Confederated Tribes of Colville Indian Reservation,* clause IV, C 2, 10.

15. Rootless in the Botanical Garden

1. Sullivan, *The Thoreau You Don't Know.*
2. Schwartz, "Nature's Masterclass."
3. Kretzer, "Butterfly Releases."
4. Wohlleben, *Hidden Life of Trees.*
5. Cohen, "Anthem."
6. Liu, *Urban Farming Practice.*
7. Mosaicultures Internationales, *Terre D'Espérance,* 59.
8. "The Chief Seattle Myth," 1.
9. "Bright Lights, Big Cities."
10. Gupta, "Chimp Traditions."
11. Liu, *Urban Farming Practice,* 120–68.
12. Orange, *There There,* 11.
13. Simpson, "Why White People Love Franz Boas," in Blackhawk and Wilner, *Indigenous Visions,* 166–81.

16. Toward a Newly Re-Spirited Environmentalism

1. Ronda, "Mourning and Melancholia."
2. Wang, "Between Charity and Business."
3. Smith, *Moral Sentiments,* IV.1.10.
4. Liu, *Urban Farming Practice,* 41–45.

5. Kimmerer, "Speaking of Nature."

6. "Welcome to the Anthropocene."

7. Martin, *Meaning of the 21st Century*, 4.

8. "The Doomsday Clock."

9. "The Doomsday Clock."

10. Buhner, *Plant Intelligence and the Imaginal Realm.*

11. Meier, "Beating the Big Dry."

12. Kimmerer, "Tallgrass."

13. Robbins, "Native Knowledge."

14. "ECOLOGIA's 'Sustainable Fibers' Program."

15. College of Menominee Nation.

16. Tempus, "People's Forest," 32.

17. Corn, "Weight of the World."

Conclusion

1. Bower, "Denisovans Emerged," 27.

2. Pomedli, *Living with Animals,* xi–xxi.

3. Slater and Yarbrough, *Gender and Sexuality.*

4. "Doctrine of Discovery," 5.

5. Green, "Stage Set for Assimilation," 95–133.

6. Pokagon, "The Red Man's Rebuke."

7. Parezo and Fowler, *Anthropology,* 150.

8. Lapier and Beck, *City Indian,* 12, 152.

9. "Cherokee Nation Faces Scrutiny"; Staples, "Black Seminole Indians"; Keilman, "Bloodlines."

10. Chin, "Red Law?"

11. "Vermont State School for the Feeble Minded."

12. G. F., "Controversies"; Bendary, "Mainstream Media"; Elliott and Brodwin, "Identity"; Estes, "Native American."

13. Kimmerer, *Braiding Sweetgrass.*

BIBLIOGRAPHY

"Aboriginal Peoples in Canada: Key Results from the 2016 Census." Statistics Canada (website). https://www150.statcan.gc.ca/n1/daily -quotidien/171025/dq171025a-eng.htm. Accessed August 6, 2019.

"The American Indian and Alaska Native Population: 2010 Census Briefs." United States Census Bureau (website). https://www.census.gov/content /dam/Census/library/publications/2012/dec/c2010br-10.pdf. Accessed August 6, 2019.

Anderson, Lars. *Carlisle vs. Army: Jim Thorpe, Dwight Eisenhower, Pop Warner (and the Forgotten Story of Football's Greatest Battle)*. New York: Random House, 2007.

Axtell, James. *The Invasion Within: The Contest of Cultures in Colonial North America*. New York: Oxford University Press, 1985.

Barker, Joanne. "Recognition." *American Studies* 46, nos. 3/4 (Fall–Winter 2005): 133–161.

Begay, Chrystal, and Tinesha Zandamela. "Sexual Assault on Native American Reservations in the U.S." Ballard Center for Economic Self-Reliance, Brigham Young University, Ballard Brief (website). http://ballardbrief.org /read/sexual-assault-on-native-american-reservations-in-the-us.

Bendary, Jennifer, "Mainstream Media Is Blowing Its Coverage of Elizabeth Warren's DNA Test" HuffPost (website), January 4, 2019. https://www .huffpost.com/entry/elizabeth-warren-dna-test-native-american_n_5c19 550fe4b0432554c512bb.

Benton, Sherrole. "Grand Entry: A New Ceremony Derived From the Old West." *Tribal College Journal* 8, no. 3 (Winter 1997).

Benton-Banai, Edward. *A Mishomis Book (Mishomis Coloring Books)*. 5 vols. (1975). Minneapolis: University of Minnesota Press, 2016.

———. *The Mishomis Book: The Voice of the Ojibway*. (1988). Minneapolis: University of Minnesota Press, 2010.

Blackhawk, Ned, and Isaiah Lorado Wilner, eds. *Indigenous Visions: Rediscovering the World of Franz Boas*. New Haven: Yale University Press, 2018.

Bonaparte, Darren. *A Lily among Thorns: The Mohawk Repatriation of Kateri Tekahkwí:tha*. Ahkwesáhsne Mohawk Territory: Wampum Chronicles, 2009.

"Boustrophedon." Wikipedia (website). https://en.wikipedia.org/wiki/Boustrophedon. Accessed August 6, 2019.

Bower, Bruce. "Denisovans Emerged from the Shadows." *Science News*, 196, no. 11 (December 21, 2019).

"Bright Lights, Big Cities: Lights and Windows Are Deadly Hazards for Birds." Bird Conservation Network (website). http://www.bcnbirds.org/window.html. Accessed August 6, 2019.

Buhner, Stephen Harrod. *Plant Intelligence and the Imaginal Realm: Into the Dreaming Earth*. Rochester, Vt.: Bear & Co., 2014.

———. *The Secret Teachings of Plants: In the Direct Perception of Nature*. Rochester, Vt.: Bear & Co., 2004.

Burke, Edmund. *Reflections on the Revolution in France*. (1790). New Rochelle, N.Y.: Arlington, 1965.

Carlisle Indian School Digital Resource Center, Dickinson University (website). http://carlisleindian.dickinson.edu/student_records. Accessed February 2, 2020.

Catholic Ecology, An Advocacy and Information Organization (website). https://catholicecology.net. Accessed February 3, 2020.

Chauchetière, Claude, S. J. *Narrative of the Mission of Sault St. Louis, 1667–1685*. Kahnawake, Quebec: Kanienkehaka Raotitiohkwa Press, 1981.

"Chaco Canyon." Ancient Wisdom (website). http://www.ancient-wisdom.com/mexicochaco.htm. Accessed August 6, 2019.

"Cherokee Nation Faces Scrutiny for Expelling Blacks." All Things Considered, National Public Radio, digital archive, September 19, 2011. https://www

.npr.org/2011/09/19/140594124/u-s-government-opposes-cherokee
-nations-decision.

"The Chief Seattle Myth." *ECOLOGIA Newsletter* 15 (May/June 1991): 1,
4–6.

Chin, Jeremiah. "Red Law, White Supremacy: Cherokee Freedmen, Tribal
Sovereignty, and the Colonial Feedback Loop," *John Marshall Law
Review* 47 (Summer 2014): 1227–68. https://asu.academia.edu/JerChin.

Clarren, Rebecca, and Jason Begay. "Confronting the 'Native Harvey
Weinsteins': When Indigenous Women Are Harassed at Work, Gaps
in Tribal Law Can Leave Them in a Precarious Gray Area." *The
Nation*, April 23, 2018. https://www.thenation.com/article/archive
/confronting-the-native-harvey-weinsteins/.

Cobb, Daniel M. *Native Peoples of North America*. DVD. The Great Courses,
Chantilly, Va.: Teaching Company, 2016.

Cohen, Leonard. "Anthem." *The Future*. CD. 1992.

College of Menominee Nation Sustainable Development Institute (website). http://www.sustainabledevelolpmentinstitute.org. Accessed
August 14, 2019.

Cooley, Charles Horton. *Human Nature and the Social Order*. New York:
Charles Scribner's Sons, 1902.

Corn, David. "Weight of the World: When You Can See Disaster Unfolding,
and Nobody Listens, What Happens?" *Mother Jones*, July–August 2019.

Davis, Natalie Zemon. *Society and Culture in Early Modern France*. Stanford,
Calif.: Stanford University Press, 1975.

"The Doctrine of Discovery, 1493." Gilder Lehrman Institute for American
History (website), 2012. https://www.gilderlehrman.org/sites/default/files
/inline-pdfs/04093_FPS.pdf.

"The Doomsday Clock." *Bulletin of the Atomic Scientists*. https://thebulletin
.org/doomsday-clock. Accessed August 14, 2019.

"ECOLOGIA's 'Sustainable Fibers' Program." ECOLOGIA (website). http://
www.ecologia.org/china09/fibers.html. Accessed August 14, 2019.

Elliott, Carl, and Paul Brodwin, "Identity and Genetic Ancestry Tracing."
British Medical Journal 325 (December 21–28, 2002): 1469–71.

Estes, Roberta. "Native American and First Nations DNA Testing: Buyer Beware."
DNA eXplained (website), January 27, 2017. https://dna-explained

.com/2017/01/27/native-american-and-first-nations-dna-testing-buyer-beware.

Fournelle, André. *États de choc.* Art Public, Ville de Montreal (website). https://artpublic.ville.montreal.qc.ca/en/oeuvre/etats-de-choc. Accessed February 2, 2020.

Gadoua, Renee K. "Native Americans Divided over Mohawk Saint Kateri Tekakwitha." *Syracuse Post Standard,* October 15, 2012. https://www.syracuse.com/news/index.ssf/2012/10/native_americans_divided_over.html.

Geary, Patrick. *Furta Sacra: Thefts of Relics in the Central Middle Ages.* Princeton, N.J.: Princeton University Press, 1990.

G. F. "The Controversies over Claims to Native American Ancestry: Tribal Nations Look to History and Culture, Not DNA, for Enrolment." *The Economist,* October 25, 2018. https://www.economist.com/the-economist-explains/2018/10/25/the-controversies-over-claims-to-native-american-ancestry.

Gong Zizhen. "Sick Plum Blossom" ("Bing Mei Guan Ji"). English translation. https://testmecards.wordpress.com/2014/11/10/sick-plum-blossom-translation-from-bingmeiguanji. Accessed August 22, 2019.

Green, Christopher T. "A Stage Set for Assimilation." *Winterthur Portfolio: A Journal of American Material Culture* 51, nos. 2/3 (Summer/Autumn 2017): 95–133.

Gupta, Sujata. "Chimp Traditions Are under Threat." *Science News,* April 13, 2019.

Gutiérrez, Ramón. "The Politics of Theater in Colonial New Mexico: Drama and the Rhetoric of Conquest." In *Reconstructing a Chicano/a Literary Heritage: Hispanic Colonial Literature of the Southwest,* edited by Maria Herrera-Sobek. Tucson: University of Arizona Press, 1993.

"The Hampton Indian School: Another Denial of the Charges of Dr. Childs." *The New York Times,* July 4, 1889. https://www.nytimes.com/1889/07/04/archives/the-hampton-indian-school-another-denial-of-the-charges-of-dr.html.

Harjo, Joy. *Crazy Brave: A Memoir.* New York: Norton, 2012.

Hoffman, Walter James. *The Midewiwin: Or Grand Medicine Society of the Ojibwa.* Part of the *Seventh Annual Report of the Bureau of Ethnology.* (1891). Whitefish, Mont.: Kessinger, 2018.

Hollins, Elizabeth Jay, ed. *Peace Is Possible: A Reader for Laymen.* New York: Grossman, 1966.

Holmes, Joan, and Associates. "The St. Lawrence Seaway Expropriations on the Kahnawake (Caughnawaga) Reserve No. 14 (1954–1978)." Report prepared by Joan Holmes & Associates, Inc. for the Mohawk Council of Kahnawake and the Specific Claims Branch, Department of Indian Affairs and Northern Development, August 1999. http://kahnawakeclaims .com/wp-content/uploads/2014/11/Seaway-ExecSumm-Aug1999 .pdf.

Horton, Robert. "Where Does the Word Boozhoo Come From?" Net News Ledger (website). http://www.netnewsledger.com/2013/11/28/word -boozhoo-come. Accessed August 6, 2019.

"Hungry Full Wolf Moon Howls Outside in Frigid January–Or Does It?" *Indian Country Today,* January 26, 2013. https://newsmaven.io/indian countrytoday/archive/hungry-full-wolf-moon-howls-outside-in-frigid -january-or-does-it-uPo9nk5HskG6PlFtfcOutw. Accessed August 7, 2019.

Jackson, Joe. *Black Elk: The Life of an American Visionary.* London: Picador, 2016.

Jenkins, Sally. *The Real All Americans: The Team That Changed a Game, a People, a Nation.* New York: Doubleday, 2007.

Jones, Dennis. "The Etymology of the Anishinaabe." https://www.coursehero .com/file/p2so1vl5/In-The-Etymology-of-the-Anishinaabe-published-the -same-year. Accessed August 6, 2019.

Kahnawake Quebec Shrine of St. Kateri (website). http://kateritekakwitha. net. Accessed August 7, 2019.

Kateri Center, Kahnawake (website). http://www.lily-of-the-mohawks.com /center.htm. Accessed August 7, 2019.

Keilman, John. "Bloodlines Drawn over Money," *Chicago Tribune,* April 4, 2002. https://www.chicagotribune.com/news/ct-xpm-2002-04 -04-0204040303-story.html.

"Killing Wolves." Historic Ipswich on the Massachusetts North Shore (web-site). https://historicipswich.org/2016/10/25/killing-wolves. Accessed August 7, 2019.

Kimmerer, Robin Wall. *Braiding Sweetgrass: Indigenous Wisdom, Scientific*

Knowledge, and the Teachings of Plants. Minneapolis: Milkweed Editions, 2013.

———. *Gathering Moss: A Natural History of Mosses.* Corvallis: Oregon State University Press, 2003.

———. "Speaking of Nature." *Orion Magazine*, March/April 2017.

———. "Tallgrass." November 26, 2018. https://www.littletoller.co.uk/the -clearing/tallgrass-by-robin-wall-kimmerer.

Klein, Naomi. *This Changes Everything: Capitalism versus the Climate.* New York: Simon & Schuster, 2014.

Kretzer, Michelle. "Butterfly Releases at Weddings and Other Events are Bad for Animals." June 24, 2018. https://www.peta.org/blog/butterfly-release -wedding. Accessed August 9, 2019.

LaDuke, Winona. *All Our Relations: Native Struggles for Land and Life.* Chicago: Haymarket, 2015.

Lapier, Rosalyn R., and David R. M. Beck. *City Indian: Native American Activism in Chicago, 1893–1894.* Lincoln: University of Nebraska Press, 2015.

"Lily of the Mohawks: Kateri's Life." Saint Francis Xavier Mission, Kahnawake (website). http://kateritekakwitha.net/kateris-trail. Accessed August 7, 2019.

"Saint Kateri Tekakwitha Feast Day." Loyola Press: A Jesuit Ministry (web-site). https://www.loyolapress.com/our-catholic-faith/saints/saints-sto-ries-for-all-ages/saint-kateri-tekakwitha. Accessed August 7, 2019.

Lind-Riehl, Jennifer F., Audrey L. Mayer, Adam M. Wellstead, and Oliver Gailing. "Hybridization, Agency Discretion, and Implementation of the U.S. Endangered Species Act." *Conservation Biology* 30, no. 6 (December 2016). https://onlinelibrary.wiley.com/action/doSearch?ContribAuthor Stored=Wellstead%2C+Adam+M&.

Liu, Yang. *Analysis of Urban Farming Practice through the Lens of Metabolic Rift: Case Studies at the City of Chengdu in China and at the City of Freiburg in Germany.* Albert-Ludwigs-Universität, Freiburg, Germany. Ph.D. dissertation, 2019.

Martin, Debra. "Anthropology Alum Explores Evidence of Ancient Violence." Department of Anthropology, University of Massachusetts, Amherst (website). https://www.umass.edu/anthro/news/anthropology

-alum-explores-evidence-ancient-violence. Accessed August 9, 2019.

Martin, James. *The Meaning of the 21st Century: A Vital Blueprint for Ensuring Our Future.* New York: Riverhead, 2006.

Massey, Charles. *Call of the Reed Warbler: A New Agriculture, A New Earth.* White River Junction, Vt.: Chelsey Green, 2017.

McCaa, Robert. "The Peopling of Mexico from Origins to Revolution." In *A Population History of North America,* edited by Michael R. Haines and Richard H. Steckel, 241–304. Cambridge, U.K.: Cambridge University Press, 2000.

Meier, Johannes. "Beating the Big Dry: How an Australian Cattle Farm Is Fighting Drought by Reviving Ancient Landscapes." *Plough Quarterly Magazine,* May 6, 2019. https://www.plough.com/en/topics/justice/environment/beating-the-big-dry.

Mertus, Julie A. *Bait and Switch: Human Rights and U.S. Foreign Policy.* Abington-on-Thames, U.K: Routledge, 2008.

Miller, Scott E. "DNA Barcoding and the Renaissance of Taxonomy." *Proceedings of the National Academy of Sciences of the United States,* March 2007. https://www.pnas.org/content/pnas/104/12/4775.full.pdf.

Mosaicultures Internationales. *Terre D'Espérance/Land of Hope.* Official album. Montreal: Mosaicultures Internationales, 2013.

"Narrative of Andrew J. Vieau Jr." In *Collections of the State Historical Society of Wisconsin*, vol. 11, edited by Reuben G. Thwaites, 219. Madison, Wisc.: Democrat Printing Co., 1888. Cited by John Boatman, "Jacques Vieau: A Son of Montreal and a Father of European Wisconsin. Another Perspective on the French and Native Peoples." Milwaukee: University of Wisconsin, 1997.

"Native American Headdresses." Native Languages of the Americas (website). http://www.native-languages.org/headdresses.htm. Accessed August 10, 2019.

"Neanderthal Mother, Denisovan Father! Hybrid Fossil." *Science Daily,* August 22, 2018. https://www.sciencedaily.com/releases/2018/08/180822131002.htm.

Neihardt, John G. *Black Elk Speaks: Being the Life Story of a Holy Man of the Oglala Sioux.* (1932). Albany: State University of New York Press, 2008.

Orange, Tommy. *There There.* New York: Knopf, 2018.

Parezo, Nancy J., and Don D. Fowler. *Anthropology Goes to the Fair: The 1904 Louisiana Purchase Exposition*. Lincoln: University of Nebraska Press, 2007.

Pokagon, Simon. "The Red Man's Rebuke." Internet Archive, Smithsonian Collection (website). https://archive.org/details/redmanquotsrebu-00Poka. Accessed January 13, 2020.

Pomedli, Michael. *Living with Animals: Ojibwe Spirit Powers*. Toronto: University of Toronto Press, 2014.

"Powwows in Europe." Native American Association of Germany (NAAoG; website). http://www.naaog.de/powwows-in-europe.html. Accessed January 12, 2020.

"Prouville de Tracy, Alexandre de, Marquis." Dictionary of Canadian Biography (website). http://www.biographi.ca/en/bio/prouville_de _tracy_alexandre_de_1E.html. Accessed August 8, 2019.

"Relics." Kateri Center (website). http://katericenter.com/english/E6R-RELICS.html. Accessed August 7, 2019.

Robbins, Jim. "Native Knowledge: What Ecologists Are Learning from Indigenous People." *Yale Environment* 360. April 26, 2018. https://e360 .yale.edu/features/native-knowledge-what-ecologists-are-learning-from -indigenous-people.

Ronda, Margaret. "Mourning and Melancholia in the Anthropocene." Post45 (website), June 10, 2013. http://post45.research.yale.edu/2013/06 /mourning-and-melancholia-in-the-anthropocene.

Saint Kateri Conservation Center (website). http://www.kateri.org. Accessed August 7, 2019.

Saint Kateri Interpretative Center in Kahnawake (website). http:// kateritekakwitha.net/latest-news/interpretive-center. Accessed August 7, 2019.

"Saint Kateri Tekakwitha." Canadian Conference of Catholic Bishops (website). http://www.cccb.ca/site/eng/church-in-canada-and-world/catholic -church-in-canada/indigenous-peoples/3263-blessed-kateri-tekakwitha. Accessed August 9, 2019.

"St. Kateri Tekakwitha." Our Lady of Martyrs Shrine (website). https://www .ourladyofmartyrsshrine.org/st-kateri-tekakwitha. Accessed August 9, 2019.

"St. Kateri Takakwitha, Mohawk Saint." *Encyclopedia Britannica*. https://www
.britannica.com/biography/Saint-Kateri-Tekakwitha. Accessed August 9,
2019.

Sainte-Marie, Buffy. "Universal Soldier." YouTube (website). https://www
.youtube.com/watch?v=j6imjvgJFvM. Accessed August 10, 2019.

Salam, Maya. "Native American Women Are Facing a Crisis." *The New York
Times*, April 4, 2019. https://www.nytimes.com/2019/04/12/us/native
-american-women-violence.html.

Schenck, Theresa. "The Algonquian Totem and Totemism: A Distortion of
the Semantic Field." *Papers of the Twenty-eighth Algonquian Conference*,
vol. 28: 341–53. Winnipeg: University of Manitoba, 1997.

Schwartz, Susan. "Nature's Masterclass: 5 Things You Should Know about Butterflies
Go Free." *Montreal Gazette*. March 14, 2019. https://montrealgazette.com/news
/local-news/natures-master-class-up-to-2000-butterflies-go-free-at
-botanical-garden. Accessed August 7, 2019.

Simpson, Audra. "Why White People Love Franz Boas; or The Grammar
of Indigenous Dispossession." In Blackhawk and Wilner, *Indigenous
Visions*, 166–81.

Shoemaker, Nancy. "Kateri Tekakwitha's Tortuous Path to Sainthood."
In *Negotiators of Change: Historical Perspectives on Native American
Women*, edited by Nancy Shoemaker, 49–71. New York: Routledge,
2012.

Slater, Sandra, and Fay A. Yarbrough, eds. *Gender and Sexuality in Indigenous
North America, 1400–1850*. Columbia: University of South Carolina
Press, 2012.

Smith, Adam. *The Theory of Moral Sentiments*. (1759). London: Penguin,
2010.

Staples, Brent. "The Black Seminole Indians Keep Fighting for Equality in the
American West." *The New York Times*, November 18, 2003. https://www
.nytimes.com/2003/11/18/opinion/editorial-observer-black-seminole
-indians-keep-fighting-for-equality-american.html. Accessed January 12,
2020.

Sullivan, Robert. *The Thoreau You Don't Know: What the Prophet of
Environmentalism Really Meant*. New York: HarperCollins, 2009.

Takemura, Alison F. "Wolf Species Are Part Coyote: Genomic Analysis

Reveals Wolves and Coyotes Have Hybridized, Potentially Complicating Wolves' Protection under the U.S. Endangered Species Act." *The Scientist*, July 28, 2016. https://www.the-scientist.com/the-nutshell /wolf-species-are-part-coyote-33123.

Taleb, Nassim Nicholas. *The Black Swan: The Impact of the Highly Improbable*. London: Penguin, 2008.

"Tekakwitha, Kateri." *Dictionary of Canadian Biography* (website). http://www .biographi.ca/en/bio/tekakwitha_1E.html. Accessed August 9, 2019

Tempus, Alexandra. "The People's Forest: How the Menominee Are Facing Climate Change." *Orion Magazine*, autumn 2018.

"Thanks to Twenty-first Century Crowd Sourcing, a Relic of a Seventeenth-century Saint Can Now Come Home." Catholic Ecology (website). February 1, 2016. https://catholicecology.net/blog/saint-kateri-relic -rescued.

Treuer, David. *The Heartbeat of Wounded Knee*. New York: Riverhead, 2019.

———. *Rez Life: An Indian's Journey Through Reservation Life*. New York: Grove, 2012.

———. "Writing Culture: Some Thoughts on Difference, Appropriation, Politics, and Race in Modern Writing." Lecture, August 20, 2018, Bread Loaf Writers Conference, Ripton, Vermont. https://midd.hosted.panopto.com /Panopto/Pages/Viewer.aspx?id=9a59c577-37cc-4d73-8ea4- a94400ffe540.

Twain, Mark. *The War Prayer*. (1923). New York: Harper & Row, 1968.

United States v. Confederated Tribes of Colville Indian Reservation. U.S. Ninth Circuit Court. https://caselaw.fiindlaw.com/us-9th-circuit/1525561. html. Accessed August 15, 2019.

Van Horn, Gavin. *The Way of Coyote: Shared Journeys in the Urban Wilds*. Chicago: University of Chicago Press, 2018.

"Vermont State School for the Feeble Minded." Eugenics Survey of Vermont: Participants and Partners, Vermont Eugenics: A Documentary History (website). http://www.uvm.edu/~eugenics/vssf.html. Accessed February 12, 2020.

Vukelich, Jim. "Ojibwe Word of the Day." Youtube (website). November 13, 2017. https://www.youtube.com/watch?v=yxMvqqn_B-A&feature =youtu.be.

Wang, Hairong. "Between Charity and Business: Chinese Social Entrepreneurs Seek to Solve Social Problems by Using a Business Approach." *Beijing Review* 45 (November 10, 2011). http://www .bjreview.com/nation/txt/2011-11/07/content_404150.htm.

"Welcome to the Anthropocene." http://www.anthropocene.info. Accessed August 14, 2019.

Williams, Florence. *The Nature Fix: Why Nature Makes Us Happier, Healthier, and More Creative.* New York: Norton, 2017.

Wilner, Isaiah Lorado. "Transformation Masks." In Blackhawk and Wilner, *Indigenous Visions,* 3–41.

Wilson, Edward O. *Biophilia: The Human Bond with Other Species.* Cambridge, Mass.: Harvard University Press, 1984.

Wohlleben, Peter. *The Hidden Life of Trees,* Vancouver, B.C.: Greystone, 2015.

INDEX

Page numbers in *italics* indicate illustrations.

Books of Related Interest

Walking on the Wind
Cherokee Teachings for Harmony and Balance
by Michael Tlanusta Garrett

The Cherokee Full Circle
A Practical Guide to Ceremonies and Traditions
by J. T. Garrett and Michael Tlanusta Garrett

Medicine of the Cherokee
The Way of Right Relationship
by J. T. Garrett and Michael Tlanusta Garrett

Earth Spirit Dreaming
Shamanic Ecotherapy Practices
by Elizabeth E. Meacham, Ph.D.
Foreword by Christopher M. Bache, Ph.D.

Dancing with Raven and Bear
A Book of Earth Medicine and Animal Magic
by Sonja Grace

Shamanic Alchemy
The Great Work of Inner Transformation
by James Endredy

Narrative Medicine
The Use of History and Story in the Healing Process
by Lewis Mehl-Madrona, M.D., Ph.D.

Bird Medicine
The Sacred Power of Bird Shamanism
by Evan T. Pritchard

INNER TRADITIONS • BEAR & COMPANY
P.O. Box 388 • Rochester, VT 05767
1-800-246-8648 • www.InnerTraditions.com

Or contact your local bookseller